the BiZARRO ENCYCLOPEDIA OF FILM | VOLUME 1

THE BIZARRO ENCYCLOPEDIA OF FILM (VOL. I)

JOHN SKIPP &
HEATHER DRAIN

FUNGASM PRESS
an imprint of Eraserhead Press
PO Box 10065
Portland, OR 97296

www.fungasmpress.com
facebook/fungasmpress

ISBN: 978-1-62105-295-1
Copyright © 2019 by John Skipp and Heather Drain
Cover illustrations copyright © 2019 Paula Rozelle Hanback
Interior graphics by Paula Rozelle Hanback and Vecteezy

Printed in the USA.

DEDICATIONS

Skipp:
To all the video stores I've loved and lost,
and to the last brave ones remaining.

Heather:
This book is dedicated to the people who not only raised me,
but have always encouraged me to be a true individual, a writer,
and to love what I love...even when it freaked them out!
I love you, Mom and Pappy. Thank you for being the best.

Paula:
To my amazing kidlet, who has taught me more
than all other teachers combined.

TABLE OF CONTENTS

WHAT THE HELL IS BIZARRO FILM?
(AND WHY DO YOU KEEP CALLING IT THAT?)
AN INFORMATIVE INTRODUCTION
BY JOHN SKIPP

**BALLYHOO, BRILLIANCE, BOLLOCKS,
BRAVADO & BIZARRO!**
A BONUS MINI-INTRO
BY HEATHER DRAIN

A WORD ABOUT THE ARTWORK
(FOR FOLKS WHO CARE ABOUT SUCH THINGS)
BY PAULA ROZELLE HANBACK

PART ONE
**THE ULTIMATE BIZARRO
VIDEO STORE**

INTRO
CULT
CHILDREN'S
FANTASY & SCIENCE FICTION
HORROR
COMEDY
DRAMA
ACTION/THRILLER
MUSICALS
FOREIGN/ARTHOUSE
DOCUMENTARIES
ADULT

CANDIDE ON SPEED
SCREWBALL SEX COMEDIES ON ACID
IN ALEX DE RENZY'S *PRETTY PEACHES* TRILOGY
Heather Drain

PLATES OF SHRIMP AND OTTO PARTS
THE LIFE OF *REPO MAN* IS ALWAYS INTENSE
John Skipp

THE BAUM WE DESERVE
BIZARRO FOR KIDS, THE OLD-FASHIONED WAY,
AND THE GLORIOUS *RETURN TO OZ*
John Skipp

THE GAS OF GRACE AND SORROW
AND THE SOUL-PLUMBING ECSTASY OF *SWISS ARMY MAN*
John Skipp

PARTING IS SUCH SWEET SORROW
THAT IT TOTALLY SUCKS
LLOYD AND BILLY GOT THEIR GUNN
IN THE TIMELESS *TROMEO AND JULIET*
John Skipp

GOD IN GOLD LAME
ROCK N ROLL RELIGIOUS PARABLES
COMPLETE WITH TALKING SNAKES IN
TIMOTHY CAREY'S *THE WORLD'S GREATEST SINNER*
Heather Drain

WHAT THE HELL IS BIZARRO FILM?
(AND WHY DO YOU KEEP CALLING IT THAT?)

AN INFORMATIVE INTRODUCTION
BY JOHN SKIPP

In the world of art-o-tainment (roughly translated as "art that's entertaining", or "entertainment that is artfully rendered"), the naming of genres is a matter of profound significance.

Not because it's actually meaningful or even *accurate*, half the time, but because it's helpful in sifting through the ever-mounting avalanche of all that's been made, and finding the sorts of things you might like. Kind of like putting labels on stacks of cans on a grocery store shelf, and arranging them in sections.

If you're nuts for kidney beans, lima beans might not do the trick, but at least you're in the right vicinity. Coming home with a can of Frisky Feast Premium Cat Food, on the other hand, might really fuck up your chili recipe.

LABELS COME IN HANDY! That's all I'm sayin'.

So we've got our standard demarcations. Comedy. Drama. Action. Fantasy. Science fiction. Horror. Foreign. Documentary. Musicals. Porn. And let's not forget the Children's section!

1

This is all well and good.

But in the course of all that, there are those amazing movies that utterly slip through the cracks. Neither fish nor fowl, kidney bean nor cat food, they defy definition because *they're too fucking weird.*

It's a frequent condition in art-o-tainment of all forms, because so much of the coolest shit bridles at the very *notion* of containment. Labels, like laws, are made to be broken.

And as for those renegade art-o-tainers who refuse to play by the rules?

What do you call them, and the strange things they make?

Back around 2006, the term "Bizarro fiction" emerged as a fresh category of outsider weirdo lit. Spearheaded, quite naturally, by outsider weirdos (Carlton Mellick III, D. Harlan Wilson, and Chris Genoa among them), the goal was to create a scene for writers whose work deliberately confounded genre, and therefore had no existing market in which to sell their crazy wares.

They marketed themselves as the "fiction of weird"—weirdness being the active ingredient—and explained Bizarro as "the literary equivalent of the cult section in a really good video store."

This was an explanation that resonated hard for me, because I always loooooved the cult section of a really good video store, back when video stores still existed. It would instantly be the first place I headed, after a quick glance at the new releases. And I very quickly gauged whether this store was for me by the quality and range of what I found.

So what's a cult movie? By definition, it finds its way to the cult section by either

a) not fitting into any other category, or

b) being so weird that so matter what genre it was originally intended for—horror, crime, musical, sci-fi, romance, fantasy, art, drama, children, you name it—the end result was so weird in execution that it got kicked off the normal bus. Exiled to the cult hinterlands.

In every case, it's *the nature of the choices the filmmakers make* that defines its Bizarro cultitude. Sometimes it's exemplary genius (David Lynch, Guy Maddin, Federico Fellini, Alejandro Jodorowsky). Sometimes it's extraordinarily well-meaning incompetence (Ed Wood, *Birdemic: Shock and Terror, Manos: The Hands of Fate*).

Weirdness comes at us in oh-so-many ways. It is the View Askew: the shattering of norm-o-scopic pop culture formulas and modalities, where the same old stories are told the same old ways. Somewhere in the telling—be it story or performance, camera placement or *mis-en-scene*—something weird and special happened.

Sometimes it's overt (Aggressive Bizarro) and sometimes it's covert (let's call it Stealth Bizarro). As suggested above, there's an enormous difference between Intentional Bizarro and Accidental Bizarro.

But the more I thought about the cult section, the more I realized it was really just *the maximum security wing* of the motion picture art-o-tainment madhouse where we house all our collective cultural fantasies. (Only porn is segregated more, with an age-specific curtained entryway that says, "And here's where the people get naked and fuck out loud, you perverts! YOU KNOW YOU WANT IT!")

Meanwhile, the entire video store was *crawling* with all kinds of spectacular weirdness that somehow managed to stay out of Cult Jail. Eluding the dragnet by successfully masquerading itself as some other, more respectable genre. Sneaking the weirdness in, and getting away with it, by nailing just enough popular tropes (with enough big names) to appeal to that genre's wider audience.

And the more I thought about it, the more I realized that yes, Bizarro is an outsider genre, absolutely. But the forces that propel it are *everywhere,* subversively insinuating themselves into even some of the world's most popular, successful movies. Are, in fact, the secret ingredients that make those movies so cool. Make them stand out from the pack. Make them, in fact, *Bizarro mainstream movies.*

At that point, I realized how important it was to bring together the insiders and the outsiders, through their common love and the code word BIZARRO. Connect those dots. And facilitate avid devotees of the cinematic strange as they wandered down the aisles, flush with searching curiosity. Seeking out those things they might truly respond to next.

You want a label? You GOT a label!

From this moment forward, let us call it Bizarro film.

That's when I contacted Heather Drain: a fantastic, grinningly punk-as-fuck writer and glowing, encyclopedic champion of all the cool cinematic outsider greatness that might otherwise be lost and forgotten. Her huge heart, casually-personal yet detail-intensive gnostic style, and unmistakable love of all the weirdo gold that glistens before us, unseen, stood her out from the rest of her rigorous peers like the yellow umbrella in a sea of black in *Harold and Maude* (1971). Directed by Hal Ashby. Written by Colin Higgins. And, incidentally, *Bizarro as fuck!*

And the more we talked, the more it came clear that we had to do this book together. Attacking it from every possible angle.

So here's what we're gonna do.

Soon as I'm done yammering here, Heather's gonna stop by and say hi. Then we're gonna lay out THE ENTIRE VIDEO STORE, section by section. Starting with Cult, the self-proclaimed center of the maelstrom. Then moving through Children's (where our shared stories begin), through Fantasy and Science Fiction

THE BIZARRO ENCYCLOPEDIA OF FILM

(where our imagined pasts and futures collide), through the worst-case scenario that is Horror, on through Comedy, and Drama, and Action, and all that other shit I laid out before.

By the time we're done, there will *roughly 1,650 titles.* And believe me, we're just scraping the surface of the depths. That's why this is Volume I.

Then, and *only* then, will we dig into a a couple dozen particular films that help define what Bizarro film means, by example. Respectively plucking out handfuls of personal favorites. Explaining why we love them. What they bring to the Bizarro party. And why that matters.

So THERE YOU GO! That's the ride you're about to embark on. Hope you have fun, and find easily hundreds of films you're personally delighted to discover, if you hadn't already.

Yer fungasmic pal on the forever trail,
Skipp

BALLYHOO, BRILLIANCE, BOLLOCKS, BRAVADO & BIZARRO!

A BONUS MINI-INTRO
BY HEATHER DRAIN

There is the weird. The strange. The unknown. The outre, even. And then?
There is Bizarro. You may be sitting there thinking, what's the difference
between cult, arthouse or psychotronic cinema versus Bizarro? Well imagine
your garden variety cult or arthouse film snorting a line of pure Z-grade trucker
speed but yet, having enough heart to bring out the inner Mary Pickford from
even the coldest and blackest of hearts. A true blue Bizarro film is one of a
singular vision and elements that make it the porridge that Goldilocks chose.
Well, if Goldilocks was a Go-Go dancer who twirls her tassels to the Musique
Concrete stylings of Pierre Schaeffer. (If THAT film existed? It would totally be
in this book.)

Art and artists that live, either by design or exquisite accident, outside of the
parameters of safety, have been the light that has attracted my inner moth-
person since I was a little girl. Going into what I like to call "fringe culture"
writing professionally as an adult, it is not only a pleasure to delve into these
shadowy nooks and crannies, but a moral imperative. Being a misfit elf means
you gotta give love and attention and respect to your fellow misfit elves.

7

THE BIZARRO ENCYCLOPEDIA OF FILM

Not all of the films we will be covering are blatant misfit elves but what is more status quo busting than the subversively weird? Either way, from your head to your groin and ultimately your heart, these are the movies that will snake their way into your DNA and never quite leave.

Enough of my ballyhoo. On with the show!

A WORD ABOUT THE ARTWORK
(FOR FOLKS WHO CARE ABOUT SUCH THINGS)

BY PAULA ROZELLE HANBACK

Those of us who came of age in the Eighties and Nineties still remember the cherished Friday Night ritual of going to the video store. For me, as an artist, what I remember most about those trips are the murals painted on the walls.

From stunningly realistic to hilariously skewed, video store murals were perhaps the earliest example of what we would now call *fan art*. The most iconic examples were, of course, the Hollywood Video murals, painted by A.D. Cook between 1989 and 1995. Originally the murals were all hand-painted on-site in the stores. They averaged ten feet in height and as much as 20 feet in length. Eventually, Cook began painting the murals in his studio on huge canvases that were then installed in the stores.

When John Skipp asked me to create the cover art for THE BIZARRO ENCYCLOPEDIA OF FILM in the style of those old video store murals, I jumped at the chance. The Hollywood Video murals were a huge inspiration, as were the many young artists currently bringing back the traditional, hand-painted montage movie poster. Kyle Lambert's work for STRANGER THINGS is among the best-known in this new-old genre.

THE BIZARRO ENCYCLOPEDIA OF FILM

The cover art for THE BIZARRO ENCYCLOPEDIA OF FILM is based on literally dozens of publicity photos and screenshots lovingly curated by the ever-effervescent Heather Drain. Like Kyle Lambert, I do most of my actual arting on computer these days. I worked on a Mac laptop using a Wacom tablet, and later on a Microsoft Surface Pro, using Adobe Photoshop and Clip Studio Paint. Every inch of the cover was lovingly hand-painted (and re-painted) by me—there is no photo manipulation—it's all the Real Deal. The software and hardware have advanced to a point where working with them is almost indistinguishable from traditional media—except, of course, for the UNDO feature.

I hope you enjoy this book, which has been a monumental labor of love for all of us, as well as an artistic trip down memory lane.

PRH

PART ONE

THE ULTIMATE
BIZARRO VIDEO STORE

LADIES AND/OR GENTLEMEN, AND OTHERS! *Please allow us to welcome you inside the video store of our dreams, wherein every motion picture is designed to take you somewhere weird, and most likely leave you there!*

At first glance, it's just like any other video store: brightly lit, laid out in long rows of racks and shelves, and packed to the rafters with movies galore. The same old sectional categories apply, with big ol' signs to show you the lay of the land, steer you clearly in the direction you seek.

But because this work-in-progress has been carefully curated—with the help of our many, many movie-loving friends—every single one of these films passes our personal Bizarro test.

This, of course, makes it substantially smaller than most video stores of yore, where they'd just let in ANY old movie the studios chose to squirt out. No insult intended for the reams upon reams of normative fare that have entertained many for generations. But, frankly, you can find that stuff anywhere. In fact, it's almost impossible to avoid.

As Frank Zappa once said, "The mainstream comes to you. But you have to go to the underground."

That said: you may be surprised by the sheer number of ostensibly "normal" films that made it in here. So while you won't find High Noon, Die Hard, *or* A League of Their Own *on the shelves (all genuinely terrific, if you like those sorts of things), you will find* It's a Wonderful Life, Beetlejuice, *and* The Lego Movie, *so you should be okay!*

Fans of the DC and Marvel comic universes may be appalled by the absence of a Superhero section (or proper representation in the Action section).. But believe us when we tell you: any movie where super-powered heroes and villains with flamboyant costumes and funny names kick the shit out of each other, THAT'S BIZARRO AS HELL. In fact, we owe the word to Superman and his creators. It's just not our thing. But please consider yourselves in.

Likewise for Bollywood, Anime, and god-only-knows how many other film forms we're aware of, but have no expertise in. We know we've barely scratched the surface of the silent era, pre-code Hollywood, and much of the rest of the world. These are among the many things we hope to expand upon in Volume Two and beyond, with your help. THANK YOU FOR YOUR HELP!

Our ultimate goal is to fill the Ultimate Bizarro Video Store with every single film on Earth that fits the criteria, broad as that may be. Your one-stop shopping for the full range of mind-bending strangeness the cinema world has to offer.

Now let's get down to the sections, shall we? ALLOW US TO SHOW YOU AROUND!

And make yourselves at home. You may be roaming for hours.

Or —if you're like us—for the rest of your life! (JS)

THE BIZARRO ENCYCLOPEDIA OF FILM

*Imagine a portal to a multitude of worlds that could thrill, terrify, tantalize
and wholesale befuddle you—awaiting your seeking eyes in the middle of a
sunbleached stripmall next to a tanning salon and a chow-mein joint that might
be a front for illegal gambling. Being a child of the 1980's in a small working
class town in Nowheresville, Arkansas, the video store was MY Disneyland.
Rows and rows of cover art greeted my eyes in some of the least exciting
buildings ever. Stripmalls as far as the eyes could see, but it didn't matter. Every
section was a microcosm of my first instinctual love-cinema and the more
obscure, strange and forbidden the title? The absolute better. Going to rent
a movie always felt like the ultimate treasure hunt. Sometimes you might find
the riches of Davy Jones Locker (ie. Alejandro Jodorowsky's* Santa Sangre)
*and other times you might find a dead jellyfish draped upon a crushed can of
Natural Ice Light (IE. 1985's shit-tastic* Fraternity Vacation. *Just say no, kids.
Just. Say. No.) But the risk was part of the fun.*

*One of the goals with this list and book is to give you that thrill of something
blazingly new. A Bizarro film is a film that loves you enough to not give you
what it thinks you want. Go to the multi-plex if you want a dead-eyed stripper
dryly grinding your lonely nethers. Come here if you want it fresh, hot, fun and
most importantly, never-ever dull. Open your mind, smell the day old popcorn
that's over by the front counter, you know the one that is framed with a giant
cardboard standee of Susan Tyrrell as Queen Doris from* Forbidden Zone *and
enormous pixie sticks, don't mind the flickering fluorescent lights and gird your
loins baby! It's gonna be a smooth ride. (HD)*

CULT

Cult is a term that has a buffet of scary-blending-into-creepy associations when it comes to religion, but with cinema? Glory glory, hallelujah! Cult cinema, while more broadly associated with a handful of films that have a smallish but devoted following, has more of a unique meaning here in the Bizarro Video Store. The first time I discovered a hip enough video store to have a legit Cult section was in the early 90's and my eyes went wide and my mind went pop. In the video store setting, Cult was less obvious titles like Rocky Horror Picture Show *and more like titles too weird and esoteric to find a home anywhere else. From 60's Psychedelic-schlock (a term used with love, by the way, in this book) to Z-Grade inanity and sexploitation gems to genre-busters that are so singularly their own beast that they are the art-equivalent to nuclear fission. Given the nature of this book, there will be titles in other sections that you might be like "Hey! Shouldn't that be in Cult?" Here's the beautiful thing. You're probably right but so are we. Genre categories are fun guidelines but it is not science. If you want something to get upset about, just read the news or mull over the musical career of Rick Dees. (HD)*

2,000 MANIACS (1964)
Written and directed by Herschell Gordon Lewis.

ACCIÓN MUTANTE (1993)
Directed by Álex de la Iglesia. Written by Jorge Guerricaechevarría and Álex de la Iglesia.

THE AMAZING TRANSPLANT (1970)
Written and directed by Doris Wishman.

AN AMERICAN HIPPIE IN ISRAEL (1972)
Directed by Amos Sefer. Written by Amos Sefer and Baruch Verthaim.

ANDY WARHOL'S BAD (BAD) (1977)
Directed by Jed Johnson. Written by Pat Hackett and George Abagnalo.

ANGEL ANGEL DOWN WE GO (1969)
Written and directed by Robert Thom.

ANOTHER DAY, ANOTHER MAN (1966)
Written and directed by Doris Wishman.

ANTIBIRTH (2016)
Written and directed by Danny Perez.

ARISE: THE SUBGENIUS VIDEO (1992)
Directed by Cordt Holland, Douglass Smith (as Rev. Ivan Stang). Written by Paul Mavrides, Harry S. Robins, Rev. Ivan Stang.

THE ASTRO-ZOMBIES (1968)
Directed by Ted V. Mikels. Written by Ted V. Mikels, Wayne Rogers.

ATTACK OF THE KILLER TOMATOES (1978)
Directed by John De Bello. Written by Costa Dillon, John De Bello, J. Stephen Peace and Rick Rockwell.

THE BABY (1973)
Directed by Ted Post. Written by Abe Polsky.

BAD GIRLS GO TO HELL (1965)
Written and directed by Doris Wishman.

Why should Bogart Peter Stuyvesant go to war and kill strangers, when the pickings are better in his own bedroom?

ANGEL ANGEL DOWN WE GO

JENNIFER JONES JORDAN CHRISTOPHER · HOLLY NEAR · LOU RAWLS · CHARLES AIDMAN · RODDY McDOWALL COLOR

BAD TASTE (1987)
Directed by Peter Jackson. Written by Peter Jackson, Tony Hiles.

BASKET CASE (1982)
Written and directed by Frank Henenlotter.

BAT PUSSY (1973)
Directed by ?, Written by ? (None credited)

BEAVER TRILOGY (1979-1985)
Written and directed by Trent Harris.

BEYOND THE VALLEY OF THE DOLLS (1970)
Directed by Russ Meyer. Written by Roger Ebert and Russ Meyer.

BIBLE! (1974)
Written and directed by Wakefield Poole.

BIKINI BEACH (1964)
Directed by William Asher, Written by William Asher, Leo Townsend and Robert Dillon.

BIRDEMIC: SHOCK AND TERROR (2010)
Written and directed by James Nguyen.

BLACK DEVIL DOLL FROM HELL (1984)
Written and directed by Chester Novell Turner.

BLACKEST HEART /THE GERMAN CHAINSAW MASSACRE (1990)
Written and directed by Christoph Schlingensief.

BLOOD FEAST (1963)
Directed by Herschell Gordon Lewis. Written by Allison Louise Downe.

BLOOD FREAK (1972)
Directed by Brad F. Grinter and Steve Hawkes. Written by Brad F. Grinter and Steve Hawkes.

BODY MELT (1993)
Directed by Philip Brophy. Written by Philip Brophy (screenplay), Rod Bishop (screenplay), Philip Brophy (short stories).

BRAIN DAMAGE (1988)
Written and directed by Frank Henenlotter.

BRAND UPON THE BRAIN! (2006)
Directed by Guy Maddin. Written by Guy Maddin, Louis Negin, George Toles.

BRIDE OF THE MONSTER (1955)
Directed by Edward D. Wood, Jr. Written by Edward D. Wood, Jr. and Alex Gordon.

CAREFUL (1992)
Directed by Guy Maddin. Written by Guy Maddin, George Toles.

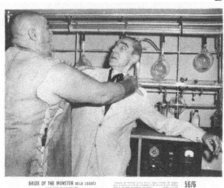

CHATTERBOX (1977)
Directed by Tom DeSimone. Written by Mark Rosin, Norman Yonemoto and Tom DeSimone.

CHILLERAMA (2011)
Written and directed by Adam Rifkin. Tim Sullivan, Adam Green, and Joe Lynch.

19

THE BIZARRO ENCYCLOPEDIA OF FILM

CHRISTMAS EVIL
Written and directed by Lewis Jackson.

CLASS OF NUKE 'EM HIGH (1986)
Directed by Richard W. Haines and Lloyd Kaufman (as Samuel Weil). Written by Richard W. Haines, Mark Rudnitsky, Lloyd Kaufman, and Stuart Strutin. Story by Richard W. Haines.

COCKHAMMER (2009)
Written and directed by Kevin Strange.

THE CORPSE GRINDERS (1971)
Directed by Ted V. Mikels. Written by Arch Hall Sr. and Joseph Cranston.

COWARDS BEND THE KNEE (2003)
Directed by Guy Maddin. Written by Guy Maddin and George Toles.

THE DARK BACKWARD (1991)
Written and directed by Adam Rifkin.

DAY OF THE BEAST (1995)
Directed by Álex de la Iglesia. Written by Jorge Guerricaechevarría, Álex de la Iglesia.

DEADLY WEAPONS (1974)
Directed by Doris Wishman. Written by Judy J. Kushner.

DESPERATE LIVING (1977)
Written and directed by John Waters.

A DIRTY SHAME (2004)
Written and directed by John Waters.

DOUBLE AGENT 73 (1974)
Directed by Doris Wishman. Written by Judy J. Kushner (Story) and Doris Wishman.

DR. CALIGARI (1989)
Directed by Stephen Sayadian. Written by Stephen Sayadian and Jerry Stahl.

EBOLA SYNDROME (1996)
Directed by Herman Yau. Written by Ting Chau.

EL TOPO (1970)
Written and directed by Alejandro Jodorowsky.

ERASERHEAD (1977)
Written and directed by David Lynch.

EXECUTIVE KOALA (2005)
Directed by Minoru Kawasaki. Written by Minoru Kawasaki, Masakazu Migita.

THE EXOTIC ONES (1968)
Written and directed by Ron Ormond.

FASTER PUSSYCAT! KILL! KILL! (1965)
Directed by Russ Meyer. Written by Jackie Moran, Russ Meyer.

FEAR AND LOATHING IN LAS VEGAS (1998)
Directed by Terry Gilliam. Written by Terry Gilliam and Tony Grisoni, with additional credits to Alex Cox and Tod Davies, from the book by Hunter S. Thompson.

FEMALE TROUBLE (1974)
Written and directed by John Waters.

FLESH GORDON (1974)
Directed by Michael Benveniste. Howard Zieme. Written by Michael Benveniste.

THE FLESH TRILOGY (1967-68)
Written and directed by Michael Findlay.

FREAKS (1932)
Directed by Tod Browning. Written by Clarence Aaron 'Tod' Robbins.

FRITZ THE CAT (1972)
Written and directed by Ralph Bakshi, based on characters by Robert Crumb.

FUNKY FOREST: THE FIRST CONTACT (2005)
Written and directed by Katsuhito Ishii, Hajime Ishimine, and Shunichiro Miki

GEEK MAGGOT BINGO (1983)
Directed by Nick Zedd. Written by Nick Zedd and Robert Kirkpatrick.

GINGER (1971)
Written and directed by Don Schain.

GLEN OR GLENDA (1953)
Written and directed by Edward D. Wood, Jr.

GONE WITH THE POPE (1975, 2010)
Written and directed by Duke Mitchell.

GORE GORE GIRLS (1972)
Directed by Herschell Gordon Lewis. Written by Alan J. Dachman.

GREASER'S PALACE (1972)
Written and directed by Robert Downey, Sr.

THE GREASY STRANGLER (2016)
Directed by Jim Hosking. Written by Jim Hosking and Toby Harvard.

HAUSU (1977)
Directed by Nobuhiko Obayashi. Written by Chiho Katsura, Chigumi Obayashi (story).

THE BIZARRO ENCYCLOPEDIA OF FILM

HEAD (1968)
Directed by Bob Rafelson. Written by Bob Rafelson and Jack Nicholson.

HEAVY TRAFFIC (1973)
Written and directed by Ralph Bakshi.

THE HOLY MOUNTAIN (1973)
Directed by Alejandro Jodorowsky. Written by Alejandro Jodorowsky.

ILSA: SHE WOLF OF THE SS (1975)
Directed by Don Edmonds. Written by John C.W. Saxton (as Jonah Royston).

THE INCREDIBLY STRANGE CREATURES WHO STOPPED LIVING AND BECAME MIXED UP ZOMBIES (1964)
Directed by Ray Dennis Steckler. Written by Gene Pollock, Robert Silliphant and E.M. Kevke.

INDECENT DESIRES (1968)
Written and directed by Doris Wishman.

INVITATION TO RUIN (1968)
Directed by Kurt Richter. Written by Max Conrad.

JIZZLY BEAR (2015)
Written and directed by Josh Malerman.

KUSO (2017)
Directed by Flying Lotus. Written by Flying Lotus, David Firth, and Zack Fox.

LADY TERMINATOR (1989)
Directed by H. Tjut Djalil. Written by Karr Kruinowz.

THE LEMON GROVE KIDS MEET THE MONSTERS (1965)
Directed by Ray Dennis Steckler. Written by Jim Harmon, Ron Haydock, E. M. Kevke and Ray Dennis Steckler.

LET'S VISIT THE WORLD OF THE FUTURE (1973)
Written and directed by Douglass Smith (aka Rev. Ivan Stang).

LIVE FREAKY, DIE FREAKY (2006)
Written and directed by John Roecker.

THE LOST SKELETON OF CADAVRA (2001)
Written and directed by Larry Blamire.

THE LOVE WITCH (2016)
Written and directed by Anna Biller.

THE LUSTING HOURS (1967)
Directed by John and Lem Amero. Written by (presumably) John and Lem Amero.

MANOS, THE HANDS OF FATE (1966)
Directed by Harold P. Warren. Written by Harold P. Warren.

ASTRA PRODUCTIONS PRESENT "ORGY OF THE DEAD" R.Q.S. DISTRIBUTION IN GORGEOUS AND SHOCKING ASTRAVISION SEXICOLOR

MESA OF LOST WOMEN (1953)
Directed by Ron Ormond and Herbert Tevos. Written by Herbert Tevos.

MULTIPLE MANIACS (1970)
Written and directed by John Waters.

MUSCLE BEACH PARTY (1964)
Directed by William Asher. Written by William Asher and Robert Dillon.

NIGHT OF THE LEPUS (1972)
Directed by William F. Claxton. Written by Don Halliday, Gene R. Kearney, and Russell Braddon (novel).

NUDE ON THE MOON (1961)
Directed by Doris Wishman. Written by Doris Wishman and Jack Caplan (idea).

NYMPHS ANONYMOUS (1968)
Directed by Manuel Conde. Written by Jean Van Hearn.

ORGY OF THE DEAD (1965)
Directed by Stephen C. Apostolof. Written by Edward D. Wood Jr.

THE PINK ANGELS (1972)
Directed by Larry G. Brown. Written by Margaret McPherson.

PINK FLAMINGOS (1972)
Written and directed by John Waters.

PLAN NINE FROM OUTER SPACE (1959)
Written and directed by Edward D. Wood, Jr.

POLYESTER (1981)
Written and directed by John Waters.

POOR WHITE TRASH 2 AKA SCUM OF THE EARTH (1974)
Directed by S.F. Brownrigg. Written by Mary Davis and Gene Ross (additional dialogue).

THE BIZARRO ENCYCLOPEDIA OF FILM

PUTNEY SWOPE (1969)
Written and directed by
Robert Downey, Sr.

PSYCH OUT (1968)
Directed by Robert Rush. Written by
E. Hunter Willett, Betty Ulius, Betty
Tusher (uncredited).

RAT PFINK A BOO-BOO (1966)
Directed by Ray Dennis Steckler.
Written by Ron Haydock and Ray
Dennis Steckler.

RED SPIRIT LAKE (1993)
Directed by Charles Pinion. Written by
Annabelle Lee,
Charles Pinion.

REPO MAN (1984)
Written and directed by
Alex Cox.

RETURN OF THE KILLER TOMATOES! (1988)
Directed by John De
Bello. Written by Stephen
Andrich, John De Bello,
Costa Dillon, and J.
Stephen Peace.

ROBOT MONSTER (1953)
Directed by Phil Tucker.
Written by Wyott Ordung.

ROCK AND ROLL HIGH SCHOOL (1979)
Directed by Alan Arkush and Joe
Dante. Written by Richard Whitley,
Russ Dvonch, and Joseph McBride,
story by Alan Arkush and Joe Dante.

ROCK AND ROLL NIGHTMARE (1987)
Directed by John Fasano.
Written by Jon Mikl Thor.

THE ROOM (2003)
Written and directed by
Tommy Wiseau.

RUBBER (2010)
Written and directed by
Quentin Dupieux.

THE RULING CLASS (1972)
Directed by Peter Medak.
Written by Peter Barnes,
from his stage play.

SANTO VS. LAS MUJERES VAMPIRO (1962)
Directed by Alfonso
Corona Blake. Written
by Antonio Orellana,
Fernando Osés, and
Rafael García Travesi.

SCARE THEIR PANTS OFF (1968)
Written and directed by John Maddox.

THE BIZARRO ENCYCLOPEDIA OF FILM

SCHIZOPOLIS (1996)
Written and directed by
Steven Soderbergh.

SCREAMPLAY (1985)
Directed by Rufus Butler Seder.
Written by Ed Greenberg and Rufus
Butler Seder.

SEIZURE (1974)
Directed by Oliver Stone. Written by
Edward Mann and Oliver Stone.

SHATTER DEAD (1994)
Written and directed by
Scooter McCrae.

SHOWGIRLS (1995)
Directed by Paul Verhoeven. Written
by Joe Eszterhas.

THE SINFUL DWARF (1973)
Directed by Vidal Raski. Written by
Harlan Asquith and William Mayo.

SKIDOO (1968)
Directed by Otto Preminger.
Written by Doran William Cannon.

SPERMULA (1976)
Written and directed by
Charles Matton.

SPIDER BABY (1967)
Written and directed by Jack Hill.

SPIRAL/UZUMAKI (2000)
Directed by Higuchinsky. Written by
Junji Ito, Kengo Kaji, Takao Nitta, and
Chika Yasuo.

SSSSSSSSSSSS (1973)
Directed by Bernard L. Kowalski.
Written by Hal Dresner and
Daniel C. Striepeke.

STRAIGHT TO HELL (1986)
Directed by Alex Cox. Written by
Alex Cox and Dick Rude.

STREET TRASH (1987)
Directed by James M. Muro. Written
by Roy Frumkes.

SUPERVIXENS! (1975)
Written and directed by Russ Meyer.

SWISS ARMY MAN (2016)
Written and directed by Dan Kwan,
Daniel Scheinert

**TALES FROM THE GIMLI HOSPITAL
(1988)**
Written and directed by Guy Maddin.

TERROR FIRMER (1999)
Directed by Lloyd Kaufman. Written
by Patrick Cassidy, Douglas Buck,
Lloyd Kaufman and James Gunn.

TERROR OF TINY TOWN (1938)
Directed by Sam Newfield. Written by
Fred Myton and Clarence Marks.

THOUSAND PLEASURES (1968)
Directed by Michael Findlay. Written
by Berla L. Moke.

THE TOXIC AVENGER (1984)
Directed by Lloyd Kaufman and Michael Herz. Written by Lloyd Kaufman and Joe Ritter.

TRAILER TOWN (2003)
Written and directed by Giuseppe Andrews.

TRASH HUMPERS (2009)
Written and directed by Harmony Korine.

TRIBULATION 99 (1992)
Written and directed by Craig Baldwin.

TROLL 2 (1990)
Directed by Claudio Fragrasso. Written by Rossella Drudi and Claudio Fragrasso.

TROMEO AND JULIET (1996)
Directed by Lloyd Kaufman. Written by James Gunn, Lloyd Kaufman, Andrew Deemer, Jason Green, Phil Rivo, and William Shakespeare.

TWISTED ISSUES (1988)
Directed by Charles Pinion. Written by Stephen L. Antczak (as Steve Antczack), Charles Pinion.

THE ULTIMATE DEGENERATE (1969)
Written and directed by Michael Findlay.

UNITED TRASH (1996)
Directed by Christoph Schlingensief. Written by Christoph Schlingensief and Oskar Roehler.

UP! (1976)
Directed by Russ Meyer. Written by Russ Meyer (as B. Callum), Roger Ebert, (as Reinhold Timme), Anthony-James Ryan (as Jim Ryan).

VEGAS IN SPACE (1991)
Directed by Phillip R. Ford. Written by Doris Fish (screenplay), Miss X (screenplay), Phillip R. Ford (screenplay), Raymond Keebaugh (additional dialogue), Sandelle Kincaid (additional dialogue).

VIVA (2007)
Written and directed by Anna Biller.

WE AWAIT (1996)
Directed by Charles Pinion Written by Charles Pinion, Ellen Smithy, John Walsh.

WEASELS RIP MY FLESH (1979)
Written and directed by Nathan Schiff.

WILD IN THE STREETS (1968)
Directed by Barry Shear. Written by Robert Thom.

THE MANIAC MAGICIAN WHOSE MONSTROUS TRICKS ACTUALLY WORK!

SCENES SO FAR BEYOND ANY YOU'VE EVER SEEN THAT NO DESCRIPTION IS POSSIBLE!

IN DEVASTATING COLOR

THE WIZARD OF GORE

From HERSCHELL GORDON LEWIS, Director of BLOOD FEAST and 2000 MANIACS!

THE WIZARD OF GORE (1970)
Directed by Herschell Gordon Lewis. Written by Allen Kahn.

THE WIZARD OF GORE (2007)
Directed by Jeremy Kasten. Written by Zach Chassler.

CHILDREN'S

I've always adored the fact that most stories written for children—and certainly almost all stories written by children—are inescapably Bizarro in nature. Because let's face it: when we come into this world, pretty much EVERYTHING is weird. Trying to make sense of it is a full-time job for the budding human, and the connections we draw are as randomly intuited as a grownup on a boatload of LSD, as scrambled as our first box of crayons from the second we get our hands on it.

And as we grow up, there's almost nothing more fun than telling insane stories to our children, or any other kids within making-shit-up range. Dr. Seuss was my first art hero, making me fall in love with both words and pictures; and the mad tales he wove made as much sense or more than anything else my parents or sisters said. When I had my own kids, those were the first books they got. And now that I've got grandkids? GUESS WHO GOT DR. SEUSS?

Bottom line: the second animals and inanimate objects start talking, the Bizarro meter's running. And though huge parts of our cultural machinery are devoted to beating our sense of wonder to death by the time we're out of high school, there's something beautiful about the fact that we feel duty-bound to feed that imagination first.

And Bizarro is the thing that feeds us our first stories. As such, in many ways, it is our foundational storytelling modality. Something to keep in mind, as we move toward more "adult" fare in the many aisles to come. (JS)

THE BIZARRO ENCYCLOPEDIA OF FILM

THE 5,000 FINGERS OF DR. T (1953)
Directed by Roy Rowland. Written by Dr. Seuss and Alan Scott.

THE ADVENTURES OF TIN TIN (2011)
Directed by Steven Spielberg, Written by Herge and Steven Moffat.

ALICE IN WONDERLAND (1949)
Directed by Dallas Bower. Written by Henry Myers, Albert Lewin, Edward Eliscu, from the novel by Lewis Carroll.

ALICE IN WONDERLAND (1951)
Directed by Clyde Geronimi, Wilfred Jackson, and Hamilton Luske. Written by Lewis Carroll.

ALL DOGS GO TO HEAVEN (1989)
Directed by Don Bluth, Gary Goldman, and Dan Kuenster. Written by Don Bluth, Ken Cromar, Gary Goldman, Larry Leker, Linda Miller, Monica Parker, John Pomeroy, Guy Shulman, David Steinberg, David N. Weiss.

ANTZ (1998)
Directed by Eric Darnell, Tim Johnson. Written by Todd Alcott, Chris Weitz, and Paul Weitz.

ATLANTIS (2001)
Directed by Gary Trousdale, Kirk Wise. Written by Tab Murphy and Kirk Wise.

BEDKNOBS AND BROOMSTICKS (1971)
Directed by Robert Stevenson. Written by Ralph Wright, Ted Berman, Bill Walsh, Don DaGradi, Mary Norton, and Ken Anderson.

BEETLEJUICE (1988)
Directed by Tim Burton. Written by Michael McDowell, Larry Wilson, and Warren Skaaren.

THE BLACK CAULDRON (1985)
Directed by Ted Berman and Richard Rich. Written by Lloyd Alexander and David Jonas.

THE BLACK HOLE (1979)
Directed by Gary Nelson. Written by Jeb Rosebrook, Bob Barbash, Richard H. Landau, Jeb Rosebrook and Gerry Day.

THE BRAVE LITTLE TOASTER (1987)
Directed by Jerry Rees. Written by Thomas M. Disch, Jerry Rees, Joe Ranft and Brian McEntee.

THE BIZARRO ENCYCLOPEDIA OF FILM

BRIDGE TO TARABITHIA (1985)
Directed by Eric Till. Written by Katherine Paterson and Nancy Sackett.

THE BOX TROLLS (2014)
Directed by Graham Annable and Anthony Stacchi. Written by Irena Brignull, Adam Pava, Alan Snow, Anthony Stacchi, Phil Dale, and Vera Brosgol.

A BUG'S LIFE (1998)
Directed by John Lasseter and Andrew Stanton. Written by John Lasseter, Andrew Stanton, Joe Ranft, Don McEnery, and Bob Shaw.

CARS (2006)
Directed by John Lasseter and Joe Ranft. Written by John Lasseter, Joe Ranft, Jorgen Klubien, Dan Fogelman, Kiel Murray, Phil Lorin, and Jorgen Klubien.

CHICKEN LITTLE (2005)
Directed by Mark Dindal. Written by Steve Bencich, Ron J. Friedman, and Ron Anderson. Story by Mark Dindal and Mark Kennedy. Additional material (of various sorts) by Ronald L. Baird, David Gerson, Sara Parriott, Josann McGibbon, David Reynolds, and Sandra Tsing Loh.

CHICKEN RUN (2000)
Directed by Peter Lord and Nick Park. Written by Peter Lord, Nick Park, Karey Kirkpatrick, Mark Burton, and John O'Farrell.

A CHRISTMAS STORY (1983)
Directed by Bob Clark. Written by Jean Shepherd, Leigh Brown, Bob Clark, from the novel "In God We Trust, All Others Pay Cash" by Jean Shepherd.

CHRONICLES OF NARNIA (2005)
Directed by Andrew Adamson. Written by Ann Peacock, Andrew Adamson, Christopher Markus, Stephen McFeely, and C.S. Lewis.

CLOUDY WITH A CHANCE OF MEATBALLS (2009)
Directed by Phil Lord and Christopher Miller. Written by Phil Lord, Christopher Miller, Judi Barrett, Ron Barrett and Rob Greenberg.

CORALINE (2009)
Directed by Henry Selick. Written by Henry Selick and Neil Gaiman.

THE CORPSE BRIDE (2005)

Directed by Tim Burton, Mike Johnson. Written by Tim Burton, Carolos Grangel, John August, Caroline Thompson, and Pamela Pettler.

THE CROODS (2013)

Directed by Kirk De Micco and Chris Sanders. Written by Chris Sanders, Kirk De Micco and John Cleese.

CRY WILDERNESS (1987)

Directed by Jay Schlossberg-Cohen. Written by Philip Yordan.

THE CURSE OF THE WERE-RABBIT (WALLACE AND GROMIT) (2005)

Directed by Steve Box and Nick Park. Written by Steve Box, Nick Park, Mark Burton and Bob Baker.

DARK CRYSTAL (1982)

Directed by Jim Henson and Frank Oz. Written by David Odell and Jim Henson.

DESPICABLE ME (2010)

Directed by Pierre Coffin and Chris Renaud. Written by Cinco Paul, Ken Daurio, and Sergio Pablos.

DROP DEAD FRED (1991)

Directed by Ate de Jong. Written by Elizabeth Livingston, Carlos Davis, and Anthony Fingleton.

DUMBO (1941)

Directed by Samuel Armstrong, Norman Ferguson, Wilfred Jackson, Jack Kinney, Bill Roberts, Ben Sharpsteen, and John Elliotte. Written by Joe Grant and Dick Huemer.

EDWARD SCISSORHANDS (1990)

Directed by Tim Burton. Written by Caroline Thompson, story by Tim Burton and Caroline Thompson.

EPIC (2013)

Directed by Chris Wedge. Written by James V. Hart and William Joyce.

THE EMPEROR'S NEW GROOVE (2000)

Directed by Mark Dindal. Written by Chris Williams and Mark Dindal.

ESCAPE TO WITCH MOUNTAIN (1975)

Directed by John Hough. Written by Robert M. Young and Alexander Key.

FANTASIA (1940)

Directed by James Algar (segment "The Sorcerer's Apprentice", uncredited), Samuel Armstrong (segments "Toccata and Fugue in D Minor", "The Nutcracker Suite", uncredited), Ford Beebe Jr. (segment "The Pastoral Symphony", uncredited), Norman Ferguson (segment "Dance of the Hours", uncredited), Jim Handley (segment "The Pastoral Symphony", uncredited), T. Hee (segment "Dance of the Hours", uncredited), Wilfred Jackson (segment "Night on Bald Mountain/Ave Maria", uncredited), Hamilton Luske (segment "The Pastoral Symphony", uncredited), Bill Roberts (segment "Rite of Spring", uncredited), Paul Satterfield (segment "Rite of Spring", uncredited), Ben Sharpsteen (uncredited). Written by Joe Grant (story direction), Dick Huemer (story direction), Lee Blair (story development, segment "Toccata and Fugue in D Minor"), Elmer Plummer (story development, segment "Toccata and Fugue in D Minor"), Phil Dike (story development, segment "Toccata and Fugue in D Minor"), Sylvia Moberly-Holland (story development, segment "The Nutcracker Suite"), Norman Wright (story development, segment "The Nutcracker Suite"), Albert Heath (story development, segment "The Nutcracker Suite"), Bianca Majolie (story development, segment "The Nutcracker Suite"), Graham Heid (story development, segment "The Nutcracker Suite"), Perce Pearce (story development, segment "The Sorcerer's Apprentice"), Carl Fallberg (story development, segment "The Sorcerer's Apprentice"), William Martin (story development and research, segment "Rite of Spring"), Leo Thiele (story development and research, segment "Rite of Spring"), Robert Sterner (story development and research, segment "Rite of Spring"), John McLeish (story development and research, segment "Rite of Spring"), Otto Englander (story development, segment "The Pastoral Symphony"), Webb Smith (story development, segment "The Pastoral Symphony"), Erdman Penner (story development, segment "The Pastoral Symphony"), Joseph Sabo (story development, segment "The Pastoral Symphony"), Bill Peet (story development, segment "The Pastoral Symphony"), Vernon Stallings (story development, segment "The Pastoral Symphony"), Campbell Grant (story development, segment "Night on Bald Mountain/Ave Maria"), Arthur Heinemann (story development, segment "Night on Bald Mountain/Ave Maria"), Phil Dike (story development, segment "Night on Bald Mountain/Ave Maria")

FANTASTIC MR. FOX (2009)

Directed by Wes Anderson. Written by Roald Dahl, Wes Anderson and Noah Baumbach.

THE BIZARRO ENCYCLOPEDIA OF FILM

FRANKENWEENIE (2012)
Directed by Tim Burton. Written by
Leonard Ripps, Tim Burton and John
August.

FLUSHED AWAY (2006)
Directed by David Bowers and Sam
Fell. Written by Dick Clement and Ian
La Frenais.

FROZEN (2013)
Directed by Chris Buck and Jennifer
Lee. Written by Jennifer Lee, Hans
Christian Anderson, Chris Buck, and
Shane Morris.

GHOSTBUSTERS (1984)
Directed by Ivan Reitman. Written by
Dan Aykroyd and Harold Ramis.

THE GOOD DINOSAUR (2015)
Directed by Peter Sohn. Written by
Bob Peterson and Peter Sohn.

GREMLINS (1984)
Directed by Joe Dante. Written by
Christopher Columbus.

**GREMLINS 2: THE NEW BATCH
(1990)**
Directed by Joe Dante. Written by
Christopher Columbus, Charles S.
Haas (as Charlie Haas).

HAPPY FEET (2006)
Directed by George Miller, Warren
Coleman and Judy Morris. Written
by George Miller, John Collee, Judy
Morris, and Warren Coleman.

HERCULES (1997)
Directed and written by Ron Clements
and John Musker.

THE HOBBIT (animated film) (1977)
Directed by Jules Bass and Arthur
Rankin Jr. Written by J.R.R. Tolkien
and Romeo Muller.

HOCUS POCUS (1993)
Directed by Kenny Ortega.Written
by David Kirschner, Mick Garris and
Neil Cuthbert.

HOME (2015)
Directed by Tim Johnson. Written by
Tom J. Astle, Matt Ember, and
Adam Rex.

HOODWINKED (2005)
Directed and written by Cory Edwards,
Todd Edwards, and Tony Leech.

HOTEL TRANSYLVANIA (2012)
Directed by Genndy Tartakovsky.
Written by Peter Baynham, Robert
Smigel, Todd Durham, Dan Hageman
and Kevin Hageman.

**HOW TO TRAIN YOUR DRAGON
(2010)**
Directed by Dean DeBlois and Chris
Sanders. Written by William Davies,
Dean DeBlois, Chris Sanders, Cressida
Cowel and Adam F. Goldberg.

HOWL'S MOVING CASTLE (2004)
Directed by Hayao Miyazaki.
Written by Hayao Miyazaki and Diana
Wynne Jones.

THE INCREDIBLES (2004)
Directed and written by Brad Bird.

INSIDE OUT (2015)
Directed and written by Pete Docter and Ronnie Del Carmen.

IRON GIANT (1999)
Directed by Brad Bird. Written by Tim McCanlies, Brad Bird and Ted Hughes

JAMES AND THE GIANT PEACH (1996)
Directed by Henry Selick. Written by Roald Dahl, Karey Kirkpatrick, Jonathan Roberts, and Steve Bloom.

JIMMY THE BOY WONDER (1966)
Directed by Herschell Gordon Lewis. Written by Hal Berg.

KUBO AND THE TWO STRINGS
Directed by Travis Knight. Written by Marc Haimes, Chris Butler and Shannon Tindle.

KUNG FU PANDA (2008)
Directed by Mark Osborne and John Stevenson. Written by Jonathan Aibel, Glenn Berger, Ethan Reiff and Cyrus Voris.

LABYRINTH (1986)
Directed by Jim Henson. Written by Dennis Lee, Jim Henson, and Terry Jones.

THE LAST UNICORN (1982)
Directed by Jules Bass and Arthur Rankin Jr. Written by Peter S. Beagle.

THE LEGO MOVIE (2014)
Directed by Phil Lord and Christopher Miller. Written by Phil Lord, Christopher Miller, Dan Hageman and Kevin Hageman.

LILO AND STITCH (2002)
Directed by Dean DeBlois and Chris Sanders. Written by Chris Sanders.

LITTLE NEMO (1989)
Directed by Masami Hata and William T. Hurtz. Written by Chris Columbus, Richard Outten, Jean Giraud, Yutaka Fukioka, and Winsor McCay.

LITTLE MONSTERS (1989)
Directed by Richard Greenberg. Written by Terry Rossio and Ted Elliot.

THE BIZARRO ENCYCLOPEDIA OF FILM

THE LORAX (2012)
Directed by Chris Renaud and Kyle Balda. Written by Dr. Seuss and Cinco Paul.

MALEFICENT (2014)
Directed by Robert Stromberg. Written by Linda Woolverton and Charles Perrault.

MATILDA (1996)
Directed by Danny Devito. Written by Roald Dahl and Nicholas Kazan.

MEET THE ROBINSONS (2007)
Directed by Stephen J. Anderson. Written by Jon Bernstein and Michelle Bochner Spitz.

MEGAMIND (2010)
Directed by Tom McGrath. Written by Alan Schoolcraft and Brent Simons.

MINIONS (2015)
Directed by Kyle Balda and Pierre Coffin. Written by Brian Lynch.

MIRRORMASK (2005)
Directed by Dave McKean. Written by Neil Gaiman and Dave McKean

MOANA (2016)
Directed by Ron Clements, Don Hall, John Musker, and Chris Williams. Written by Jared Bush.

MONSTER HOUSE (2006)
Directed by Gil Kenan. Written by Dan Harmon, Rob Schrab, and Pamela Pettler.

MONSTERS INC (2001)
Directed by Pete Docter, David Silverman, and Lee Unkrich. Written by Pete Docter, Jill Culton, Jeff Pidgeon, Ralph Eggleston, Andrew Stanton, and Daniel Gerson.

MONSTERS VS. ALIENS (2009)
Directed by Rob Letterman and Conrad Vernon. Written by Maya Forbes and Wallace Wolodarsky.

MR. PEABODY AND MR. SHERMAN (2014)
Directed by Rob Minkoff. Written by Jay Ward and Craig Wright.

MY NEIGHBOR TOTORO (1988)
Directed and written by Hayao Miyazaki.

A MOUSE AND HIS CHILD (1977)
Directed by Charles Swenson, Fred Wolf. Written by Russell Hoban (novel), Carol Monpere (screenplay)

MUPPETS FROM SPACE (1999)
Directed by Tim Hill. Written by Jerry Juhl, Joey Mazzarino, and Ken Kaufman.

THE BIZARRO ENCYCLOPEDIA OF FILM

MUPPETS TAKE MANHATTAN (1984)
Directed by Frank Oz. Written by Tom Patchett, Jay Tarses and Frank Oz.

THE NEVERENDING STORY (1984)
Directed by Wolfgang Petersen. Written by Wolfgang Petersen, Herman Weigel, Michael Ende, and Robert Easton.

THE NIGHTMARE BEFORE CHRISTMAS (1993)
Directed by Henry Selick. Written by Tim Burton, Michael McDowell, and Caroline Thompson.

PAGEMASTER (1984)
Directed by Pixote Hunt and Joe Johnston. Written by David Kirschner and David Casci.

PARANORMAN (2012)
Directed by Chris Butler and Sam Fell. Written by Chris Butler.

THE PEANUT BUTTER SOLUTION (1985)
Directed by Michael Rubbo. Written by Vojtech Jasný, Andrée Pelletier, Louise Pelletier, and Michael Rubbo.

PEE-WEE'S BIG ADVENTURE (1985)
Directed by Tim Burton. Written by Phil Hartman, Paul Reubens.

PERCY JACKSON SERIES (2013)
Directed by Thor Freudenthal. Written by Marc Guggenheim and Rick Riordian.

PETE'S DRAGON (1977)
Directed by Don Chafey. Written by Malcolm Marmorstein, story by Seton I. Miller and S.S. Fields.

PETE'S DRAGON (2016)
Directed by David Lowery. Written David Lowery and Toby Halbrooks.

PINNOCHIO (1940)
Directed by Norman Ferguson and T. Hee. Written by Carlo Collodi and Ted Sears.

PONYO (2008)
Directed and written by Hayao Miyazaki.

PRINCESS MONONOKE (1997)
Directed and written by Hayao Miyazaki.

PUFF THE MAGIC DRAGON (1978)
Directed by Charles Swenson and Fred Wolf. Written by Romeo Muller.

RETURN TO OZ (1985)
Directed by Walter Murch. Written by Walter Murch, Gill Dennis, based on the books by L. Frank Baum.

RETURN FROM WITCH MOUNTAIN (1978)
Directed by John Hough. Written by Malcolm Marmorstein and Alexander Key.

THE BIZARRO ENCYCLOPEDIA OF FILM

RISE OF THE GUARDIANS (2012)
Directed by Peter Ramsey. Written by
David Lindsay-Abaire and
William Joyce.

ROBIN HOOD (1973)
Directed by Wolfgang Reitherman.
Written by Larry Clemmons and
Ken Anderson.

SANTA CLAUS (1959)
Directed by René Cardona.
Written by Adolfo Torres Portillo and
René Cardona.

**SANTA CLAUS CONQUERS THE
MARTIANS (1964)**
Directed by Nicholas Webster.
Written by Glenville Mareth and
Paul L. Jacobson.

THE SECRET OF NIMH (1982)
Directed by Don Bluth. Written by
Don Bluth, Robert C. O'Brien,
Gary Goldman, John Pomeroy, and
Will Finn.

SHREK SERIES (2001)
Directed by Andrew Adamson and
Vicky Jenson. Written by William
Steig and Ted Elliot.

**SOMETHING WICKED THIS WAY
COMES (1983)**
Directed by Jack Clayton. Written by
Ray Bradbury.

SPACE JAM (1996)
Directed by Joe Pytka. Written by Leo
Benvenuti and Steve Rudnick.

SPIRITED AWAY (2001)
Written and directed by Hayao
Miyazaki.

**THE SPONGEBOB MOVIE: SPONGE
OUT OF WATER (2015)**
Directed by Paul Tibbitt and Mike
Mitchell. Written by Glenn Berger and
Jonathan Aibel.

**THE SPONGEBOB SQUAREPANTS
MOVIE (2004)**
Directed by Stephen Hillenburg and
Mark Osborne. Written by Stephen
Hillenberg.

STORKS (2016)
Directed by Nicholas Stoller and Doug
Sweetland. Written by Nicholas Stoller.

TANGLED (2010)
Directed by Nathan Greno and Byron
Howard. Written by Dan Fogelman
and Jacob Grimm.

THE TALE OF DESPEREAUX (2008)
Directed by Sam Fell and Robert
Stevenhagen. Written by Kate
DiCamillo and Will McRobb.

TIME BANDITS (1981)
Directed by Terry Gilliam. Written by
Michael Palin, Terry Gilliam.

TITAN A.E. (2000)
Directed by Don Bluth and Gary
Goldman. Written by Hans Bauer and
Randall McCormick.

THE BIZARRO ENCYCLOPEDIA OF FILM

A TOWN CALLED PANIC (2009)
Written and directed by Stephane Aubier and Vincent Patar.

TOY STORY SERIES (1995)
Directed by John Lasseter. Written by John Lasseter and Pete Docter.

TREASURE PLANET (2002)
Directed by Ron Clements and John Musker. Written by Robert Louis Stevenson and Ron Clements.

TRON (1982)
Directed and written by Steven Lisberger.

TURBO (2013)
Directed by David Soren. Written by Darren Lemke and Robert D. Siegel.

UP (2009)
Directed and written by Pete Docter and Bob Peterson.

WALL-E (2008)
Directed by Andrew Stanton. Written by Andrew Stanton and Pete Docter.

WATERSHIP DOWN (1978)
Directed by Martin Rosen. Written by Martin Rosen and Richard Adams (novel).

WHERE THE WILD THINGS ARE (2009)
Directed by Spike Jonze. Written by Spike Jonze and Dave Eggers.

WHO FRAMED ROGER RABBIT (1988)
Directed by Robert Zemeckis

WILLIE WONKA AND THE CHOCOLATE FACTORY (1971)
Directed by Herschell Gordon Lewis. Written by Roald Dahl, from his book "Charlie and the Chocolate Factory".

WIND IN THE WILLOWS (1983)
Directed by Mark Hall and Chris Taylor. Written by Kenneth Grahame and Rosemary Anne Sisson.

THE WITCHES (1990)
Directed by Nicolas Roeg. Written by Roald Dahl and Allan Scott.

WIZARD OF OZ (1939)
Directed by Victor Fleming, George Cukor, Mervyn LeRoy, Norman Taurog, and King Vidor.

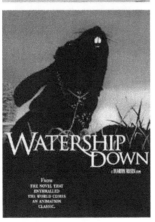

THE BIZARRO ENCYCLOPEDIA OF FILM

WONDERFUL LAND OF OZ (1969)
Directed by Barry Mahon. Written by Barry Mahon and L. Frank Baum (novel)

WRECK-IT RALPH (2012)
Directed by Rich Moore. Written by Rich Moore and Phil Johnston.

YOKAI MONSTERS: SPOOK WARFARE (1968)
Directed by Yoshiyuki Kuroda. Written by Tetsuro Yoshida.

THE GREAT YOKAI WAR
Directed by Takashi Miike. Written by Hiroshi Aramata, Takashi Miike, Mitsuhiko Sawamura, and Takehiko Itakura.

ZOOTOPIA (2016)
Directed by Byron Howard, Rich Moore, and Jared Bush. Written by Byron Howard, Rich Moore, Jared Bush, Jim Reardon, Josie Trinidad, Phil Johnston and Jennifer Lee.

FANTASY & SCIENCE FICTION

Fantasy, as a rule, draws its power from our mythic past. Faerie tales, legends, religious and spiritual iconography mark the transition from "Children's stories" to more complex attempts at making sense of the universe at large.

Science fiction, on the other hand, is a much more recent and forward-looking genre, using past and present as launching pads for projecting into the future. And it's always struck me as strange that the two were so often sandwiched together.

But honestly? Robots and aliens are the elves and demons of tomorrow. And the nascent A.I. that awaits us is every bit as potentially all-knowing and terrifying as the gods that many of us still love and fear.

So here are our fantasized projections of our pasts and futures, laid out together in full Bizarro regalia. Because if this shit isn't weird, I don't know what is. (JS)

2001: A SPACE ODYSSEY (1968)
Directed by Stanley Kubrick. Written by Stanley Kubrick and Arthur C. Clarke.

THE ADVENTURES OF BARON MUNCHAUSEN (1988)
Directed by Terry Gilliam. Written by Charles McKeown, Terry Gilliam.

THE ADVENTURES OF BUCKAROO BANZAI ACROSS THE EIGHTH DIMENSION (1984)
Directed by W.D. Richter. Written by Earl Mac Rauch.

AELITA QUEEN OF MARS (1924)
Directed by Yakov Protazanov. Written by Aleksai Fajko, Fyodor Otsep and Aleksei Tolstoy (story).

AKIRA (1988)
Directed by Katsuhiro Ôtomo. Written by Katsuhiro Ôtomo. Izo Hashimoto, from Katsuhiro Ôtomo's graphic novel.

ALIEN (1979)
Directed by Ridley Scott. Written by Dan O'Bannon. Story by Dan O'Bannon and Ronald Shusett.

ALIEN FROM LA (1988)
Directed by Albert Pyun. Written by Debra Ricci, Regina Davis and Albert Pyun.

ALIENS (1986)
Written and directed by James Cameron. Story by James Cameron, David Giler, and Walter Hill, from characters created by Dan O'Bannon and Ronald Shusett.

ALTERED STATES (1980)
Directed by Ken Russell. Written by Paddy Chayefsky (as Sidney Aaron), from his novel.

BARBARELLA (1968)
Directed by Roger Vadim. Written by Terry Southern, Roger Vadim, from the comics by Jean-Claude Forest, Claude Brulé, Vittorio Bonicelli, Clement Biddle Wood, Brian Degas, and Tudor Gates.

BEYOND THE BLACK RAINBOW (2010)
Written and directed by Panos Cosmatos.

BIG-ASS SPIDER (2013)
Directed by Mike Mendez. Written by Gregory Gieras.

BLADE RUNNER (1982)
Directed by Ridley Scott. Written by Hampton Fancher and David Webb Peoples (as David Peoples), from the novel *Do Androids Dream of Electric Sheep?* by Philip K. Dick.

THE BRAIN THAT WOULDN'T DIE (1962)
Directed by Joseph Green. Written by Joseph Green (screenplay and original story), Rex Carlton (original story)

BRAINSTORM (1983)
Directed by Douglas Trumbull. Written by Robert Stitzel, Philip Frank Messina, story by Bruce Joel Rubin.

BRAZIL (1985)
Directed by Terry Gilliam. Written by Terry Gilliam, Tom Stoppard, Charles McKeown.

BREAD AND CIRCUS (2003)
Written by directed by Martin Loke.

CHILDREN OF MEN (2006)
Directed by Alfonso Cuarón. Written by Alfonso Cuarón, Timothy J. Sexton, David Arata, Mark Fergus, Hawk Ostby, from the novel by P. D. James.

CITY OF LOST CHILDREN (1995)

Directed by Marc Caro and Jean-Pierre Jeunet. Written by Gilles Adrien, Jean-Pierre Jeunet and Marc Caro.

CLASS OF 1999 (1990)

Directed by Mark L. Lester. Written by Mark L. Lester (story), C. Courtney Joyner, John Skipp (uncredited), Craig Spector (uncredited), and Abbe Wool (uncredited).

A CLOCKWORK ORANGE (1971)

Written and directed by Stanley Kubrick, from the novel by Anthony Burgess.

CLOUD ATLAS (2012)

Directed by Tom Tykwer, Lana Wachowski, Lilly Wachowski. Written by Lana Wachowski, Tom Tykwer, and Lilly Wachowski, from the novel by David Mitchell.

COMMUNION (1989)

Directed by Philippe Mora. Written by Whitley Strieber (book and screenplay).

THE COMPANY OF WOLVES (1984)

Directed by Neil Jordan. Written by Angela Carter and Neil Jordan, from Carter's books.

THE CURIOUS DR. HUMPP (1969)

Directed and written by Emilio Vieyra.

THE DARK CRYSTAL (1982)

Directed by Jim Henson, Frank Oz. Written by David Odell, story by Jim Henson.

DARK STAR (1974)

Directed by John Carpenter. Written by John Carpenter and Dan O'Bannon.

DEATH POWDER (1986)

Written and directed by Shigeru Izumiya.

DEMON CITY SHINJUKU (1988)

Directed by Yoshiaki Kawajiri. Written by Hideyuki Kikuchi (novel), Kaori Okamura.

THE DIABOLICAL DR. Z (1966)

Directed by Jess Franco (as J. Franco). Written by Jess Franco and Jean-Claude Carriere.

THE BIZARRO ENCYCLOPEDIA OF FILM

DISTRICT NINE (2009)
Directed by Neill Blomkamp. Written by Neill Blomkamp, Terri Tatchell.

ESCAPE FROM TOMORROW (2013)
Written and directed by Randy Moore.

ETERNAL SUNSHINE OF THE SPOTLESS MIND (2004)
Directed by Michel Gondry. Written by Charlie Kaufman, story by Charlie Kaufman, Michel Gondry and Pierre Bismuth.

EXISTENZ (1999)
Written and directed by David Cronenberg.

EXORCIST II: THE HERETIC (1977)
Directed by John Boorman. Written by William Goodhart, from characters created by William Peter Blatty.

THE FALL (2006)
Directed by Tarsem Singh (as Tarsem). Written by Dan Gilroy, Nico Soultanakis, and Tarsem Singh, from the screenplay *Yo Ho Ho* by Valeri Petrov (as Valery Petrov).

FANTASTIC PLANET (1973)
Directed by René Laloux. Written by Roland Topor and René Laloux, from the novel by Stefan Wul.

THE FIFTH ELEMENT (1997)
Directed by Luc Besson. Written by Luc Besson, Robert Mark Kamen, story by Luc Besson.

FLASH GORDON (1980)
Directed by Mike Hodges. Written by Lorenzo Semple Jr., Michael Allin and Alex Raymond (character creator)

GALAXY QUEST (1999)
Directed by Dean Parisot. Written by David Howard and Robert Gordon, story by David Howard.

GHOSTS OF MARS (2001)
Directed by John Carpenter. Written by John Carpenter and Larry Sulkis.

GINSENG KING (1989)
Directed by Ru-Tar Rotar.

GODZILLA VS HEDORAH (1971)
Directed by Yoshimitsu Banno. Written by Yoshimitsu Banno and Takeshi Kimura

GOKE, BODY SNATCHER FROM HELL (1968)
Directed by Hajime Sato. Written by Kyuzo Kobayashi, Susumu Takaku.

GRAVITY (2013)
Directed by Alfonso Cuarón. Written by Alfonso and Jonas Cuarón.

HARDWARE (1990)
Directed by Richard Stanley. Written by Steve MacManus, Kevin O'Neill, Richard Stanley and Michael Fallon.

HEADS OF CONTROL: THE GORAL BAHEAU BRAIN EXPEDITION (2006)
Written and directed by Pat Tremblay.

HELLACIOUS ACRES: THE CASE OF JOHN GLASS (2011)
Written and directed by Pat Tremblay.

THE HOST (2006)
Directed by Joon-ho Bong (as Joon Ho Bong). Written by Joon-ho Bong (as Joon Ho Bong), Won-jun Ha (as Jun-won Ha), and Chul-hyun Baek.

ICE FROM THE SUN (1999)
Written and directed by Eric Stanze.

IDAHO TRANSFER (1973)
Directed by Peter Fonda. Written by Thomas Matthiesen (story and screenplay).

INVADERS FROM MARS (1953)
Directed by William Cameron Menzies. Written by Richard Blake.

INVADERS FROM MARS (1986)
Directed by Tobe Hooper. Written by Don Jakoby, Dan O'Bannon, and based on screenplay by Richard Blake.

INVASION FROM INNER EARTH (1974)
Directed by Bill Rebane. Written by Barbara J. Rebane.

INVASION OF THE BEE GIRLS (1973)
Directed by Denis Sanders. Written by Nicholas Meyer.

INVASION OF THE BODY SNATCHERS (1956)
Directed by Don Siegel. Written by Daniel Mainwaring, from the novel *Body Snatchers* by Jack Finney.

INVASION OF THE BODY SNATCHERS (1978)
Directed by Philip Kaufman. Written by W.D. Richter, from the novel *Body Snatchers* by Jack Finney.

IT! THE TERROR FROM BEYOND SPACE (1958)
Directed by Edward L. Cahn. Written by Jerome Bixby.

IT CONQUERED THE WORLD (1956)
Directed by Roger Corman. Written by Lou Rusoff.

IT'S A WONDERFUL LIFE (1946)
Directed by Frank Capra. Written by Frances Goodrich, Albert Hackett, and Frank Capra.

JOHN DIES AT THE END (2012)
Written and directed by Don Coscarelli, from the book by David Wong.

JOURNEY TO THE WEST: CONQUERING THE DEMONS (2013)
Directed by Stephen Chow. Written by Stephen Chow, Derek Kwok, Xin Huo, Yun Wang, Fung Chih Chiang, Lu Zheng Wu, Lee Sheung Shing, and Y.Y. Kong.

THE KILLER SHREWS (1959)
Directed by Ray Kellogg. Written by Jay Simms.

KILLERS FROM SPACE (1954)
Directed by W. Lee Wilder. Written by William Raynor and Myles Wilder (story).

THE LAST CIRCUS (2012)
Written and directed by Álex de la Iglesia.

LEGEND (1985)
Directed by Ridley Scott. Written by William Hjortsberg.

LIFEFORCE (1985)
Directed by Tobe Hooper. Written by Dan O'Bannon, Don Jakoby, Michael Armstrong (uncredited), Olaf Pooley (uncredited), and based on the novel *Space Vampires* by Colin Wilson.

LIQUID DREAMS (1991)
Directed by Mark S. Manos. Written by Zack Davis and Mark S. Manos.

LIQUID SKY (1982)
Directed by Slava Tsukerman. Written by Slava Tsukerman. Anne Carlisle and Nina V. Kerova.

LOGAN'S RUN (1976)
Directed by Michael Anderson. Written by David Zelag Goodman, from the novel by William F. Nolan and George Clayton Johnson.

LOOPER (2012)
Written and directed by Rian Johnson.

THE MAN WHO FELL TO EARTH (1976)
Directed by Nicolas Roeg. Written by Paul Mayerberg, from the novel by Walter Tevis.

THE MERMAID (2016)
Directed by Stephen Chow. Written by Stephen Chow, Hing-Ka Chan, Chi Keung Fung, Miu-Kei Ho, Ivy Kong, Si-Cheun Lee, Zhengyu Lu, and Kan-Cheung Tsang.

MIDNIGHT IN PARIS (2011)
Written and directed by Woody Allen.

THE MILDEW FROM PLANET

XONADER (2015)
Directed by Giulio De Santi, Neil Meschino. Written by Giulio De Santi, Dave Fogerson, Tiziana Machella, Neil Meschino.

NEW ROSE HOTEL (1998)
Directed by Abel Ferrara. Written by Christ Zois, Abel Ferrara, based on the short story by William Gibson.

NIGHT TIDE (1961)
Written and directed by Curtis Harrington.

EL NIÑO DE LA LUNA (1989)
Written and directed by Agustí Villaronga.

THE OMEGA MAN (1971)
Directed by Boris Sagal. Written by John William Corrington, Joyce Hooper Corrington (as Joyce H. Corrington), and (uncredited) William Peter Blatty. From the novel *I Am Legend* by Richard Matheson.

THE OUTRAGEOUS BARON MUNCHAUSEN (1961)
Directed by Karel Zeman. Written by Karel Zeman, Josef Kainar, Jirí Brdecka.

PAN'S LABYRINTH (2006)
Written and directed by Guillermo del Toro

PLANET OF THE APES (1968)
Directed by Franklin J. Schaffner. Written by Rod Serling and Michael Wilson, from the book by Pierre Boulle.

THE PRINCESS BRIDE (1987)
Directed by Rob Reiner. Written by William Goldman, from his book.

THE PURPLE ROSE OF CAIRO (1985)
Written and directed by Woody Allen.

QUEEN OF BLOOD (1966)
Written and directed by Curtis Harrington.

THE BIZARRO ENCYCLOPEDIA OF FILM

RADIOACTIVE DREAMS (1985)
Written and directed by Albert Pyun.

ROBOCOP (1987)
Directed by Paul Verhoeven. Written by Edward Nuemeier and Michael Miner.

ROBOGEISHA (2009)
Written and directed by Noboru Iguchi.

ROUJIN Z (1991)
Directed by Hiroyuki Kitakubo. Written by William Flanagan (subtitle translation), Katsuhiro Otomo.

A SCANNER DARKLY (2006)
Written and directed by Richard Linklater, from the novel by Philip K. Dick.

SNOWPIERCER (2013)
Directed by Joon Ho Bong. Written by Joon Ho Bong and Kelly Masterson.

SOYLENT GREEN (1973)
Directed by Richard Fleischer. Written by Stanley R. Greenberg, from the novel *Make Room! Make Room!* by Harry Harrison.

STARSHIP TROOPERS (1997)
Directed by Paul Verhoeven. Written by Edward Nuemeier, from the novel by Robert Heinlein.

TANK GIRL (1995)
Directed by Rachel Talalay. Written by Tedi Sarafian, based on the comics by Alan Martin and Jamie Hewlett.

TERMINATOR 2: JUDGMENT DAY (1991)
Directed by James Cameron. Written by James Cameron and William Wisher Jr.

TETSUO (1989)
Written and directed by Shin'ya Tsukamoto.

THESE ARE THE DAMNED (1962)
Directed by Joseph Losey. Written by Evan Jones, based on the novel *Children of Light* by H. L. Lawrence.

THEY LIVE (1988)
Written and directed by John Carpenter, from the short story "Eight O' Clock in the Morning" by Ray Nelson.

TROLLHUNTER (2010)
Written and directed by André Øvredal.

THE BIZARRO ENCYCLOPEDIA OF FILM

TURBO KID (2015)
Written and directed by
François Simard, Anouk
Whissell, and Yoann-
Karl Whissell.

**TWELVE MONKEYS
(1995)**
Directed by Terry
Gilliam. Written by
David Webb Peoples (as
David Peoples) and Janet
Peoples, from the short
film *Le Jetée* by Chris
Marker.

**THE VALLEY OF
GWANGI (1969)**
Directed by Jim
O'Connolly. Written by
William Bast and Julian
Moore.

**VANISHING WAVES
(2012)**
Directed by Kristina
Buozyte. Written by
Kristina Buozyte, Bruno
Samper.

WARNING FROM SPACE (1956)
Directed by Koji Shima. Written by
Jay Cipes (English dialogue), Gentaro
Nakajima (novel), Hideo Oguni,
Edward Palmer (English dialogue).

WESTWORLD (1973)
Written and directed by
Michael Crichton.

**THE WORLD'S END
(2013)**
Directed by Edgar
Wright. Written by Edgar
Wright and Simon Pegg.

**X: THE MAN WITH
X-RAY EYES (1963)**
Directed by Roger
Corman. Written by
Robert Dillon and Ray
Russell.

**ZONTAR, THE THING
FROM VENUS (1966)**
Directed by Larry
Buchanan. Written by
Hillman Taylor and Larry
Buchanan.

ZOTZ! (1962)
Directed by William
Castle. Written by Ray
Russell (screenplay) and
Walter Karig (novel).

HORROR

Here's where the shit hits the fan, both mythologically and in gruesomely practical terms. Because whether past or future, for kids or grownups, horror is the fiction of worst-case scenarios. The nightmare zone. Where the Bad Things Happen. And the monsters dwell.

It should go without saying that zombies, werewolves, vampires, ghosts, Lovecraftian monstrosities, and all the wickedest hellscape tropes of fantasy and science fiction are Bizarro as fuck. But once you add psychological horror to the mix, all bets are off. Because madness — the mind darkly askew, drawing all the wrong connections, and executing from there — is a trillion times worse than Godzilla. Unless, of course, Godzilla actually steps on your head.

It should be duly noted that only porn is more looked-down-upon than horror in the genre sweepstakes. Both show us the things we're told we shouldn't be looking at. Even though sex and mayhem are primary selling points for EVERY other genre.

In the end, I think of horror as an ingredient rather than a genre. Much as I regard Bizarro. It's a "Gusto-Adding Flavor"!

But horror as a genre is vast and sprawling, finding a million ways to lean into that nightmare that haunts to the bone. It's my second-favorite genre, tied with its flip-side: Comedy. And much of the best horror does both, flipping laffs and tragedy.

As we plumb our fear of the unknown. The weirdest shit there is. (J.S.)

THE BIZARRO ENCYCLOPEDIA OF FILM

Everything John wrote above hits the nail on the head perfectly here, but as a former monster kid, I had to chime in. The appeal of horror to both children and adults alike is equal parts of the fear-adrenaline-thrill ride as it is a chance to rip open our minds and explore the darker elements of our world and very nature with imagination being the ruler above all. For the sensitive especially, a genre like horror can actually give a chance to make some strange peace with the real horrors of waking life. The canvas of horror can equally explore the grue-filled and shadowy halls of beauty too, creating a tapestry of all that both compels and repulses. (H.D.)

1408 (2007)
Directed by Mikael Hafstrom. Written by Scott Alexander and Larry Karaszewski.

THE ABOMINABLE DR. PHIBES (1971)
Directed by Robert Fuest. Written by James Whiton and William Goldstein.

THE ADDICTION (1995)
Directed by Abel Ferrara. Written by Nicholas St. John.

AMER (2009)
Written and directed by Héléne Cattet, Bruno Forzani.

AMERICAN MUMMY (2014)
Directed by Charles Pinion. Written by Charles Pinion and Greg Salman.

Dr. Phibes has Great Vibes

and complete dedication to his lifework, which is MURDER in the Nth Degree. Lovely Vulnavia (right) is his cheerful sidekick who cleans his electrodes, checks his oil, plugs him in and turns him on. Although Phibes is entirely synthetic Vulnavia— Hoo Boy!— isn't.

JAMES H. NICHOLSON and SAMUEL Z. ARKOFF present
VINCENT PRICE
JOSEPH COTTEN
the abominable
dr. phibes

HUGH GRIFFITH ▼ and TERRY-THOMAS
VIRGINIA NORTH

AMERICAN PSYCHO (2000)
Directed by Mary Harron. Written by Mary Harron and Guinevere Turner, from the novel by Bret Easton Ellis.

AN AMERICAN WEREWOLF IN LONDON (1981)
Written and directed by John Landis.

ANGEL HEART (1987)
Directed by Alan Parker. Written by Alan Parker, from the novel *Falling Angel* by William Hjortsberg.

ANGST (1983)
Directed by Gerald Kargl. Written by Zbigniew Rybczynski and Gerald Kargl.

ASYLUM (1972)
Directed by Roy Ward Baker. Written by Robert Bloch.

THE BIZARRO ENCYCLOPEDIA OF FILM

AT MIDNIGHT I'LL TAKE YOUR SOUL (1964)
Directed by Jose Mojica Marins. Written by Jose Mojica Marins and Magda Mei.

THE AWFUL DR. ORLOF (1962)
Written and directed by Jess Franco.

THE BABADOOK (2014)
Written and directed by Jennifer Kent.

BAD CHANNELS (1992)
Directed by Ted Nicolaou. Written by Charles Band (original idea), Jackson Barr (screenplay).

A BAY OF BLOOD aka TWITCH OF THE DEATH NERVE (1971)
Directed by Mario Bava. Written by Mario Bava, Filippo Ottoni, Giuseppe Zaccariello, Sergio Canevari, and Gene Luotto.

BEN (1972)
Directed by Phil Karlson. Written by Gilbert Ralston (as Gilbert A. Ralston), from characters created by Stephen Gilbert.

THE BEYOND (1981)
Directed by Lucio Fulci. Written by Dardano Sachetti, Giorgio Mariuzzo and Lucio Fulci.

THE BLACK CAT (1934)
Directed by Edgar G. Ulmer. Written by Peter Ruric, Edgar G. Ulmer and Edgar Allan Poe (based on story).

BLACK CHRISTMAS (1974)
Directed by Bob Clark. Written by Roy Moore.

BLACULA (1972)
Directed by William Crain. Written by Joan Torres and Raymond Koenig.

BLOOD & DONUTS (1995)
Directed by Holly Dale. Written by Andrew Rai Berzins.

BLOOD FOR DRACULA (1974)
Written and directed by Paul Morrissey.

BLOODBATH (1966)
Written and directed by Jack Hill and Stephanie Rothman

THE BLOODY APE (1997)
Directed Keith J. Crocker. Written by Keith J. Crocker and George Reis.

BOTTLED FOOLS/HELLEVATOR (2004)
Written and directed by Hiroki Yamaguchi.

THE BIZARRO ENCYCLOPEDIA OF FILM

THE BOXER'S OMEN (MO) (1983)
Directed by Chih-Hung Kuei. Written by Chih-Hung Kuei and On Szeto.

BRIDE OF FRANKENSTEIN (1935)
Directed by James Whale. Written by William Hurlbut, John L. Balderston (adapted by) and Mary Shelley (novel).

THE BROOD (1979)
Written and directed by David Cronenberg.

BRUISER (2000)
Written and directed by George A. Romero.

BUBBA HO-TEP (2002)
Written and directed by Don Coscarelli.

BURIAL GROUND (1981)
Directed by Andrea Bianchi. Written by Piero Regnoli.

THE CABIN IN THE WOODS (2012)
Directed by Drew Goddard. Written by Drew Goddard and Joss Whedon.

THE CABINET OF DR. CALIGARI (1920)
Directed by Robert Wiene. Written by Carl Mayer and Hans Janowitz.

CANNIBAL HOLOCAUST (1980)
Directed by Ruggero Deodato. Written by Gianfranco Clerci.

CARNIVAL OF SOULS (1962)
Directed by Herk Harvey. Written by John Clifford.

CASTLE OF THE LIVING DEAD (1964)
Directed by Warren Kiefer, Luciano Ricci, and Michael Reeves (uncredited). Written by Warren Kiefer, Fede Arnaud (Italian version), and Michael Reeves (uncredited).

CASTLE OF THE LIVING DEAD

THE CAT AND THE CANARY (1927)
Directed by Paul Leni. Written by John Willard (play), Robert F. Hill, Alfred A. Cohn and Walter Anthony (title)

THE CAT AND THE CANARY (1978)
Directed by Radley Metzger. Written by Radley Metzger and John Willard (play).

A CAT IN THE BRAIN (1990)
Directed by Lucio Fulci. Written by Lucio Fulci, Giovanni Simonelli, and Antonio Tentori. Story by Lucio Fulci and Giovanni Simonelli.

CAT PEOPLE (1942)
Directed by Jacques Tourneur. Written by DeWitt Bodeen.

CAT PEOPLE (1982)
Directed by Paul Schrader. Written by Alan Ormsby and DeWitt Bodeen (story).

CHAINED (2012)
Written and directed by Jennifer Lynch, from a screenplay by Damian O'Donnell.

CHILDREN SHOULDN'T PLAY WITH DEAD THINGS (1972)
Directed by Bob Clark (as Benjamin Clark). Written by Alan Ormsby and Bob Clark (as Benjamin Clark.)

C.H.U.D. (1984)
Directed by Douglas Cheek. Written by Parnell Hall and Shepard Abbott.

C.H.U.D. II: BUD THE CHUD (1989)
Directed by David Irving. Written by Ed Naha.

THE COMEDY OF TERRORS (1962)
Directed by Jacques Tourneur. Written by Richard Matheson.

THE CONVENT (2000)
Directed by Mike Mendez. Written by Chaton Anderson.

CORRUPTION (1968)
Directed by Roger Hartford-Davis. Written by Donald Ford and Derek Ford.

CRAWLSPACE (1986)
Written and directed by David Schmoeller.

CREATURE FROM THE BLACK LAGOON (1954)
Directed by Jack Arnold. Written by Harry Essex, Arthur Ross, and Maurice Zimm (stor).

THE CREATURE WALKS AMONG US (1956)
Directed by John Sherwood. Written by Arthur A. Ross (as Arthur Ross).

CREEPSHOW (1982)
Directed by George A. Romero. Written by Stephen King.

CURSE OF THE FACELESS MAN (1958)
Directed by Edward L. Cahn. Written by Jerome Bixby.

DAGON (2001)
Directed by Stuart Gordon. Written by Dennis Paoli, based on the work of H.P. Lovecraft.

DARKNESS (1993)
Written and directed by Lief Jonker.

DAWN OF THE DEAD (1978)
Written and directed by George A. Romero.

DAY OF THE DEAD (1985)
Written and directed by George A. Romero.

DEAD ALIVE (aka BRAIN DEAD) (1992)
Directed by Peter Jackson. Written by Peter Jackson, Stephen Sinclair and Fran Walsh.

THE DEAD ZONE (1983)
Directed by David Cronenberg. Written by Jeffrey Boam, from the novel by Stephen King.

DEADGIRL (2008)
Directed by Marcel Sarmiento and Gadi Harel. Written by Trent Haaga.

DEATH GAME (1977)
Directed by Peter S. Traynor. Written by Anthony Overman and Michael Ronald Ross.

DEATHDREAM (1974)
Directed by Bob Clark. Written by Alan Ormsby, inspired by the short story "The Monkey's Paw" by W.W. Jacobs.

DEEP RED (1975)
Directed by Dario Argento. Written by Dario Argento and Bernardino Zapponi.

DEMENTIA 13 (1963)
Directed by Francis Ford Coppola. Written by Francis Ford Coppola, Jack Hill.

DEMONS (1985)
Directed by Lamberto Bava. Written by Lamberto Bava, Dario Argento, Franco Ferrini, and Dardano Sacchetti, from a story by Sacchetti.

THE DEVIL'S MESSENGER (1961)
Directed by Herbert L. Strock, Curt Siodmak (uncredited). Written by Leo Guild.

DIARY OF THE DEAD (2007)
Written and directed by George A. Romero.

DR. PHIBES RISES AGAIN (1972)
Directed by Robert Fuest. Written by Robert Fuest, Robert Blees, James Whiton (characters) and William Goldstein (characters).

DR. TERROR'S HOUSE OF HORRORS (1965)
Directed by Freddie Francis. Written by Milton Subotsky.

DON'T LOOK IN THE BASEMENT (1973)
Directed by S.F. Brownrigg. Written by Tim Pope.

DRACULA (1931)
Directed by Tod Browning. Written by Garrett Fort, from the novel by Bram Stoker and stage play by Hamilton Deane and John L. Balderson.

DRACULA (1931)
Directed by George Melford, Enrique Tovar Avalos (uncredited). Written by Baltasar Fernandez Cue, from the novel by Bram Stoker and stage play by Hamilton Deane and John L. Balderson.

THE DRACULA SAGA (1973)
Directed by Leon Klimovsky. Written by Emilio Martinez Lazaro.

DREAMCATCHER (2003)
Directed by Lawrence Kasdan. Written by William Goldman and Lawrence Kasdan, from the novel by Stephen King.

THE DRILLER KILLER (1979)
Directed by Abel Ferrara. Written by Nicholas St. John.

THE DUNWICH HORROR (1970)
Directed by Daniel Haller. Written by Curtis Hanson, Henry Rosenbaum, Ronald Silkosky, based on the story by H. P. Lovecraft.

DUST DEVIL (1992)
Written and directed by Richard Stanley.

EATEN ALIVE (1976)
Directed by Tobe Hooper. Written by Alvin L. Fast, Mohammed Rustam and Kim Henkel.

EVILSPEAK (1981)
Directed by Eric Weston. Written by Joseph Garofalo (screenplay), Eric Weston (screenplay), Joseph Garofalo (story).

EQUINOX (1970)
Directed by Jack Woods, Mark Thomas McGee (co-director, uncredited), Dennis Muren (uncredited). Written by Mark Thomas McGee (story), Jack Woods.

ETERNAL EVIL OF ASIA (1995)
Directed by Man Kei Chin. Written by Man Kei Chin.

THE EVIL DEAD (1981)
Written and directed by Sam Raimi.

EVIL DEAD II (1987)
Written and directed by Sam Raimi.

EVILSPEAK (1981)
Directed by Eric Weston. Written by Joseph Garofalo and Eric Weston, from a story by Joseph Garofalo.

EXCISION (2012)
Written and directed by Richard Bates Jr.

THE EXORCIST (1973)
Directed by William Friedkin. Written by William Peter Blatty.

THE EXORCIST III (1990)
Written and directed by William Peter Blatty, from his novel *Legion*.

EXTE: HAIR EXTENSIONS (2007)
Directed by Sion Sono. Written by Sion Sono (screenplay), Masaki Adachi (screenplay), Makoto Sanada (screenplay), Sion Sono (story).

EYES OF FIRE (1983)
Written and directed by Avery Crounse.

EYES WITHOUT A FACE (1960)
Directed by Georges Franju. Written by Pierre Boileau, Thomas Narcejac, Jean Redon, Claude Sautet, and Pierre Gascar

FASCINATION (1979)
Written and directed by Jean Rollin.

FATAL FRAMES (1996)
Directed by Al Festa. Written by Al Festa. Alessandro Monese and Mary Rinaldi (dialogue).

FEAST OF FLESH (1967)
Directed by Emilio Vieyra. Written by Jack Curtis (English dubbed dialogue), Antonio Rosso and Emilio Vieyra.

FEMALE VAMPIRE (1975)
Directed by Jess Franco. Written by Jess Franco and Josyane Gibert (dialogue).

FIRESTARTER (1984)
Directed by Mark L. Lester. Written by Stanley Mann, from the novel by Stephen King.

FLESH FOR FRANKENSTEIN (1973)
Written and directed by Paul Morrissey.

THE FLY (1958)
Directed by Kurt Neumann. Written by James Clavell, from the short story by George Langelaan.

THE FLY (1986)
Directed by David Cronenberg. Written by David Cronenberg and Charles Edward Pogue, from the short story by George Langelaan.

FRANKENSTEIN (1931)
Directed by James Whale. Written by Garrett Fort, Francis Edward Faragoh, John L. Balderston (based upon composition by), Peggy Webling (adapted from the play by) and Mary Shelley (from the novel by.)

FRENZY (1972)
Directed by Alfred Hitchcock. Written by Anthony Shaffer, from the novel by Arthur La Burn.

FRIGHT SHOW AKA CINEMAGIC (1985)
Directed by Damon Santostefano. Written by Eddie Brill, Chris Phillips, Jonathan Mostow, Gregory J. Keller, Jeffrey Baker, Frank Kerr, and Richard Taylor.

FROM A WHISPER TO A SCREAM (1987)
Directed by Jeff Burr. Written by C. Courtney Joyner, Darin Scott, and Jeff Burr. Additional material by Mike Malone.

FROM BEYOND (1986)
Directed by Stuart Gordon. Written by Dennis Paoli, Stuart Gordon, Brian Yuzna, and H.P. Lovecraft (short story).

FROM DUSK TILL DAWN (1996)
Directed by Robert Rodriguez. Written by Quentin Tarantino. Story by Robert Kurtzman.

FROM DUSK TILL DAWN 2: TEXAS BLOOD MONEY (1999)
Directed by Scott Spiegel. Written by Scott Spiegel and Duane Whitaker. Story by Scott Spiegel and Boaz Yakin.

FROM DUSK TILL DAWN 3: THE HANGMAN'S DAUGHTER (1999)
Directed by P.J. Pesce. Written by Alvaro Rodriguez. Story by Alvaro Rodriguez and Robert Rodriguez.

THE FUNHOUSE (1981)
Directed by Tobe Hooper. Written by Lawrence Block (as Larry Block).

FUNNY GAMES (1997)
Written and directed by Michael Haneke.

GERMAN ANGST (2015)
Directed by Jörg Buttgereit (segment "Final Girl"), Michal Kosakowski (segment "Make a Wish"), Andreas Marschall (segment "Alraune"). Written by Jörg Buttgereit (segment "Final Girl"), Goran Mimica (segment "Make a Wish"), Michal Kosakowski (segment "Make a Wish"), Andreas Marschall (segment "Alraune").

GET OUT (2017)
Written and directed by Jordan Peele.

GINGER SNAPS (2000)
Directed by John Fawcett. Written by John Fawcett and Karen Walton.

A GIRL WALKS HOME ALONE AT NIGHT (2014)
Written and directed by Anna Lily Amirpour.

GIRLY (1970)
Directed by Freddie Francis. Written by Brian Comport (screenplay), Maisie Mosco (play).

THE GORILLA (1939)
Directed by Allan Dwan. Written by Ralph Spence (play), Rian James (screenplay), Sid Silvers (screenplay).

GOTHIC (1986)
Directed by Ken Russell. Written by Stephen Volk , from stories by Lord Byron and Percy Bysshe Shelley..

GOZU (2003)
Directed by Takashi Miike. Written by Sakichi Sato (screenplay).

GRADUATION DAY (1981)
Directed by Herb Freed. Written by Herb Freed, Anne Marisse, and David Baughn (story).

GRAPES OF DEATH (1978)
Directed by Jean Rollin. Written by Jean-Pierre, Jean Rollin and Christian Meunier.

GRAVE OF THE VAMPIRE (1972)
Directed by John Hayes. Written by David Chase and John Hayes (screen treatment).

HALLOWEEN (1978)
Directed by John Carpenter. Written by John Carpenter and Debra Hill.

HALLOWEEN III: SEASON OF THE WITCH (1982)
Written and directed by Tommy Lee Wallace.

HARD ROCK ZOMBIES (1985)
Directed by Krishna Shah. Written by David Allen Ball and Krishna Shah.

HARVEST LAKE (2016)

Written and directed by Scott Schirmer.

THE HAUNTING (1963)

Directed by Robert Wise. Written by Nelson Gidding, from the novel *The Haunting of Hill House* by Shirley Jackson.

HE NEVER DIED (2015)

Written and directed by Jason Crawczyk,

HEADLESS (2015)

Directed by Arthur Cullipher. Written by Nathan Erdel and Todd Rigney (based on characters and situations created by).

HELL OF THE LIVING DEAD (1980)

Directed by Bruno Mattei, Claudio Fragasso. Written by Claudio Fragasso (story and screenplay), José María Cunillés (story and screenplay).

HELLRAISER (1987)

Written and directed by Clive Barker.

THE HIDEOUS SUN DEMON (1959)

Directed by Robert Clarke, Tom Boutross (co-director). Written by E.S. Seeley Jr. (screenplay), Doane R. Hoag (additional dialogue), Robert Clarke (based on an original idea by), Phil Hiner (based on an original idea by).

THE HILLS HAVE EYES (1977)

Written and directed by Wes Craven.

THE HILLS HAVE EYES (2006)

Directed by Alexandre Aja. Written by Alexandre Aja and Grégory Levasseur, based on the movie by Wes Craven.

THE HILLS RUN RED (2009)

Directed by Dave Parker. Written by David J. Schow and John Dombrow, story by Don Carchietta.

THE HITCHER (1986)

Directed by Robert Harmon. Written by Eric Red.

HOBGOBLINS (1988)

Written and directed by Rick Sloane.

HOMICIDAL (1961)
Directed by William Castle. Written by Robb White.

HORRORS OF MALFORMED MEN (1969)
Directed by Teruo Ishii. Written by Teruo ishii (screenplay), Masahiro Kakefuda (screenplay), Rampo Edogawa (novel), Bobby White (subtitles).

HORRORS OF SPIDER ISLAND (BODY IN THE WEB) (1960)
Directed by Fritz Böttger. Written by Fritz Böttger, Eldon Howard, and Albert G. Miller.

HOUSE OF 1,000 CORPSES (2003)
Written and directed by Rob Zombie.

THE HOUSE THAT DRIPPED BLOOD (1971)
Directed by Peter Duffell. Written by Robert Bloch.

THE HOUSE THAT SCREAMED (1970)
Directed by Narciso Ibáñez Serrador. Written by Narciso Ibáñez Serrador and Juan Tébar.

HOUSEBOUND (2014)
Written and directed by Gerard Johnstone.

THE HOWLING (1981)
Directed by Joe Dante. Written by John Sayles and Terence H. Winkless, from the novel by Gary Brandner.

THE HUMAN CENTIPEDE: FIRST SEQUENCE (2009)
Written and directed by Tom Six.

THE HUMAN CENTIPEDE: FINAL SEQUENCE (2015)
Written and directed by Tom Six.

THE HUMAN CENTIPEDE: FULL SEQUENCE (2011)
Written and directed by Tom Six.

I AM NIGHTMARE (2014)
Directed by M. dot Strange.

I DRINK YOUR BLOOD (1970)
Directed by David E. Durston. Written by David E. Durston.

I SAW THE DEVIL (2010)
Directed by Jee-woon Kim. Written by Jee-woon Kim and Hoon-jung Park.

INFERNO (1980)
Written and directed by Dario Argento.

INSIDE (2007)
Written and directed by Alexandre Bustillo and Julien Maury.

INTRUDER (1989)
Written and directed by Scott Spiegel. Story by Lawrence Bender and Scott Spiegel.

THE BIZARRO ENCYCLOPEDIA OF FILM

INVASION OF THE BLOOD FARMERS (1972)
Directed by Ed Adlum. Written by Ed Adlum and Ed Kelleher.

ISLAND OF LOST SOULS (1932)
Directed by Erle C. Kenton. Written by Waldemar Young, Philip Wylie and H.G. Wells (Novel.)

they planted the LIVING and harvested the DEAD!

INVASION OF THE BLOOD FARMERS

IT FOLLOWS (2014)
Written and directed by David Robert Mitchell.

IT'S ALIVE (1974)
Written and directed by Larry Cohen.

JACKALS (2017)
Directed by Kevin Greutert. Written by Jared Rivet.

JACOB'S LADDER (1990)
Directed by Adrian Lyne. Written by Bruce Joel Rubin.

JANIE (1970)
Directed by Michael Findlay (film is credited to Jack Bravman). Written by James Foley.

JUAN OF THE DEAD (2011)
Written and directed by Alejandro Brugués.

KILLER CONDOM (1996)
Directed by Martin Walz. Written by Ralf Konig, Martin Walz, and Mario Kramp.

KILLER KLOWNS FROM OUTER SPACE (1988)
Directed by Stephen Chiodo. Written by Stephen and Charles Chiodo.

KILLER TONGUE (1996)
Written and directed by Alberto Sciamma.

LADY FRANKENSTEIN (1971)
Directed by Mel Welles and Aureliano Luppo (uncredited). Written by Edward Di Lorenzo and Dick Randall (original story).

LAIR OF THE WHITE WORM (1988)
Written and directed by Ken Russell.

LAND OF THE DEAD (2005)
Written and directed by George A. Romero.

THE LAST HORROR FILM (1982)
Directed by David Winters. Written by Judd Hamilton, David Winters and Tom Klassen

THE BIZARRO ENCYCLOPEDIA OF FILM

LAST HOUSE ON DEAD END STREET (1977)
Written and directed by Roger Watkins (as Brian Laurence and Victor Yanos. respectively).

LATE PHASES (2014)
Directed by Adrian Garcia Bogliano. Written by Eric Stolze.

LEMORA: A CHILD'S TALE OF THE SUPERNATURAL (1973)
Directed by Richard Blackburn. Written by Richard Blackburn

LET'S SCARE JESSICA TO DEATH (1971)
Directed by John D. Hancock (as John Hancock). Written by John D. Hancock (as Ralph Rose), Lee Kalcheim (as Norman Jonas).

THE LEGEND OF HELL HOUSE (1973)
Directed by John Hough. Written by Richard Matheson, from his novel *Hell House*.

LIPS OF BLOOD (1975)
Directed by Jean Rollin. Written by Jean-Loup Philippe and Jean Rollin

LITTLE SHOP OF HORRORS (1960)
Directed by Roger Corman. Written by Charles B. Griffith.

THE LORDS OF SALEM (2012)
Written and directed by Rob Zombie.

THE LOVED ONES (2009)
Written and directed by Sean Byrne.

MANHUNTER (1986)
Directed by Michael Mann. Written by Michael Mann and Thomas Harris (Novel)

MANIAC (1934)
Directed by Dwain Esper. Written by Hildegarde Stadie.

MANIAC (1980)
Directed by William Lustic. Written by C.A. Rosenberg and Joe Spinell.

MANIAC (2012)
Directed by Frank Khalfoun. Written by Alexandre Aja, Gregory Levasseur, and based on the original screenplay by Joe "The Man" Spinell.

MANIAC COP (1988)
Directed by William Lustig. Written by Larry Cohen.

MANIAC COP 2 (1990)
Directed by William Lustig. Written by Larry Cohen.

THE MANSTER (1959)
Directed by George P. Breakston. Written by George P. Breakston and William J. Sheldon.

MARTIN (1977)
Written and directed by George A. Romero.

MARTYRS (2008)
Written and directed by Pascal Laugier.

THE MASQUE OF THE RED DEATH (1964)
Directed by Roger Corman. Written by Charles Beaumont, R. Wright Campbell, from a story by Edgar Allan Poe.

MAY (2002)
Written and directed by Lucky McKee.

MEATBALL MACHINE (1999)
Written and directed by Jun'ichi Yamamoto.

MESSIAH OF EVIL (1973)
Written and directed by Willard Huyck and Gloria Katz.

THE MONSTER (1925)
Directed by Roland West. Written by Roland West (stage production,) Crane Wilbur (play), Willard Mack, Albert Kenyon and C. Gardner Sullivan (titles)

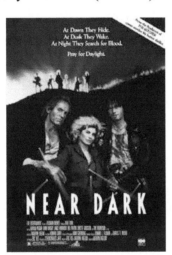

MORGIANA (1972)
Directed by Juraj Herz. Written by Vladimír Bor (writer), Alexander Grin (story), Juraj Herz (writer).

MOTEL HELL (1980)
Directed by Kevin Connor. Written by Robert Jaffe and Steven-Charles Jaffe.

MYSTICS IN BALI (1981)
Directed by H. Tjut Djalil. Written by Putra Mada (novel), Jimmy Atmaja (scenario).

NEAR DARK (1987)
Directed by Kathryn Bigelow. Written by Kathryn Bigelow and Eric Red.

NEKROMANTIK (1987)
Directed by Jörg Buttgereit. Written by Jörg Buttgereit and Franz Rodenkirchen.

NEKROMANTIK II (1991)
Directed by Jörg Buttgereit. Written by Jörg Buttgereit and Franz Rodenkirchen.

THE BIZARRO ENCYCLOPEDIA OF FILM

THE NEON DEMON (2016)
Directed by Nicolas Winding Regn. Written by Nicolas Winding Refn, Mary Laws, Polly Stenham.

NEON MANIACS (1986)
Directed by Joseph Mangine. Written by Mark Patrick Carducci.

THE NEW YORK RIPPER (1982)
Directed by Lucio Fulci. Written by Lucio Fulci, Dardano Sacchetti, Gianfranco Clerici, and Vincenzo Mannino.

NIGHT OF THE CREEPS (1986)
Written and directed by Fred Dekker.

NIGHT OF THE LIVING DEAD (1968)
Directed by George A. Romero. Written by George A Romero and John A. Russo.

THE NIGHT STALKER (1972)
Directed by John Llewellyn Moxey. Written by Richard Matheson. Story by Jeffrey Grant Rice (as Jeff Rice).

NIGHT WARNING (BUTCHER BAKER NIGHTMARE MAKER) (1982)
Directed by William Asher. Written by Steve Briemer (screenplay), Alan Jay Glueckman (screenplay and story), Boon Collins (screenplay and story).

A NIGHTMARE ON ELM STREET (1984)
Written and directed by Wes Craven.

NIGHTMARES IN A DAMAGED BRAIN (1981)
Written and directed by Romano Scavolini.

THE NINTH GATE (1999)
Directed by Roman Polanski. Written by John Brownjohn, Enrique Urbizu, Roman Polanski, based on the novel *Club Dumas* by Arturo Pérez-Reverte.

NOCTURNA (1979)
Directed by Harry Hurwitz. Written by Nai Bonet and Harry Hurwitz.

NOSFERATU (1922)
Directed by F.W. Murnau. Written by Henrik Galeen, based on the novel *Dracula* by Bram Stoker.

NOSFERATU IN VENICE (1988)
Directed by Augusto Caminito. Mario Caiano, Luigi Cozzi (uncredited), Klaus Kinski (uncredited) and Maurizio Lucidi (uncredited), Written by Alberto Alfieri, Augusto Caminito, Leandro Lucchetti and Pascale Squitieri (uncredited).

NOSFERATU THE VAMPYRE (1979)
Written and directed by Werner Herzog.

THE OLD DARK HOUSE (1932)
Directed by James Whale. Written by J.B. Priestly (novel) and Benn W. Levy

OPERA (1987)
Directed by Dario Argento. Written by Dario Argento and Franco Ferrini.

THE OREGONIAN (2011)
Written and directed by Calvin Lee Reeder.

THE OTHER (1972)
Directed by Robert Mulligan. Written by Tom Tryon (screenplay and novel).

PARENTS (1989)
Directed by Bob Balaban. Written by Christopher Hawthorne.

PHANTASM (1979)
Written and directed by Don Coscarelli.

PHENOMENA (1985)
Directed by Dario Argento. Written by Dario Argento and Franco Ferrini.

PIECES (1982)
Directed by Juan Piquer Simón. Written by Dick Randall and Roberto Loyola.

PIGS (1973)
Written and directed by Marc Lawrence.

PIN (1988)
Directed by Sandor Stern. Written by Sandor Stern, from the novel by Andrew Neiderman.

THE PIT AND THE PENDULUM (1961)
Directed by Roger Corman. Written by Richard Matheson, based on the short story by Edgar Allan Poe.

THE PIT AND THE PENDULUM (1991)
Directed by Stuart Gordon. Written by Dennis Paoli, based on the short story by Edgar Allan Poe.

PLANET TERROR (2007)
Written and directed by Robert Rodriguez.

POSSESSION (1981)
Written and directed by Andrzej Zulawski.

PSYCHO (1960)
Directed by Alfred Hitchcock. Written by Joseph Stefano, from the novel by Robert Bloch.

THE PSYCHOPATH aka EYE FOR AN EYE (1973)
Directed by Larry G. Brown. Written by Larry G. Brown and Walter Dallenbach.

PUMPKINHEAD (1988)
Directed by Stan Winston. Written by Mark Patrick Carducci and Gary Gerani. Story Mark Patrick Carducci, Stan Winston, and Richard Weinman (as Richard C. Weinman), from a poem by Ed Justin.

Q (1982)
Written and directed by Larry Cohen.

THE BIZARRO ENCYCLOPEDIA OF FILM

RABID (1977)
Written and directed by David
Cronenberg.

THE RAMBLER (2013)
Written and directed by Calvin Lee
Reeder.

THE RAVEN (1963)
Directed by Roger Corman. Written by
Richard Matheson, based on the poem
by Edgar Allan Poe.

RAVENOUS (1999)
Directed by Antonia Bird. Written by
Ted Griffin.

RE-ANIMATOR (1985)
Directed by Stuart Gordon. Written
by Dennis Paoli, William Norris, and
Stuart Gordon, from the story by H.P.
Lovecraft.

RED STATE (2011)
Written and directed by Kevin Smith.

**REDD, INC. (Inhuman Resources)
(2013)**
Directed by Daniel Krige. Written
by Anthony O'Connor and Jonathon
Green.

THE REFLECTING SKIN (1990)
Written and directed by Philip Ridley.

REPULSION (1965)
Directed by Roman Polanski. Written
by Roman Polanski, Gerard Brach,
and David Stone.

**RETURN OF THE LIVING DEAD
(1985)**
Directed by Dan O'Bannon. Written
by Rudy Ricci, John A. Russo, and
Russell Streiner.

**REVENGE OF THE CREATURE
(1955)**
Directed by Jack Arnold. Written by
Martin Berkeley. Story by William
Alland.

ROSEMARY'S BABY (1968)
Directed by Roman Polanski. Written
by Ira Levin and Roman Polanski.

SANTA SANGRE (1989)
Directed by Alejandro Jodorowsky.
Written by Alejandro Jodorowsky,
Roberto Leoni and Claudio Argento.

SCHIZOID (1980)
Written and directed by David Paulsen.

SCREAM OF FEAR (1961)
Directed by Seth Holt. Written by
Jimmy Sangster.

**SCREAM BLACULA SCREAM
(1973)**
Directed by Bob Kelijan. Written by
Joan Torres, Raymond Koenig, and
Maurice Jules. Story by Joan Torres
and Raymond Koenig.

SHATTER DEAD (1994)
Written and directed by Scooter
McCrae.

THE BIZARRO ENCYCLOPEDIA OF FILM

THE SHE-CREATURE (1956)
Directed by Edward L. Cahn. Written by Lou Rusoff and Jerry Zigmond (original idea).

SHE CREATURE (2001)
Written and directed by Sebastian Gutierrez.

SHRIEK OF THE MUTILATED (1974)
Directed by Michael Findley. Written by Ed Adlum, Ed Kelleher.

THE SILENCE OF THE LAMBS (1991)
Directed by Jonathan Demme. Written by Ted Tally, from the novel by Thomas Harris.

SISTERS (1973)
Directed by Brian De Palma. Written by Brian De Palma and Louisa Rose.

SLEEPWALKERS (1992)
Directed by Mick Garris. Written by Stephen King.

SLITHER (2006)
Written and directed by James Gunn.

SNUFFET (2014)
Directed by Dustin Mills. Written by Allison Egan, Dustin Mills, Brandon Salkil.

SOCIETY (1989)
Directed by Brian Yuzna. Written by Rick Fry and Woody Keith.

SOMETHING WEIRD (1967)
Directed by Herschell Gordon Lewis. Written by James F. Hurley.

SPIRITS OF THE DEAD (1968)
Directed by Roger Vadim, Louis Malle, and Federico Fellini. Written by Roger Vadim, Pascal Cousin, Louis Malle, Clement Biddle Wood, Daniel Boulanger, Federico Fellini, and Bernardino Zapponi, from the short stories "Metzengerstein", "William Wilson", and "Never Bet the Devil Your Head" by Edgar Allan Poe.

SPOOKIES (1986)
Directed by Genie Joseph. Thomas Doran and Brendan Faulkner, Written by Ann Burgund, Thomas Doran, Frank M. Farel and Brendan Faulkner.

SSSSSSS (1973)
Directed by Bernard L. Kowalski. Written by Hal Dresner and Daniel C. Striepeke.

THE STENDAHL SYNDROME (1996)
Directed by Dario Argento. Written by Dario Argento, Franco Ferrini, and Graziella Magherini (novel).

THE STRANGE COLOR OF YOUR BODY'S TEARS (2013)

Written and directed by Hélène Cattet and Bruno Forzani.

STRANGE CIRCUS (2005)

Written and directed by Sion Sono.

THE STUFF (1985)

Written and directed by Larry Cohen.

SUNDOWN: THE VAMPIRE IN RETREAT (1989)

Directed by Anthony Hickox. Written by John Burgess and Anthony Hickox.

SUSPIRIA (1977)

Directed by Dario Argento. Written by Dario Argento and Daria Nicolodi.

SYMPTOMS (1974)

Directed by Jose Ramon Larraz. Written by Jose Ramon Larraz, Stanley Miller, and Thomas Owen (story).

A TALE OF TWO SISTERS (2003)

Written and directed by Jee-woon Kim.

TALES FROM THE CRYPT (1972)

Directed by Freddie Francis. Written by Milton Subotsky, from stories by Al Feldstein, Johnny Craig, and William M. Gaines.

TALES FROM THE CRYPT: DEMON KNIGHT (1995)

Directed by Ernest R. Dickerson (as Ernest Dickerson). Written by Ethan Reiff, Cyrus Voris, and Mark Bishop.

TALES FROM THE HOOD (1995)

Directed by Rusty Cundieff. Written by Rusty Cundieff and Darin Scott.

TALES OF HALLOWEEN (2015)

Directed by Dave Parker, Darren Lynn Bousman, Adam Gierasch, Paul Solet, Axelle Carolyn, Lucky McKee, John Skipp and Andrew Kasch, Mike Mendez, Ryan Schifrin, and Neal Marshall. Written by Dave Parker, Clint Sears, Adam Gierasch and Jace Anderson (as Greg Commons), Mollie Millions, Lucky McKee, John Skipp and Andrew Kasch, Mike Mendez, Ryan Schifrin, and Neil Marshall.

TASTE OF BLOOD (1967)

Directed by Herschell Gordon Lewis. Written by Donald Stanford.

TENEBRE (1982)

Written and directed by Dario Argento

TERROR AT RED WOLF INN (1972)

Directed by Bud Townsend. Written by Allen Actor.

THE BIZARRO ENCYCLOPEDIA OF FILM

TERROR TOONS (2002)
Directed by Joe Castro. Written by Rudy Balli, Joe Castro, Steven J. Escobar, and Mark Villalobos.

TERRORVISION (1986)
Written and directed by Ted Nicolaou.

THE TEXAS CHAIN SAW MASSACRE (1974)
Directed by Tobe Hooper. Written by Tobe Hooper and Kim Henkel.

THE TEXAS CHAINSAW MASSACRE 2 (1986)
Directed by Tobe Hooper. Written by L.M. Kit Carson and Tobe Hooper.

THEATRE OF BLOOD (1973)
Directed by Douglas Hickox. Written by Anthony Greville-Bell and Stanley Mann.

THEY CAME FROM WITHIN (SHIVERS) (1975)
Written and directed by David Cronenburg.

THE THING (1982)
Directed by John Carpenter. Written by Bill Lancaster, from the short story "Who Goes There?" by John W. Campbell, Jr.

THE THING THAT COULDN'T DIE (1958)
Directed by Will Cowan. Written by David Duncan.

THINGS (1993)
Directed by Dennis Devine, Eugene James, Jay Woelfel. Written by Mike Bowler, Dennis Devine, Steve Jarvis, Jay Woelfel.

THIS NIGHT I WILL POSSESS YOUR CORPSE (1967)
Directed by Jose Mojica Marins. Written by Jose Mojica Marins and Aldenora De Sa Porto.

THE TINGLER (1959)
Directed by William Castle. Written by Robb White.

TINTORERA: KILLER SHARK (1977)
Directed by René Cardona Jr. Written by René Cardona Jr., Christina Schuch and Ramón Bravo (novel).

TOKYO GORE POLICE (2008)
Directed by Yoshihiro Nishimura. Written by Kengo Kaji, Maki Mizui and Yoshihiro Nishimura.

TOMIE (1999)
Directed by Ataru Oikawa. Written by Junji Ito (comic), Ataru Oikawa.

TOURIST TRAP (1979)
Directed by David Schmoeller. Written by David Schmoeller and J. Larry Carroll.

TRACK OF THE MOON BEAST (1976)
Directed by Richard Ashe. Written by Bill Finger, Charles Sinclair.

THE BIZARRO ENCYCLOPEDIA OF FILM

TRAIN TO BUSAN (2016)
Directed by Sang-ho Yeon. Written by Joo-Suk Park and Sang-ho Yeon.

TRILOGY OF TERROR (1975)
Directed by Dan Curtis. Written by Richard Matheson and William F. Nolan.

TROUBLE EVERY DAY (2001)
Directed by Claire Dennis. Written by Claire Dennis and Jean-Pol Fargeau.

TUSK (2014)
Written and directed by Kevin Smith.

TWO EVIL EYES (1990)
Directed by Dario Argento and George Romero. Written by Dario Argento, Franco Ferrini, George A. Romero, and Edgar Allan Poe (stories.)

VAMPIRE CIRCUS (1972)
Directed by Robert Young. Written by Judson Kinberg.

VAMPIRE GIRL VS. FRANKENSTEIN GIRL (2009)
Directed by Yoshihiro Nishimura, Naoyuki Tomomatsu. Written by Daichi Nagisa (screenplay), Naoyuki Tomomatsu (screenplay), Shungiku Uchida.

VAMPYRES (1974)
Directed by José Ramón Larraz. Written by Diana Daubeney.

THE VANISHING (1988)
Directed by George Sluizer. Written by Tim Krabbé, based on the novel. Adapted by George Sluizer.

VENUS IN FURS (1969)
Directed by Jess Franco. Written by Jess Franco and Malvin Wald.

A VIRGIN AMONG THE LIVING DEAD (1973)
Directed by Jess Franco. Written by Jess Franco and Paul D'Ales (French Dialogue).

VIDEODROME (1983)
Written and directed by David Cronenberg.

THE VVITCH: A NEW ENGLAND FOLK TALE (2015)
Written and directed by Robert Eggers.

THE WASP WOMAN (1959)
Directed by Roger Corman and Jack Hill (uncredited). Written by Leo Gordon and Kinta Zertuche (story).

WAXWORKS (1988)
Written and directed by Anthony Hickox.

WAXWORKS (1924)
Directed by Paul Leni and Leo Birinski. Written by Henrik Galeen.

WHERE THE DEAD GO TO DIE (2012)
Written and directed by Jimmy ScreamerClauz.

WHITE OF THE EYE (1987)
Directed by Donald Cammell. Written by China Kong (as China Cammell) and Donald Cammell, from the novel by Andrew Klaven and Laurence Klaven (writing as Margaret Tracy).

WHOEVER SLEW AUNTIE ROO? (1972)
Directed by Curtis Harrington. Written by David D. Osborn, Robert Blees, Jimmy Sangster, and Gavin Lambert.

WILLARD (1971)
Directed by Daniel Mann. Written by Gilbert Ralston, based on the novel by Stephen Gilbert.

WILLARD (2003)
Directed by Glen Morgan. Written by Glen Morgan, based on the original Gilbert Ralston screenplay and the novel by Stephen Gilbert.

WILD ZERO (1999)
Directed by Tetsuro Takeuchi. Written by Satoshi and Tetsuro Takeuchi.

WITCHFINDER GENERAL (1968)
Directed by Michael Reeves. Written by Michael Reeves, Tom Baker, Louis M. Heyward (additional dialogue), based on the novel by Ronald Bassett and uncredited poem by Edgar Allan Poe.

THE WITCHING (1993)
Written and directed by Matthew Jason Walsh.

ZOMBIE (1979)
Directed by Lucio Fulci. Written by Elisa Briganti.

ZOMBIE ASS (2011)
Directed by Noboru Iguchi. Written by Tadayoshi Kubo, Ao Murata, and Jun Tsugita.

COMEDY

Comedy is a hothouse for Bizarro, because things are rarely funny unless something is totally wrong. And indeed, this playfulness is often used to distinguish Bizarro for other, more characteristically somber approaches to the Weird.

Comedy also has the opportunity to take the piss out of every other genre, another uniquely Bizarro calling card. By being able to make fun of everything, including itself, it has perhaps the widest range short of the Cult section itself (which also contains tons of comedy).

What I loved most about compiling this section was clocking how many of these films are just one inch *from winding up in Cult, but always seemed to show up in Comedy by the skin of their teeth, and corrective marketing. That way, it doesn't have to be funny; it just has to* try to be!

No doubt, some of the weirdest shit that ever existed was made in an attempt to make us laugh. And there is much to laugh both with and at in this sprawling section. (JS)

ADAPTATION (2002)
Directed by Spike Jonze, Written by Susan Orlean (book), Charlie Kaufman (screenplay).

AFTER HOURS (1985)
Directed by Martin Scorsese, Written by Joseph Minion.

ALL OF ME (1984)
Directed by Carl Reiner. Written by Phil Alden Robinson and Henry Olek, based on the unpublished novel *Me Two* by Edwin Davis.

THE BIZARRO ENCYCLOPEDIA OF FILM

AIRPLANE! (1980)
Written and directed by Jim Abrahams, David Zucker.

AMAZON WOMEN ON THE MOON (1987)
Directed by Joe Dante, Carl Gottlieb, Peter Horton, John Landis and Robert K. Weiss. Written by Michael Barrie and Jim Mulholland.

AMERICAN RASPBERRY (1977)
Directed by Bradley R. Swirnoff. Written by John Baskin, Stephen Feinberg, Roger Shulman and Bradley R. Swirnoff.

A NIGHT AT THE OPERA (1935)
Directed by Sam Wood, Edmund Goulding. Written by George S. Kaufman, Morrie Ryskind.

AQUA TEEN HUNGER FORCE COLON MOVIE FILM FOR THEATERS (2007)
Written and directed by Mat Maiellaro and Dave Willis.

BABY DOLL (1956)
Directed by Elia Kazan. Written by Tennessee Williams.

BAD SANTA (2003)
Directed by Terry Zwigoff. Written by Glenn Ficarra and John Requa.

BALL OF FIRE (1941)
Directed by Howard Hawks. Written by Charles Brackett and Billy Wilder. Story by Billy Wilder and Thomas Monroe.

BANANAS (1971)
Directed by Woody Allen. Written by Woody Allen, Mickey Rose.

BASEKETBALL (1998)
Directed by David Zucker. Written by David Zucker, Robert LoCash, Lewis Friedman and Jeff Wright.

BEING JOHN MALKOVICH (1999)
Directed by Spike Jonez. Written by Charlie Kaufman.

BEETLEJUICE (1988)
Directed by Tim Burton. Written by Michael McDowell (story), Larry Wilson (story), Michael McDowell (screenplay), Warren Skaaren (screenplay).

BEING THERE (1979)
Directed by Hal Ashby. Written by Jerzy Kosinski, from his novel.

BETTER OFF DEAD (1985)
Written and directed by Savage Steve Holland.

THE BIZARRO ENCYCLOPEDIA OF FILM

THE BIG LEBOWSKI (1998)
Written and directed by Joel Coen, Ethan Coen.

THE BIG PICTURE (1989)
Directed by Christopher Guest. Written by Christopher Guest, Michael McKean, and Michael Vorhol.

BILL AND TED'S BOGUS JOURNEY (1991)
Directed by Peter Hewitt. Written by Chris Matheson, Ed Solomon.

BILL AND TED'S EXCELLENT ADVENTURE (1989)
Directed by Stephen Herek. Written by Chris Matheson, Ed Solomon.

BONED (2015)
Written and directed by Laura Lee Bahr.

THE BOOB TUBE (1975)
Written and directed by Christopher Odin.

BORAT: CULTURAL LEARNINGS OF AMERICA FOR MAKE GLORIOUS NATION OF KAZAKHSTAN (2006)
Directed by Larry Charles. Written by Sacha Baron Cohen, Anthony Hines.

THE BRADY BUNCH MOVIE (1995)
Directed by Betty Thomas. Written by Sherwood Schwartz, Laurice Elehwany.

BREWSTER MCCLOUD (1970)
Directed by Robert Altman. Written by Doran William Cannon.

BRINGING UP BABY (1938)
Directed by Howard Hawks. Written by Dudley Nichols, Hagar Wilde.

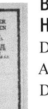

BRITANNIA HOSPITAL (1982)
Directed by Lindsay Anderson. Written by Davis Sherwin.

BUBBLE BOY (2001)
Directed by Blair Hayes. Written by Cinco Paul and Ken Daurio.

CABIN BOY (1994)
Written and directed by Adam Rifkin. Story by Adam Rifkin and Chris Elliott.

CANDY (1968)
Directed by Christian Marquand. Written by Buck Henry, from the book by Mason Hoffenberg and Terry Southern.

THE BIZARRO ENCYCLOPEDIA OF FILM

THE CENSUS TAKER (1984)
Directed by Bruce R. Cook. Written by Bruce R. Cook and Gordon M. Smith.

CHEECH AND CHONG'S NEXT MOVIE (1980)
Directed by Tommy Chong. Written by Tommy Chong and Cheech Marin.

CHUCK AND BUCK (2000)
Directed by Miguel Arteta. Written by Mike White.

CLUE (1985)
Directed by Jonathan Lynn. Written by John Landis and Jonathan Lynn.

COLD FEET (1989)
Directed by Robert Dornhelm. Written by Thomas McGuane and Jim Harrison.

CRACKING UP (1977)
Directed by Rowby Goren and Chuck Staley. Written by Ace Trucking Company, Peter Bergman, Credibility Gap, Neal Israel and Phil Proctor.

CRIMEWAVE (1985)
Directed by Sam Raimi. Written by Joel and Ethan Coen, Sam Raimi.

DEAD MEN DON'T WEAR PLAID (1982)
Directed by Carl Reiner. Written by Carl Reiner, George Gipe, and Steve Martin.

DEATH BECOMES HER (1992)
Directed by Robert Zemeckis. Written by Martin Donovan and David Koepp.

DEATHROW GAMESHOW (1987)
Directed by Mark Pirro. Written by Mark Pirro and Alan Gries.

DECONSTRUCTING HARRY (1997)
Written and directed by Woody Allen.

DR. STRANGELOVE OR HOW I STOPPED WORRYING AND LEARNED TO LOVE THE BOMB (1964)
Directed by Stanley Kubrick. Written by Stanley Kubrick, Terry Southern.

DOGMA (1999)
Written and directed by Kevin Smith.

DOWN BY LAW (1986)
Written and directed by Jim Jarmusch.

THE BIZARRO ENCYCLOPEDIA OF FILM

DUCK SOUP (1933)
Directed by Leo McCarey. Written by Bert Kalmar, Harry Ruby.

DUCK, YOU SUCKER! (1973)
Directed by Sergio Leone. Written by Luciano Vincenzoni, Sergio Donati, and Sergio Leone. Story by Sergio Donati and Sergio Leone.

EARTH GIRLS ARE EASY (1988)
Directed by Julien Temple. Written by Julien Temple, Charlie Coffey and Terrance E. McNally.

EAT THE RICH (1987)
Directed by Peter Richardson. Written by Peter Richardson and Pete Richens.

EATING RAOUL (1982)
Directed by Paul Bartel. Written by Paul Bartel and Richard Blackburn.

THE FACE WITH TWO LEFT FEET (JOHN TRAVOLTO) (1979)
Directed by Neri Parenti. Written by Massimo Franciosa (writer), Neri Parenti (writer), Giovanni Simonelli.

THE FAT SPY (1966)
Directed by Joseph Cates. Written by Matthew Andrews.

FEAR OF A BLACK HAT (1993)
Written and directed by Rusty Cundieff.

A FISH CALLED WANDA (1988)
Directed by Charles Crichton and John Cleese (uncredited). Written by John Cleese. Story by John Cleese and Charles Chrichton.

FREAKED (1993)
Directed by Tom Stern, Alex Winter. Written by Tim Burns, Tom Stern, Alex Winter.

FREDDY GOT FINGERED (2001)
Directed by Tom Green. Written by Tom Green and Derek Harvie.

THE GENERAL (1926)
Directed by Clyde Bruckman and Buster Keaton. Written by Al Boasburg, Clyde Bruckman, Buster Keaton, Charles Henry Smith and George Girard Smith, based on the book *The Great Locomotive Chase* by William Pittinger.

GET CRAZY (1983)
Directed by Allan Arkush. Written by Danny Opatoshu, Henry Rosenbaum and David Taylor.

GOD BLESS AMERICA (2011)
Written and directed by Bobcat Goldthwait.

THE GROOVE TUBE (1974)
Directed by Ken Shapiro. Written by Lane Sarasohn, Ken Shapiro.

THE BIZARRO ENCYCLOPEDIA OF FILM

HAGGARD (2003)
Directed by Bam Margera. Written by Chris Aspite, Brandon DiCamillo and Bam Margera.

HAIL, CEASAR! (2016)
Written and directed by Joel and Ethan Coen.

HAIL THE CONQUERING HERO (1944)
Written and directed by Preston Sturges.

HAPPINESS (1998)
Written and directed by Todd Solondz.

HAROLD AND MAUDE (1971)
Directed by Hal Ashby. Written by Colin Higgins.

HEATHERS (1988)
Directed by Michael Lehmann. Written by Daniel Waters.

HI, MOM! (1970)
Directed by Brian De Palma. Written by Brian De Palma (story and screenplay), Charles Hirsch (story).

HIGHWAY 61 (1991)
Directed by Bruce McDonald. Written by Allan Magee, Bruce McDonald and Don McKellar.

HOLLYWOOD SHUFFLE (1987)
Directed by Robert Townsend. Written by Robert Townsend and Keenen Ivory Wayans.

HORSE FEATHERS (1932)
Directed by Norman Z. McLeod. Written by Bert Kalmar, Harry Ruby, S.J. Perelman, Will B. Johnstone.

HOW I GOT INTO COLLEGE (1989)
Directed by Savage Steve Holland. Written by Terrel Seltzer.

HOW TO GET AHEAD IN ADVERTISING (1989)
Written and directed by Bruce Robinson

HOW TO STUFF A WILD BIKINI (1965)
Directed by William Asher. Written by William Asher and Leo Townsend.

THE HUDSUCKER PROXY (1994)
Directed by Joel Coen, Ethan Coen. Written by Joel Coen, Ethan Coen, Sam Raimi.

HUMAN NATURE (2001)
Directed by Michel Gondry. Written by Charlie Kaufman.

THE BIZARRO ENCYCLOPEDIA OF FILM

IDIOCRACY (2006)
Directed by Mike Judge. Written by Mike Judge (story and screenplay), Etan Cohen (screenplay).

IN BRUGES (2008)
Written and directed by Martin McDonagh.

IT'S PAT (1994)
Directed by Adam Bernstein. Written by Julia Sweeney, Jim Emerson and Stephen Hibbert.

JACKASS: THE MOVIE (2002)
Directed by Jeff Tremaine. Written by Jeff Tremaine and Cast.

THE JERK (1979)
Directed by Carl Reiner. Written by Steve Martin, Carl Gottlieb, and Michael Elias.

JOYSTICKS (1983)
Directed by Greydon Clark. Written by Al Gomez, Mickey Epps, and Curtis Burch.

KAMIKAZE GIRLS (2004)
Directed by Tetsuya Nakashima. Written by Nobara Takemoto (novel), Tetsuya Nakashima (screenplay).

KID BLUE (1973)
Directed by James Frawley. Written by Bud Shrake.

KIDS IN THE HALL: BRAIN CANDY (1996)
Directed by Kelly Makin. Written by Norm Hiscock, Bruce McCulloch, Kevin McDonald, Mark McKinney, Scott Thompson.

KING OF HEARTS (1966)
Directed by Philippe de Broca. Written by Daniel Boulanger (scenario and dialogue), Maurice Bessy (idea) .

KINGPIN (1996)
Directed by Bobby Farrelly, Peter Farrelly. Written by Barry Fanaro, Mort Nathan.

KISS MEETS THE PHANTOM OF THE PARK (1978)
Directed by Gordon Hessler. Written by Jan Michael Sherman and Don Buday.

KUNG FU HUSTLE (2004)
Directed by Stephen Chow. Written by Stephen Chow, Kan-Cheung Tsang, Xin Huo, Man Keung Chan.

THE LAST SUPPER (1995)
Directed by Stacy Title. Written by Dan Rosen.

THE LOBSTER (2015)
Directed by Yorgos Lanthimos. Written by Yorgos Lanthimos and Efthymis Filippou

LOVE SERENADE (1996)
Written and directed by Shirley Barrett.

THE LOVED ONE (1965)
Directed by Tony Richardson. Written by Terry Southern and Christopher Isherwood, from the novel by Evelyn Waugh.

MAKING MR. RIGHT (1987)
Directed by Susan Seidelman. Written by Floyd Byars and Laurie Frank.

THE MAN WITH TWO BRAINS (1983)
Directed by Carl Reiner. Written by Steve Martin, Carl Reiner, and George Gipe.

MEET THE HOLLOWHEADS (1989)
Directed by Thomas R. Burman. Written by Thomas R. Burman, Stanley Mieses, and Lisa Morton.

MODERN VAMPIRES (1998)
Directed by Richard Elfman. Written by Matthew Bright.

MONTY PYTHON AND THE HOLY GRAIL (1975)
Directed by Terry Gilliam, Terry Jones. Written by Graham Chapman, John Cleese.

MONTY PYTHON'S THE LIFE OF BRIAN (1979)
Directed by Terry Jones. Written by Graham Chapman, John Cleese, Terry Gilliam, Eric Idle, Terry Jones, Michael Palin.

MONTY PYTHON'S THE MEANING OF LIFE (1983)
Directed by Terry Jones, Terry Gilliam. Written by Graham Chapman, John Cleese, Terry Gilliam, Eric Idle, Terry Jones, Michael Palin.

MORGAN! (1966)
Directed by Karel Reisz. Written by David Mercer.

THE BIZARRO ENCYCLOPEDIA OF FILM

MOTIVATIONAL GROWTH (2013)
Written and directed by Don Thacker.

MOTORAMA (1991)
Directed by Barry Shils. Written by Joseph Minion.

MST3K: THE MOVIE (1996)
Directed by Jim Mallon. Written by Michael J. Nelson, Trace Beaulieu, Jim Mallon, Kevin Murphy, Mary Jo Pehl, Paul Chaplin, Bridget Jones, Joel Hodgson (television series "Mystery Science Theater 3000").

MY CHAUFFEUR (1986)
Written and directed by David Beaird.

MY NAME IS NOBODY (1973)
Directed by Tonino Valeri and (uncredited) Sergio Leone. Written by Ernesto Gastaldi. Story by Fulvio Morsella and Ernesto Gastaldi, from an idea by Sergio Leone.

MYRA BRECKINRIDGE (1970)
Directed by Michael Sarne. Written by Gore Vidal (novel), Michael Sarne and David Giler.

MYSTERY TRAIN (1989)
Written and directed by Jim Jarmusch.

NACHO LIBRE (2006)
Directed by Jared Hess. Written by Jared Hess, Jerusha Hess, and Mike White.

NAPOLEON DYNAMITE (2004)
Directed by Jared Hess. Written by Jared and Jerusha Hess.

NICE DREAMS (1981)
Directed by Tommy Chong. Written by Tommy Chong and Cheech Marin.

NIGHT ON EARTH (1991)
Written and directed by Jim Jarmusch.

O BROTHER WHERE ART THOU (2000)
Directed by Joel Coen, Ethan Coen. Written by Ethan Coen, Joel Coen, loosely based on the work of Homer.

OH, GOD! (1977)
Directed by Carl Reiner. Written by Larry Gelbart and Avery Corman (novel).

ONE CRAZY SUMMER (1986)
Written and directed by Savage Steve Holland.

ORGAZMO (1997)
Written and directed by Trey Parker.

THE BIZARRO ENCYCLOPEDIA OF FILM

OUTRAGEOUS! (1977)
Directed by Richard Benner. Written by Richard Benner and Margaret Gibson Gilboord (based on story).

THE PARTY (1968)
Directed by Blake Edwards. Written by Blake Edwards and Tom and Frank Waldman.

PASS THE AMMO (1988)
Directed by David Beaird. Written by Joel and Neil Cohen.

PENN & TELLER GET KILLED (1989)
Directed by Arthur Penn. Written by Penn Jillette and Teller.

THE PLAYER (1992)
Directed by Robert Altman. Written by Michael Tolkin, from his book.

PLEASE DON'T EAT MY MOTHER! (1973)
Directed by Carl Monson. Written by Eric Norden.

A POLISH VAMPIRE IN BURBANK (1985)
Written and directed by Mark Pirro.

PRIVATE PARTS (1972)
Directed by Paul Bartel. Written by Philip Kearney, Les Rendelstein.

RAISING ARIZONA (1987)
Written and directed by Joel and Ethan Coen.

REAL GENIUS (1985)
Directed by Martha Coolidge. Written by Neal Israel, Pat Proft, and Peter Torokvei.

THE REF (1995)
Directed by Ted Demme. Written by Richard LaGravenese and Marie Weiss. Story by Marie Weiss.

REVENGE OF THE CHEERLEADERS (1976)
Directed by Richard Lerner. Written by Nathaniel Dorsky (story), Richard Lerner (story), Ted Greenwald and Ace Baandage.

ROADSIDE PROPHETS (1992)
Written and directed by Abbe Wool.

ROSELAND (1971)
Written and directed by Fredric Hobbs.

THE BIZARRO ENCYCLOPEDIA OF FILM

RUBIN & ED (1991)
Written and directed by Trent Harris.

SAFETY LAST! (1923)
Directed by Fred C. Newmeyer and Sam Taylor. Story by Hal Roach, Sam Taylor, Tim Whelan, and (uncredited) Jean C. Havez and Harold Lloyd. Titles by H.M. Walker.

SALVATION! HAVE YOU SAID YOUR PRAYERS TODAY? (1987)
Directed by Beth B. Written by Beth B. and Tom Robinson.

SCREEN TEST (1985)
Directed by Sam Auster. Written by Laura Auster and Sam Auster.

SCROOGED (1988)
Directed by Richard Donner. Written by Mitch Glazer and Michael O'Donoghue, from the novel *A Christmas Carol* by Charles Dickens.

SEEKING A FRIEND FOR THE END OF THE WORLD (2012)
Written and directed by Lorene Scafaria.

SEPTIEN (2011)
Directed by Michael Tully. Written by Robert Longstreet (story), Onur Tukel (story), Michael Tully (story).

SERIAL MOM (1994)
Written and directed by John Waters.

SEVEN PSYCHOPATHS (2012)
Written and directed by Martin McDonagh.

SHAKES THE CLOWN (1991)
Written and directed by Bobcat Goldthwait.

SIGHTSEERS (2012)
Directed by Ben Wheatley. Written by Alice Lowe and Steve Oram, additional material by Amy Jump.

SIMON (1980)
Directed by Marshall Brickman. Written by Marshall Brickman and Thomas Baum (story).

SLACKER (1991)
Written and directed by Richard Linklater.

THE BIZARRO ENCYCLOPEDIA OF FILM

SLEEPING DOGS LIE (2006)
Written and directed by Bobcat Goldthwait.

SOMETHING WILD (1986)
Directed by Jonathan Demme. Written by E. Max Frye.

SOUTH PARK BIGGER, LONGER, AND UNCUT (1999)
Directed by Trey Parker. Written by Trey Parker, Matt Stone, Pam Brady.

STEAMBOAT BILL, JR. (1928)
Directed by Charles Reisner (as Chas F. Reisner) and (uncredited) Buster Keaton. Written (uncredited) by Buster Keaton and Carl Harbaugh (story).

STRANGER THAN PARADISE (1984)
Written and directed by Jim Jarmusch

SULLIVAN'S TRAVELS (1941)
Written and directed by Preston Sturges.

SWIMMING WITH SHARKS (1994)
Written and directed by George Huang.

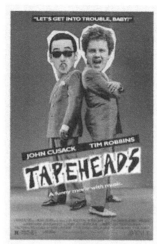

THE SUPERGRASS (1985)
Directed by Peter Richardson. Written Peter Richardson and Pete Richens.

TAPEHEADS (1988)
Directed by Bill Fishman. Written by Bill Fishman, Peter McCarthy, Jim Herzfeld and Ryan Rowe.

TEAM AMERICA (2004)
Directed by Trey Parker. Written by Trey Parker, Matt Stone, Pam Brady.

TENACIOUS D IN THE PICK OF DESTINY (2006)
Directed by Liam Lynch. Written by Jack Black, Kyle Gass, and Liam Lynch.

THIS IS THE END (2013)
Written and directed by Evan Goldberg and Seth Rogen.

TOP SECRET! (1984)
Written and directed by Jim Abrahams, David Zucker, Jerry Zucker, Martyn Burke.

THE BIZARRO ENCYCLOPEDIA OF FILM

UNFAITHFULLY YOURS (1948)
Written and directed by Preston Sturges.

UP IN SMOKE (1978)
Directed by Lou Adler and Tommy Chong (Uncredited), Written by Tommy Chong and Cheech Marin.

A VERY BRADY SEQUEL (1996)
Directed by Arlene Sanford. Written by Sherwood Schwartz (characters), Harry Elfont (story and screenplay), Deborah Kaplan (story and screenplay), James Berg (screenplay), Stan Zimmerman (screenplay).

WAITING FOR GUFFMAN (1996)
Directed by Christopher Guest. Written by Christopher Guest and Eugene Levy

WALK HARD: THE DEWEY COX STORY (2007)
Directed by Jake Kasdan, Written by Judd Apatow, Jake Kasdan.

WIENER-DOG (2016)
Written and directed by Todd Solondz.

WHERE THE BUFFALO ROAM (1980)
Directed by Art Linson. Written by John Kaye and Hunter. S. Thompson (stories).

WHERE'S POPPA? (1970)
Directed by Carl Reiner. Written by Robert Klane.

WHO FRAMED ROGER RABBIT? (1988)
Directed by Robert Zemeckis. Written by Gary K. Wolf (novel), Jeffrey Price (scrrenplay), Peter S. Seaman (screenplay).

WILDER NAPALM (1993)
Directed by Glenn Gordon Caron. Written by Vince Gilligan.

THE WITCHES OF EASTWICK (1987)
Directed by George Miller. Written by Michael Cristofer, based on the novel by John Updike.

WITHNAIL AND I (1987)
Written and directed by Bruce Robinson.

WOLFCOP (2014)
Written and directed by Lowell Dean.

WORK IS A FOUR-LETTER WORD (1968)

Directed by Peter Hall. Written by Jeremy Brooks, Henry Livings (play).

WRONG (2012)

Written and directed by Quentin Dupieux.

YOUNG FRANKENSTEIN (1974)

Directed by Mel Brooks. Written by Gene Wilder, Mel Brooks, based on characters from the novel Frankenstein by Mary Shelley.

DRAMA

Drama is commonly thought of as the grown-up section of the video store, where people who want to see serious subjects discussed seriously convene, parsing over its shelves while bypassing the more lurid and infantile sections. Which is a legit and mature response to much of the world's ceaseless knuckleheadedness.

That said, for the Bizarro explorer, many of the juiciest deep dives are to be found within this section. Because the more "serious" artists get, the more they run the risk of either a) turning into the dreaded "Melodrama", where serious issues turn cartoonish and overwrought (aka BIZARRO GOLD), or b) transitioning into Cult or Arthouse fare (a line we are wrestling with like crazy, in differentiating the three).

Bottom line—and in case you hadn't noticed by now—these categories are all over the place. *But in the spirit of doing this video store thing, I think it's worthwhile to consider these films in this context. And then put them wherever you want.*

Bottom line: David Lynch never shows up in the Cult or Arthouse sections. And that should tell you everything you need to know. (JS)

3 WOMEN (1977)
Written and directed by Robert Altman.

AMADEUS (1984)
Directed by Milos Forman. Written by Peter Shaffer, from his play.

APARTMENT ZERO (1988)
Directed by Martin Donovan. Written by Martin Donovan (story/screenplay) and David Koepp (screenplay).

THE BIZARRO ENCYCLOPEDIA OF FILM

APOCALYPSE NOW (1979)
Directed by Francis Ford Coppola.
Written by Francis Ford Coppola, John
Milius, and Joseph Conrad (book).

AUTO FOCUS (2002)
Directed by Paul Schrader. Written
by Scott Alexander and Larry
Karaszewski.

BAD BOY BUBBY (1993)
Written and directed by Rolf de Heer.

**BAD TIMING: A SENSUAL
OBSESSION (1980)**
Directed by Nicolas Roeg. Written by
Yale Udoff.

BARFLY (1987)
Directed by Barbet Schroeder. Written
by Charles Bukowski.

BARTON FINK (1991)
Written and directed by
Joel and Ethan Coen.

**BAYOU AKA POOR
WHITE TRASH (1957)**
Directed by Harold
Daniels. Written by
Edward I. Fessler

**BEASTS OF THE
SOUTHERN WILD
(2012)**
Directed by Benh
Zeitlin. Written by Lucy
Alibar and Benh Zeitlin.

BIG EYES (2014)
Directed by Tim Burton. Written
by Scott Alexander and Larry
Karaszewski.

BIRDMAN (2014)
Directed by Alejandro G. Iñárritu.
Written by Alejandro G. Iñárritu,
Nicolás Giacobone, Alexander
Dinelaris, Armando Bo, and Raymond
Carver (for his dramatized short story
"What We Talk About When We Talk
About Love").

BIRDY (1984)
Directed by Alan Parker. Written by
Sandy Kroopf and Jack Behr, from the
novel by William Wharton.

BITTER MOON (1992)
Directed by Roman Polanski. Written
by Roman Polanski, Gerard Brach,
John Brownjohn, and Jeff Gross, from
the novel by Pascal
Bruckner.

BLACK SWAN (2010)
Directed by Darren
Aronofsky. Written by
Mark Heyman, Andres
Heinz, and John J.
McLaughlin. Story by
Andres Heinz.

BLUE VELVET (1986)
Written and directed by
David Lynch.

BOOGIE NIGHTS (1997)
Written and directed by Paul
Thomas Anderson.

BORDER RADIO (1987)
Written and directed by Allison
Anders, Dean Lent and Kurt Voss.

BOXING HELENA (1993)
Directed by Jennifer Chambers Lynch.
Written by Philippe Caland (story),
Jennifer Chambers Lynch (screenplay).

THE BOYS IN THE BAND (1970)
Directed by William Friedkin. Written
by Mart Crowley.

BRIMSTONE AND TREACLE (1987)
Directed by Barry David. Written by
Dennis Potter.

**BRING ME THE HEAD OF ALFREDO
GARCIA (1974)**
Directed by Sam
Peckinpah. Written by
Sam Peckinpah and
Gordon T. Dawson (as
Gordon Dawson). Story
by Sam Peckinpah and
Frank Kowalski.

CALIGULA (1979)
Directed by Tinto
Brass. Giancarlo Lui
(uncredited) and Bob
Guccione (uncredited).
Written by Gore Vidal.

CHEAP THRILLS (2013)
Directed by E.L. Katz. Written by
David Chirchirillo and Trent Haaga.

CHILLY SCENES OF WINTER (1979)
Directed by Joan Micklin Silver.
Written by Joan Micklin Silver and
Ann Beattie (Based on Novel).

CITIZEN KANE (1941)
Directed by Orson Welles. Written
by Herman J. Mankiewicz and
Orson Welles.

CITY LIGHTS (1931)
Written and directed by
Charles Chaplin.

CLEAN, SHAVEN (1993)
Written and directed by Lodge
Kerrigan (as Lodge H. Kerrigan).

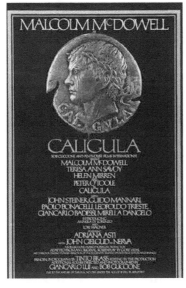

**THE COLOR OF
MONEY (1986)**
Directed by Martin
Scorsese. Written by
Richard Price, loosely
based on the novel by
Walter Tevis.

COSMOPOLIS (2012)
Written and directed by
David Cronenberg,
from the novel by
Don DeLillo.

CRAZY LOVE (1987)
Directed by Dominique Deruddere. Written by Dominique Deruddere and Mark Didden, from stories by Charles Bukowski.

DAY OF THE LOCUST (1975)
Directed by John Schlesinger. Written by Waldo Salt and Nathanael West (novel).

DEAD RINGERS (1988)
Directed by David Cronenberg. Written by David Cronenberg and Norman Snider.

THE DEVILS (1971)
Directed by Ken Russell. Written by Ken Russell, from the books *The Devils of Loudin* by Aldous Huxley and *The Devils* by John Whiting.

VANESSA REDGRAVE · OLIVER REED

LES DIABLES

DIABOLIQUE (1955)
Directed by Henri-Georges Clouzot (as H.G. Clouzot). Written by Henri-Georges Clouzot, Jérôme Géronimi, René Masson, and Frédéric Grendel, from the novel by Pierre Boileau and Thomas Narcejac.

THE DIARY OF A TEENAGE GIRL (2015)
Written and directed by Marielle Heller, from the graphic novel *The Diary of a Teenage Girl: An Account in Words and Pictures* by Phoebe Gloeckner.

DO THE RIGHT THING (1989)
Written and directed by Spike Lee.

EASY RIDER (1969)
Directed by Dennis Hopper. Written by Peter Fonda, Dennis Hopper, and Terry Southern.

ED WOOD (1994)
Directed by Tim Burton. Written by Scott Alexander and Larry Karaszewski.

EDMOND (2005)
Directed by Stuart Gordon. Written by David Mamet (adapted from his play).

THE ELEPHANT MAN (1980)
Directed by David Lynch. Written by David Lynch, Christopher De Vore, and Eric Bergren, from the books *The Elephant Man and Other Reminiscences* by Frederick Treves, and *The Elephant Man: A Study in Human Dignity* by Ashley Montagu.

ELEVEN P.M. (1928)
Directed and written by Richard Maurice.

A FACE IN THE CROWD (1957)
Directed Elia Kazan. Written by Budd Schulberg, from his short story "Your Arkansas Traveller".

FAMILY PORTRAITS: A TRILOGY OF AMERICA (2005)
Written and directed by Doug Buck.

FARGO (1999)
Written and directed by Joel and Ethan Coen.

FATHER OF THE YEAR (2012)
Written and directed by Neil Hiatt.

FIGHT CLUB (1999)
Directed by David Fincher. Written by Jim Uhls.

THE FISHER KING (1991)
Directed by Terry Gilliam. Written by Richard LaGravenese.

THE FORBIDDEN DANCE: LAMBADA (1990)
Directed by Greydon Clark. Written by Roy Langsdon and John Platt.

FRANCES (1982)
Directed by Graeme Clifford. Written by Eric Bergen, Christopher De Vore, and Nicholas Kazan.

FREEWAY (1996)
Written and directed by Matthew Bright.

FREEWAY II: CONFESSIONS OF A TRICKBABY (1999)
Written and directed by Matthew Bright.

FULL METAL JACKET (1987)
Directed by Stanley Kubrick. Written by Stanley Kubrick, Michael Herr, and Gustav Hasford, from Hasford's novel *The Short-Timers.*

THE GAME (1997)
Directed by David Fincher. Written by John Brancato and Michael Ferris.

GAMES (1967)
Directed by Curtis Harrington. Written by Gene R. Kearney (as Gene Kearney). Story by Curtis Harrington and George Edwards.

GASLIGHT (1944)
Directed by George Cukor. Written by John Van Druten, Walter Reisch, and John L. Balderston, from the play by Patrick Hamilton.

GHOST WORLD (2001)
Directed by Terry Zwigoff. Written by Daniel Clowes.

GLENGARRY GLEN ROSS (1992)
Directed by James Foley. Written by David Mamet, from his play.

THE GOLD RUSH (1925)
Written and directed by Charles Chaplin.

THE GREAT DICTATOR (1941)
Written and directed by Charles Chaplin.

THE BIZARRO ENCYCLOPEDIA OF FILM

GUMMO (1997)
Written and directed by
Harmony Korine.

THE HATEFUL EIGHT (2015)
Written and directed by Quentin
Tarantino.

HE WHO GETS SLAPPED (1924)
Directed by Victor Sjöström. Written
by Leonid Andreyev (adapted from
play), Carey Wilson, Victor Sjöström
and Marian Ainslee (titles).

**THE HEART IS DECEITFUL ABOVE
ALL THINGS (2004)**
Directed by Asia Argento. Written by
Asia Argento, Alessandro Magania,
and Laura Albert (as J.T. Leroy)
(Short Stories).

HEAVENLY CREATURES (1994)
Directed by Peter Jackson. Written by
Fran Walsh (as Frances Walsh) and
Peter Jackson.

HIGH-RISE (2015)
Directed by Ben Wheatley. Written by
Amy Jump, from the novel by
J.G. Ballard.

HOTEL NEW HAMPSHIRE (1984)
Directed by Tony Richardson. Written
by Tony Richardson, from the novel by
John Irving.

THE HUSTLER (1961)
Directed by Robert Rossen. Written by
Sidney Carroll, Robert Rossen, from
the novel by Walter Tevis.

IN A GLASS CAGE (1986)
Written and directed by Agustí
Villaronga (as Agustín Villaronga).

IN MY SKIN (2002)
Written and directed by
Marina de Van.

THE INCIDENT (1967)
Directed by Larry Peerce. Written by
Nicholas E. Baehr.

INLAND EMPIRE (2006)
Written and directed by David Lynch.

INSIGNIFICANCE (1985)
Directed by Nicolas Roeg. Written by
Terry Johnson (screenplay).

THE INVITATION (2015)
Directed by Karyn Kusama. Written
by Phil Hay and Matt Manfredi.

IT'S ALL ABOUT LOVE (2003)
Directed by Thomas Vinterberg,
Written by Mogens Rukov, |
Thomas Vinterberg.

JFK (1991)
Directed by Oliver Stone. Written
by Oliver Stone, Zachary Sklar
and based on the book *On the Trail
of the Assassins* by Jim Garrison
and *Crossfire: The Plot That Killed
Kennedy* by Jim Marrs.

JOE (1970)
Directed by John G. Avildsen. Written
by Norman Wexler.

THE BIZARRO ENCYCLOPEDIA OF FILM

JOHNNY GOT HIS GUN (1971)
Written and directed by
Dalton Trumbo.

THE KID (1921)
Written and directed by
Charles Chaplin.

KILLER JOE (2011)
Directed by William Friedkin. Written
by Tracy Letts, from his play.

KNIGHTRIDERS (1981)
Written and directed by G
eorge A. Romero.

LA STRADA (1954)
Directed by Federico Fellini. Written
by Federico Fellini, Tulio Pinelli, and
Ennio Flaiano.

LAST EXIT TO BROOKLYN (1989)
Directed by Uli Edel. Written by
Desmond Nakano, from the book by
Hubert Selby, Jr.

THE LAST MOVIE (1971)
Directed by Dennis Hopper. Written
by Dennis Hopper and Stewart Stern

THE LAST WAVE (1977)
Directed by Peter Weir. Written by
Peter Weir, Tony Morphett and
Petru Popescu.

LOLITA (1962)
Directed by Stanley Kubrick. Written
by Vladimir Nabokov, from his book.

LOLITA (1997)
Directed by Adrian Lyne. Written by
Stephen Schiff and Vladimir Nabokov
(novel).

**THE LONELINESS OF THE LONG
DISTANCE RUNNER (1962)**
Directed by Tony Richardson. Written
by Alan Sillitoe.

THE LONG GOODBYE (1973)
Directed by Robert Altman. Written
by Leigh Brackett and Raymond
Chandler (novel).

LOST HIGHWAY (1997)
Directed by David Lynch. Written by
David Lynch and Barry Gifford.

MAD LOVE (1935)
Directed by Karl Freund. Written by
Maurice Renard (novel), Florence
Crewe-Jones, Guy Endore, P.J.
Wolfson, John L. Balderston.

MAGIC (1978)
Directed by Richard Attenborough.
Written by William Goldman, from
his novel.

MAN ON THE MOON (1999)
Directed by Milos Forman. Written
by Scott Alexander and Larry
Karaszewski.

MAPS TO THE STARS (2014)
Directed by David Cronenberg.
Written by Bruce Wagner.

MASH (1970)
Directed by Robert Altman. Written by Ring Lardner Jr. and Richard Hooker (Novel).

MILLER'S CROSSING (1990)
Written and directed by Joel and Ethan Coen.

MODERN TIMES (1936)
Written and directed by Charles Chaplin.

MULHOLLAND DRIVE (2001)
Written and directed by David Lynch.

THE NAKED CIVIL SERVANT (1975)
Directed by Jack Gold. Written by Phillip Mackie, from the book by Quentin Crisp.

THE NAKED KISS (1964)
Written and directed by Samuel Fuller.

NATURAL BORN KILLERS (1994)
Directed by Oliver Stone. Written by Oliver Stone, Dan Veloz, and Richard Rutowski, from the original screenplay by Quentin Tarantino.

NETWORK (1976)
Directed by Sidney Lumet. Written by Paddy Chayefsky.

THE NIGHT PORTER (1974)
Directed by Liliana Cavani. Written by Liliana Cavani and Italo Moscati. Story by Barbara Alberti, Amedeo Pagani, Italo Moscati, and Liliana Cavani.

NIGHTCRAWLER (2014)
Written and directed by Dan Gilroy.

THE NIGHTS OF CABIRIA (1957)
Directed by Federico Fellini. Written by Federico Fellini, Ennio Flaiano, Tulio Pinelli, and Pier Paolo Pasolini.

THE NINTH CONFIGURATION (1980)
Written and directed by William Peter Blatty, from his novel *Twinkle, Twinkle, Killer Kane*.

NO COUNTRY FOR OLD MEN (2007)
Written and directed by Joel and Ethan Coen, from the novel by Cormac McCarthy.

ODD MAN OUT (1947)
Directed by Carol Reed. Written by F. L. Green and R. C. Sherriff.

ONE FLEW OVER THE CUCKOO'S NEST (1975)
Directed by Milos Forman. Written by Lawrence Hauben, Bo Goldman, based on the novel by Ken Kesey and the play adaptation by Dale Wasserman.

ONLY LOVERS LEFT ALIVE (2013)
Written and directed by Jim Jarmusch.

OUT OF THE BLUE (1980)
Directed by Dennis Hopper. Written by Leonard Yakir and Brenda Nielson.

ORLANDO (1992)
Written and directed by Sally Potter, from the novel by Virginia Woolf.

THE PAPERBOY (2012)
Directed by Lee Daniels. Written by Peter Dexter (screenplay), Lee Daniels (screenplay), Peter Dexter (based on the novel by).

PASOLINI (2014)
Directed by Abel Ferrara. Written by Maurizio Braucci, based on an idea by Abel Ferrara and Nicola Tranquillino.

THE PASSION OF DARKLY NOON (1995)
Written and directed by Philip Ridley.

PATHS OF GLORY (1957)
Directed by Stanley Kubrick. Written by Stanley Kubrick, Calder Willingham, Jim Thompson, based on the novel by Humphrey Cobb.

THE PEOPLE VS. LARRY FLYNT (1996)
Directed by Milos Forman. Written by Scott Alexander and Larry Karaszewski.

PERFORMANCE (1970)
Directed by Donald Cammell and Nicolas Roeg. Written by Donald Cammell.

PULP FICTION (1994)
Directed by Quentin Tarantino. Written by Quentin Tarantino. Stories by Quentin Tarantino and Roger Avary.

THE RAPTURE (1991)
Written and directed by Michael Tolkin.

RATBOY (1986)
Directed by Sondra Locke. Written by Rob Thompson.

REQUIEM FOR A DREAM (2000)
Directed by Darren Aronofsky. Written by Hubert Selby, Jr. and Darren Aronofsky, from the book by Hubert Selby, Jr.

RESERVOIR DOGS (1992)
Written and directed by Quentin Tarantino. (Additional radio dialogue by Roger Avary.)

RIVER'S EDGE (1986)
Directed by Tim Hunter. Written by Neal Jimenez.

THE BIZARRO ENCYCLOPEDIA OF FILM

RUMBLEFISH (1983)
Directed by Francis Ford Coppola.
Written by Francis Ford Coppola and
S.E. Hinton.

SALVADOR (1986)
Directed by Oliver Stone.
Written by Oliver Stone
and Richard Boyle.

SCARLET DIVA (2000)
Written and directed by
Asia Argento.

A SERIOUS MAN (2009)
Written and directed by
Joel and Ethan Coen.

SIGN OF THE CROSS (1932)
Directed by Cecil B. DeMille. Written
by Waldemar Young, Sidney Buchman
and Wilson Barrett (Play).

SMITHEREENS (1982)
Directed by Susan Seidelman. Written
by Ron Nyswaner, Peter Askin, and
Susan Seidelman (Story.)

SONNY BOY (1989)
Directed by Robert Martin Carroll.
Written by Graeme Whifler (original
screenplay, Peter Desberg (additional
dialogue).

STAG (1997)
Directed by Gavin Wilding. Written
by Pat Bermel and Evan Taylor.

THE STRAIGHT STORY (1999)
Directed by David Lynch. Written by
John Roach and Mary Sweeney.

SUBURBIA (1983)
Written and directed by
Penelope Spheeris.

SUGAR COOKIES (1973)
Directed by Theodore
Gershuny. Written by
Theodore Gershuny and
Lloyd Kaufman.

SUMMER OF SAM (1999)
Directed by Spike
Lee. Written by Victor
Colicchio, Michael Imperioli, and
Spike Lee.

SUNSET BOULEVARD (1950)
Directed by Billy Wilder. Written by
Billy Wilder, Charles Brackett, and
D.M. Marshman Jr.

SYNECHDOCHE NY (2008)
Written and directed by Charlie
Kaufman.

THE TENANT (1976)
Directed by Roman Polanski. Written
by Roman Polanski, Gerard Brach and
Roland Topor (novel).

THE BIZARRO ENCYCLOPEDIA OF FILM

THEY SHOOT HORSES, DON'T THEY? (1969)
Directed by Sidney Pollack. Written by James Poe and Robert E. Thompson, from the novel by Horace McCoy.

THE THIRD MAN (1949)
Directed by Carol Reed. Written by Graham Greene, based on his novel.

THRONE OF BLOOD (1957)
Directed by Akira Kurosawa. Written by Hideo Oguni, Shinobu Hashimoto, Ryuzo Kikishima, Akira Kurosawa, based on the play *Macbeth* by William Shakespeare.

TIDELAND (2005)
Directed by Terry Gilliam. Written by Tony Grisony and Terry Gilliam.

TITUS (1999)
Written and directed by Julie Taymor.

TRACKS (1976)
Written and directed by Henry Jaglom.

TRAINSPOTTING (1996)
Directed by Danny Boyle. Written by John Hodge.

TRASH (1970)
Directed by Paul Morrissey. Written by Paul Morrissey.

THE TRIP (1967)
Directed by Roger Corman. Written by Jack Nicholson.

TRUE ROMANCE (1993)
Directed by Tony Scott. Written by Quentin Tarantino.

TWIN PEAKS: FIRE WALK WITH ME (1992)
Directed by David Lynch. Written by David Lynch and Robert Engels.

TWISTER (1989)
Written and directed by Michael Almereyda, from the novel by Mary Robison.

VIBRATIONS (1968)
Written and directed by Joe Sarno.

VIBRATIONS (1996)
Written and directed by Michael Paseornek.

WAKE IN FRIGHT (1971)
Directed by Ted Kotcheff. Screenplay by Evan Jones, from the novel by Kenneth Cook.

WALKABOUT (1971)
Directed by Nicolas Roeg. Written by Edward Bond and James Vance Marshall (novel).

WALKER (1987)
Directed by Alex Cox. Written by Rudy Wurlitzer.

THE UNHOLY THREE (1925)
Directed by Tod Browning. Written by Clarence Aaron 'Tod' Robbins (story) and Waldemar Young (scenario)

WHAT'S EATING GILBERT GRAPE (1993)

Directed by Lasse Hallstrom. Written by Peter Hedges.

WHATEVER HAPPENED TO BABY JANE? (1962)

Directed by Robert Aldrich. Written by Lukas Heller, from the novel by Henry Farrell.

WHITE DOG (1982)

Directed by Samuel Fuller. Written by Samuel Fuller and Curtis Hanson, from the novel by Romain Gary.

WHO'LL STOP THE RAIN (1978)

Directed by Karel Reisz. Written by Judith Rascoe and Robert Stone, from Stone's novel *Dog Soldiers*.

WHO'S AFRAID OF VIRGINIA WOOLF? (1966)

Directed by Mike Nichols. Written by Ernest Lehman, from the play by Edward Albee.

WILD AT HEART (1990)

Written and directed by David Lynch, from the novel by Barry Gifford.

WISE BLOOD (1979)

Directed by John Huston. Written by Benedict Fitzgerald, Michael Fitzgerald, from the novel by Flannery O'Connor.

WOMEN IN LOVE (1969)

Directed by Ken Russell. Written by Larry Kramer, from the book by D.H. Lawrence.

THE WORLD ACCORDING TO GARP (1982)

Directed by George Roy Hill. Written by Steve Tesich, from the novel by John Irving.

THE WORLD'S GREATEST SINNER (1962)

Written and directed by Timothy Carey.

ACTION/THRILLER

If any genre lends itself well to balls-to-the-walls fun and the finest kind of ridiculousness, it is the Action genre. Inside every one of us is an Ed Gruberman. Who is this Ed Gruberman, you may be asking? Well, he was the frustrated martial arts student in Canadian comedy troupe's The Frantics classic "Ti Kwan Leep." (Better known to us Yanks who listened to Dr. Demento as "Boot to the Head.") The saga of Mr. Gruberman is about a man who is less interested in the spiritual and mental aspects of his chosen study and instead just wants to start "wailing on some bozos!"

That is the prime id of the human spirit right there. You are Ed Gruberman and so am I. Do I want to sometimes just see someone kick a bunch of ass and blow up things? Hell yeah! It is the most basic form of seeing the fruits of one's heroic labors. For the majority of us, if we work a crappy dayjob and witness all kinds of not-rightedness, we rarely ever get to experience any actual karma at play. Same for our various corrupt leaders. Wouldn't be great to see some money and power hungry politico whose heart was replaced with smegma and Excelsior a long time ago, get a motherfucking boot to the head? Again, hell yeah! Grab your favorite cheap beer and prepare to get your "Ti Kwan Leep" on with the following films. (HD)

68 KILL (2017)
Directed by Trent Haaga. Written by Trent Haaga, from the novel by Bryan Smith.

ACTION JACKSON (1988)
Directed by Craig R. Baxley. Written by Robert Reneau.

ARREBATO (2014)
Directed by Sandra Gugliotta. Written by Sandra Gugliotta, Sebastian Rotstein.

ASSAULT ON PRECINCT 13 (1976)
Written and directed by John Carpenter.

ATTACK THE BLOCK (2011)
Written and directed by Joe Cornish.

AVENGING ANGEL (1985)
Written and directed by Robert Vincent O'Neill.

BAD LIEUTENANT (1992)
Directed by Abel Ferrara. Written by Abel Ferrara and Zoe Lund.

BAD LIEUTENANT: PORT OF CALL NEW ORLEANS (2009)
Directed by Werner Herzog. Written by William F. Finkelstein.

BARBED WIRE DOLLS (1976)
Directed by Jess Franco. Written by Jess Franco, Connie Grau, and Christine Lembach.

BATTLE ROYALE (2000)
Directed by Kinji Fukasaku. Written by Kenta Fukasaku.

THE BEGUILED (1971)
Directed by Don Siegel. Written by Albert Maltz and Irene Kamp, from the novel *A Painted Devil* by Thomas P. Cullinan.

THE BIG RED ONE (1980)
Written and directed by Samuel Fuller.

BIRD WITH THE CRYSTAL PLUMAGE (1970)
Written and directed by Dario Argento.

BLOOD SIMPLE (1984)
Written and directed by Joel and Ethan Coen.

BLUE RUIN (2013)
Written and directed by Jeremy Saulnier.

THE BOYS NEXT DOOR (1985)
Directed by Penelope Spheeris. Written by Glen Morgan and James Wong.

BULLET (1996)
Directed by Julien Temple. Written by Mickey Rourke and Bruce Rubenstein.

BUTCH CASSIDY AND THE SUNDANCE KID (1969)
Directed by George Roy Hill. Written by William Goldman.

CAPE FEAR (1962)
Directed by J. Lee Thompson. Written by James R. Webb and John D. McDonald (novel).

CAPE FEAR (1991)
Directed by Martin Scorsese. Written by Wesley Strick, James R. Webb (earlier screenplay), and John D. McDonald (novel).

THE CAT O'NINE TAILS (1971)
Directed by Dario Argento. Written by Dario Argento, from a story by Luigi Collo, Dardano Sachetti, and (uncredited) Bryan Edgar Wallace.

THE BIZARRO ENCYCLOPEDIA OF FILM

CIRCLE OF IRON (1978)
Directed by Richard Moore. Written by Stirling Silliphant, Stanley Mann, Bruce Lee and James Coburn.

CLASS OF 1984 (1982)
Directed by Mark L. Lester. Written by Mark L. Lester, Tom Holland, John S.W. Saxton, and Barry Schneider (uncredited).

THE CRAZIES (1975)
Directed by George A. Romero. Written by George A. Romero, from an original script by Paul McCullough.

CRUISING (1980)
Directed by William Friedkin. Written by William Friedkin and Gerald Walker (novel).

CUTTER'S WAY (1981)
Directed by Ivan Passer. Written by Jeffrey Alan Fiskin and Newton Thornburg (Novel).

DANGER: DIABOLIK (1968)
Directed by Mario Bava. Written by Arduino Maiuri, Brian Degas, Tudor Gates, and Mario Bava.

DANGEROUS MEN (2005)
Written by directed by Jahangir Salehi.

DEAD TIME: KALA (2007)
Written and directed by Joko Anwar.

DEADLY PREY (1987)
Written and directed by David A. Prior.

DEATH RACE 2000 (1975)
Directed by Paul Bartel. Written by Robert Thom and Charles B. Griffith, from the story "The Racer" by Ib Melchior.

THE DEVIL'S REJECTS (2005)
Written and directed by Rob Zombie.

DISCO GODFATHER (1979)
Directed by J. Robert Wagoner. Written by J. Robert Wagoner and Cliff Roquemore.

DJANGO KILL...IF THEY LIVE, SHOOT! (1967)
Directed by Giulio Questi. Written by Franco Arcalli, Giulio Questi, and Benedetto Benedetti, from an idea by María del Carmen Martínez Román (as Ma del Carmen Roman).

DJANGO UNCHAINED (2012)
Written and directed by Quentin Tarantino.

DOLEMITE (1975)
Directed by D'Urville Martin. Written by Jerry Jones and Rudy Ray Moore.

THE BIZARRO ENCYCLOPEDIA OF FILM

DOWN TWISTED (1987)
Directed by Albert Pyun. Written by Gene O'Neill, Tom O'Neill, Noreen Turbin and Albert Pyun

DRUNKEN WUTANG (1984)
Directed by Cheung-Yan Yuen. Written by Yuen Clan (story), Kei Mai (screenplay).

DUEL (1971)
Directed by Steven Spielberg. Written by Richard Matheson, from his short story.

FANTOMAS (1964)
Directed by André Hunebelle. Written by Pierre Souvestre, Marcel Allain, Jean Halain, and Pierre Foucaud.

FEAR CITY (1984)
Directed by Abel Ferrara. Written by Nicholas St. John.

FIRECRACKER (2005)
Directed by Steve Balderson. Written by Steve Balderson and Clark Balderson (translation).

A FISTFUL OF DOLLARS (1964)
Directed by Sergio Leone. Written by Adriano Bolzoni (story,) Mark Lowell (story,) Victor Andres Catena, Sergio Leone, Jaime Comas Gil, Fernando Di Leo (uncredited), Duccio Tessari (uncredited), and Tonino Valerii.

FOR A FEW DOLLARS MORE (1965)
Directed by Sergio Leone. Written by Sergio Leone, Luciano Vincenzoni.

FOR Y'UR HEIGHT ONLY (1981)
Directed by Eddie Nicart. Written by Cora Caballes (story and scrrenplay).

FOUR OF THE APOCALYPSE (1975)
Directed by Lucio Fulci. Written by Ennio de Concini, from the short stories "The Luck of Roaring Camp" and "The Outcasts of Poker Flat" by Bret Harte.

THE FUNERAL (1996)
Directed by Abel Ferrara. Written by Nicholas St. John.

GHOST DOG: THE WAY OF THE SAMURAI (1999)
Written and directed by Jim Jarmusch.

THE GOOD, THE BAD, AND THE UGLY (1966)
Directed by Sergio Leone. Written by Sergio Leone, Luciano Vincenzoni, Agenore Incrocce, and Furio Scarpelli. Story by Sergio Leone and Luciano Vincenzoni.

GREEN ROOM (2015)
Written and directed by Jeremy Saulnier.

HIGH PLAINS DRIFTER (1973)
Directed by Clint Eastwood. Written by Ernest Tidyman.

HOLLYWOOD VICE SQUAD (1986)
Directed by Penelope Spheeris. Written by James J. Docherty.

THE BIZARRO ENCYCLOPEDIA OF FILM

ICHI THE KILLER (2001)
Directed by Takashi Miike. Written by
Sakichi Sato and Hideo Yamamoto.

INGLORIOUS BASTERDS (2009)
Written and directed by
Quentin Tarantino.

IN LIKE FLINT (1967)
Directed by Gordon Douglas. Written
by Hal Fimberg.

ISLE OF DOGS (2011)
Directed by Tammi Sutton. Written by
Seth Holt.

A HISTORY OF VIOLENCE (2005)
Directed by David Cronenberg.
Written by Josh Olson, from the
graphic novel by John Wagner and
Vince Locke.

THE HONEYMOON KILLERS (1970)
Directed by Leonard Kastle and
Donald Volkman (uncredited). Written
by Leonard Kastle.

HUDSON HAWK (1991)
Directed by Michael Lehmann.
Written by Bruce Willis, Robert Kraft,
Steven E. de Souza, and Daniel Waters.

THE HUMAN TORNADO (1976)
Directed by Cliff Roquemore. Written
by Jerry Jones, Rudy Ray Moore
(characters) and Jimmy Lynch (special
dialogue) .

KILL BILL VOL. 1-2 (2003-2004)
Written and directed by
Quentin Tarantino.

KILL LIST (2011)
Directed by Ben Wheatley. Written by
Ben Wheatley and Amy Jump.

KILLER'S KISS (1955)
Written and directed by
Stanley Kubrick.

THE KILLING (1956)
Directed by Stanley Kubrick. Written
by Stanley Kubrick, Jim Thompson
(dialogue), and Lionel White (Novel).

KING OF NEW YORK (1990)
Directed by Abel Ferrara. Written by
Nicholas St. John.

KING OF THE ANTS (2003)
Directed by Stuart Gordon. Written by
Charlie Higson.

THE LAST DINOSAUR (1977)
Directed by Alexander Grasshoff,
Tsugunobu Kotani. Written by William
Overgard.

**THE LEGEND OF DRUNKEN
MASTER (1994)**
Directed by Chia-Liang Liu. Written
by Edward Tang, Man-Ming Tong,
Kai-Chi Yuen. English adaptation by
Rod Dean.

THE LIMEY (1999)
Directed by Steven Soderbergh.
Written by Lem Dobbs.

MACHINE GIRL (2008)
Written and directed by Noboru Iguchi.

MAD FOXES (1981)
Directed by Paul Grau. Written by Paul Grau, Hans R. Walthard, Melvin Quiñones, and (uncredited) Jaime Jesûs Balcázar.

MASSACRE AT CENTRAL HIGH (1976)
Written and directed by Rene Daalder.

MEMENTO (2000)
Written and directed by Christopher Nolan, from the short story "Memento Mori" by Jonathan Nolan.

THE MIAMI CONNECTION (1987)
Directed by Woo-sang Park. Written by Woo-sang Park, Y.K. Kim, and Joseph Diamond.

MISERY (1990)
Directed by Rob Reiner. Written by William Goldman, from the novel by Stephen King.

MS .45 (1981)
Directed by Abel Ferrara. Written by Nicholas St. John.

MUDHONEY (1965)
Directed by Russ Meyer. Written by Billy Sprague and Raymond Friday Locke, based on his novel *Streets Paved With Gold.*

MUTANT GIRLS SQUAD (2010)
Directed by Noboru Iguchi, Yoshihiro Nishimura, and Tak Sakaguchi. Written by Noburu Iguchi and Jun Tsugita.

MYSTERY MEN (1999)
Directed by Kinka Usher. Written by Neil Cuthbert and Bob Burden (creator comic book series).

THE NANNY (1965)
Directed by Seth Holt. Written by Jimmy Sangster, from the novel by Marryam Modell (as Evelyn Piper).

NATURAL BORN KILLERS (1994)
Directed by Oliver Stone. Written by Quentin Tarantino, David Veloz, Richard Rutowski, and Oliver Stone.

NIGHT OF THE HUNTER (1955)
Directed by Charles Laughton. Written by James Agee, based on the novel by Davis Grubb.

OLDBOY (2003)
Directed by Chan-wook Park. Written by Chan-wook Park, Chun-hyeong Lim, and Jo-yun Hwang, from the story by Garon Tsuchiya and comic by Nobuaki Minegishi.

ONCE UPON A TIME IN AMERICA (1984)
Directed by Sergio Leone. Written by Leonardo Benvenuti, Piero De Bernardi, Enrico Medioli, Franco Arcalli, Franco Ferrini, Sergio Leone, Stuart Kaminski (additional dialogue), Ernesto Gastaldi (uncredited), based on the novel *The Hoods* by Harry Grey.

ONCE UPON A TIME IN THE WEST (1968)
Directed by Sergio Leone. Written by Sergio Leone and Sergio Donati. Story by Dario Argento, Bernardo Bertolucci, and Sergio Leone.

PERDITA DURANGO (DANCE WITH THE DEVIL) (1997)
Directed by Álex de la Iglesia. Written by Barry Gifford, David Trueba, Álex de la Iglesia, and Jorge Guerricaechevarría.

PHONE BOOTH (2002)
Directed by Joel Schumacher. Written by Larry Cohen.

PLAY MISTY FOR ME (1971)
Directed by Clint Eastwood. Written by Jo Heims and Dean Reisler. Story by Jo Heims.

RACE WITH THE DEVIL (1975)
Directed by Jack Starrett. Written by Lee Frost and Wes Bishop.

RAW FORCE (1982)
Written and directed by Edward D. Murphy.

RETURN OF CAPTAIN INVINCIBLE (1983)
Directed by Philippe Mora. Written by Steven E. de Souza, Andrew Gaty and Peter Smalley (additional dialogue)

RIKI-OH: THE STORY OF RIKI (1991)
Directed by Lam Nai-choi, Written by Lam Nai-choi and Tetsuya Saruwatari.

ROAD HOUSE (1989)
Directed by Rowdy Herrington. Written by R. Lance Hill and Hilary Henkin.

ROAR (1981)
Written and directed by Noel Marshall.

RUNAWAY TRAIN (1985)
Directed by Andrey Konchalovskiy. Written by Djorde Milicevic, Paul Zindel, Edward Bunker, Ryûzô Kikushima (uncredited), Hideo Oguni (uncredited), based on the screenplay *Boso kikansha* by Akira Kurosawa.

THE SADIST (1963)
Written and directed by James Landis.

THE BIZARRO ENCYCLOPEDIA OF FILM

SE7EN (1995)
Directed by David Fincher. Written by Andrew Kevin Walker.

THE SEVEN SAMURAI (1964)
Directed by Akira Kurosawa. Written by Akira Kurosawa, Shinobu Hashimoto, and Hideo Oguni.

SHE MOB (1968)
Directed by Harry Wuest. Written by Diana Paschal.

SHOGUN ASSASSIN (1980)
Directed by Robert Houston and Kenji Misumi. Written by Robert Houston, Kazou Koike, Goseki Kojima, and David Weisman.

SORCERER (1977)
Directed by William Friedkin. Written by Walon Green and Georges Arnaud (novel).

SOUL VENGEANCE (WELCOME HOME BROTHER CHARLES) (1975)
Written and directed by Jamaa Fanaka.

SOUTHERN COMFORT (1981)
Directed by Walter Hill. Written by Walter Hill, Michael Kane, and David Giler.

THE SPECIALS (2000)
Directed by Craig Mazin. Written by James Gunn.

SHOCK CORRIDOR (1963)
Written and directed by Samuel Fuller.

THE STEPFATHER (1987)
Directed by Joseph Ruben. Written by Donald E. Westlake, Brian Garfield (story), and Carolyn Lefcourt.

STONE COLD (1991)
Directed by Craig R. Baxley. Written by Walter Doniger.

STRAW DOGS (1971)
Directed by Sam Peckinpah. Written by Sam Peckinpah and David Zelig Goodman, from the novel *The Siege of Trencher's Farm* by Gordon M. Williams (as Gordon Williams).

STREETS OF FIRE (1984)
Directed by Walter Hill. Written by Walter Hill and Larry Gross.

SUKIYAKI WESTERN DJANGO (2007)
Directed by Takashi Miike. Written by Takashi Miike and Masa Nakamura.

SUPER (2010)
Written and directed by James Gunn.

TARGETS (1968)
Written and directed by Peter Bogdanovich.

TEARS OF THE BLACK TIGER (2000)
Written and directed by Wisit Sasanatieng.

TO LIVE AND DIE IN L.A. (1985)
Directed by William Friedkin. Written by William Friedkin and Gerald Petievich.

TWO MULES FOR SISTER SARA (1970)
Directed by Don Siegel. Written by Albert Maltz. Story by Budd Boetticher.

U-TURN (1997)
Directed by Oliver Stone. Written by John Ridley.

UNIVERSAL SOLDIER: REGENERATION (2009)
Directed by John Hyams. Written by Victor Ostrovsky.

UNIVERSAL SOLDIER: DAY OF RECKONING (2012)
Directed by John Hyams. Written by John Hyams, Doug Magnuson, and John Greenhalgh.

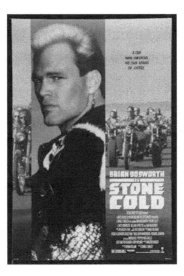

VALHALLA RISING (2009)
Directed by Nicolas Winding Refn. Written by Nicolas Winding Refn, Roy Jacobsen, and Matthew Read.

VICE SQUAD (1982)
Directed by Gary Sherman (as Gary A. Sherman). Written by Sandy Howard, Kenneth Peters, Robert Vincent O'Neill (as Robert Vincent O'Neil) and (uncredited) Gary Sherman.

THE VIOLATION OF THE BITCH (1978)
Directed by José Ramón Larraz. Written by José Ramón Larraz and Monique Pastrynn.

VORTEX (1982)
Written and directed by Scott and Beth B.

WAKE IN FRIGHT (1971)
Directed by Ted Kotcheff. Written by Evan Jones (screenplay), Kenneth Cook (based on the novel by).

THE WARRIORS (1979)
Directed by Walter Hill. Written by David Shaber, Walter Hill, based on the novel by Sol Yurick.

WHO KILLED TEDDY BEAR? (1965)

Directed by Joseph Cates. Written by Arnold Drake and Leon Tokatyan.

THE WILD BUNCH (1969)

Directed by Sam Peckinpah. Written by Sam Peckinpah and Walon Green. Story by Walon Green and Roy N. Sickner.

YAKUZA WEAPON (2011)

Directed by Tak Sakaguchi and Yudai Yamaguchi. Written by Ken Ishikawa, Yudai Yamaguchi, and Tak Sakaguchi.

THE YIN AND YANG OF MR. GO (1970)

Directed by Burgess Meredith. Written by Burgess Meredith (screenplay), Joseph Zucchero (story) and Alvin Ostroff (story.)

YOJIMBO (1961)

Directed by Akira Kurosawa. Written by Akira Kurosawa and Ryuzo Kikushima.

MUSICALS

A little song. A little dance. A little seltzer in the pants. I love the razzle dazzle as much as the next one, unless we're talking OKLAHOMA, which is a terrible musical about one of the most cursed pieces of land in the great United States, but there's something really precious when a musical goes full tilt Bizarro. The very nature of the Musical is inherently Bizarro, because music doesn't just pop up, especially randomly, in our regular lives. (Well, unless you're really, really lucky!)

The films listed here are ones that have used music with the storytelling in a spectacularly different way. Whether it is from the searingly accurate cynicism of SHOCK TREATMENT and LADIES & GENTLEMEN, THE FABULOUS STAINS to the DaDa colourforms from the heart work of Ken Russell, Bizarro Musicals are my kind of musicals. (HD)

200 MOTELS (1971)
Directed by Frank Zappa and Tony Palmer. Written by Frank Zappa, Tony Palmer, Mark Volman, Howard Kaylan and Jeff Simmons (uncredited)

ALICE IN WONDERLAND (1976)
Directed by Bud Townsend. Written by Bucky Searles and Lewis Carrol (novel)

ALL THAT JAZZ (1979)
Directed by Bob Fosse. Written by Bob Fosse and Robert Alan Aurthur

THE AMAZING MISTER BICKFORD (1987)
Directed by Frank Zappa and Bruce Bickford. Written by Frank Zappa.

AMERICAN POP (1981)
Directed by Ralph Bakshi.

THE APPLE (1980)

Directed by Menahem Golan. Written by Menahem Golan, Iris Recht and Coby Recht.

BEACH BLANKET BINGO (1965)

Directed by William Asher. Written by William Asher and Leo Townsent.

BIG TIME (1988)

Directed by Chris Blum. Written by Kathleen Brennan and Tom Waits.

BUGSY MALONE (1976)

Written and directed by Alan Parker.

BURST CITY (1982)

Directed by Gakuryu Ishii. Written by Jugatsu Toi (based on the novel by).

CANNIBAL: THE MUSICAL (1993)

Written and directed by Trey Parker.

CHA-CHA (1979)

Directed by Herbert Curiel. Written by Herbert Curiel, Herman Brood, Lene Lovich and Nina Hagen

DANDY (1988)

Directed by Peter Sempel. Written by Peter Sempel and Voltaire (novel).

DARKTOWN STRUTTERS (1975)

Directed by William Witney. Written by George Armitage.

DOGS IN SPACE (1986)

Written and directed by Richard Lowenstein.

DOWNTOWN 81 (1981)

Directed by Edo Bertoglio. Written by Glenn O'Brien

THE FIRST NUDIE MUSICAL (1976)

Directed by Mark Haggard and Bruce Kimmel. Written by Bruce Kimmel.

FORBIDDEN ZONE (1980)

Directed by Richard Elfman. Written by Richard Elfman, Matthew Bright, Nick L. Martinson, and Nicholas James (as Nick James).

THE GREAT ROCK'N'ROLL SWINDLE (1980)
Written and directed by Julien Temple.

THE HAPPINESS OF THE KATAKURIS (2001)
Directed by Takashi Miike. Written by Ai Kennedy (translation), Kikumi Yamagishi (screenplay).

HEDWIG AND THE ANGRY INCH (2001)
Written and directed by John Cameron Mitchell.

HUMAN HIGHWAY (1982)
Directed by Dean Stockwell and Neil Young. Written by Neil Young, Jeanne Field, Dean Stockwell, Russ Tamblyn and James Beshears.

INSIDE LLEWYN DAVIS (2013)
Written and directed by Joel and Ethan Coen.

JACQUES BREL IS ALIVE AND WELL AND LIVING IN PARIS (1974)
Directed by Annett Wolf, Sr. Written by Eric Blau and Mort Shuman, from their play based on the songs of Jacques Brel. Danish translation by Jorgan Hartman-Peterson (as Habakuk).

LADIES & GENTLEMEN THE FABULOUS STAINS (1982)
Directed by Lou Adler. Written by Nancy Dowd.

LISZTOMANIA (1975)
Written and directed by Ken Russell.

LITTLE SHOP OF HORRORS (1986)
Directed by Frank Oz. Written by Howard Ashman, based on the original screenplay by Charles B. Griffith.

MEET THE FEEBLES (1989)
Directed by Peter Jackson. Written by Fran Walsh, Stephen Sinclair, Danny Mulheron, and Peter Jackson.

A MIGHTY WIND (2003)
Directed by Christopher Guest. Written by Christopher Guest and Eugene Levy.

NASHVILLE (1975)
Directed by Robert Altman. Written by Joan Tewkesbury.

NUDIST COLONY OF THE DEAD (1991)
Written and directed by Mark Pirro.

ONE FROM THE HEART (1981)
Directed by Francis Ford Coppola. Written by Francis Ford Coppola, Armyan Bernstein and Luanna Anders (uncredited.)

PENNIES FROM HEAVEN (1981)
Directed by Herbert Ross. Written by Dennis Potter.

PHANTOM OF THE PARADISE (1974)
Written and directed by Brian De Palma.

THE PHYNX (1970)
Directed by Lee H. Katzin. Written by Bob Booker, George Foster, and Stan Cornyn.

PINK FLOYD: THE WALL (1982)
Directed by Alan Parker. Written by Roger Waters.

POPULATION 1 (1986)
Written and directed by Rene Daalder.

POULTRYGEIST: NIGHT OF THE CHICKEN DEAD (2006)
Directed by Lloyd Kaufman and Gabriel Friedman (uncredited). Written by Daniel Bova, Gabriel Friedman, and Lloyd Kaufman.

REPO THE GENETIC OPERA (2008)
Directed by Darren Lynn Bousman. Written by Darren Smith and Terrance Zdunich.

ROCKY HORROR PICTURE SHOW (1975)
Directed by Jim Sharman. Written by Richard O'Brien and Jim Sharman

THE SADDEST MUSIC IN THE WORLD (2003)
Directed by Guy Maddin. Written by Kazuo Ishiguro, George Toles, and Guy Maddin.

SGT. PEPPER'S LONELY HEARTS CLUB (1978)
Directed by Michael Schultz. Written by Henry Edwards and The Devil

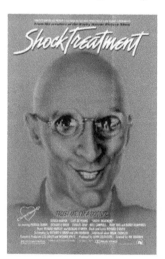

SHOCK TREATMENT (1981)
Directed by Jim Sharman. Written by Richard O'Brien and Jim Sharman.

STARSTRUCK (1982)
Directed by Gillian Armstrong. Written by Stephen MacLean.

SUPER STARLET A.D. (2000)
Written and directed by John Michael McCarthy.

THIS IS SPINAL TAP (1984)
Directed by Rob Reiner. Written by Christopher Guest, Michael McKean, Harry Shearer, and Rob Reiner.

TOMMY (1975)
Directed by Ken Russell. Written by The Who, Ken Russell and Pete Townshend.

UNDER THE CHERRY MOON (1986)
Directed by Prince and Michael Ballhaus (uncredited). Written by Becky Johnston.

VIVA (2007)
Written and directed by Anna Biller.

ZACHARIAH (2015)
Directed by Craig Zobel. Written by Nissar Modi.

ZERO PATIENCE (1993)
Written and directed by John Greyson.

FOREIGN/ARTHOUSE

Arthouse films are the ones that not only go outside the paint-by-numbers canvas of traditional filmmaking, but build their own canvas. The fabric is stretched out over frames built from branches, vision and artistic bravery. No one is going to buy a mansion making only Arthouse films. Part of the eternal appeal of Arthouse is that you get the promise of witnessing something completely different.

Foreign films have a similar appeal in the sense of you're not getting a pure film diet of the foods you're used to. The human condition unites us all, with art being one of the strongest glues, but the colors and paint strokes are different with every country and culture and thank the gods for that. Foreign and Arthouse are two of the best kinds of peanut butter and chocolate around. (HD)

8 ½ (1963)
Written and directed by Frederico Fellini.

1334 (2012)
Written and directed by Nico B.

THE 10TH VICTIM (1965)
Directed by Elio Petri. Written by Robert Sheckley (story), Tonino Guerra, Giorgio Salvioni, Ennio Flaiano and Elio Petri.

AGUIRRE, THE WRATH OF GOD (1972)
Written and directed by Werner Herzog.

ALICE (1988)
Written and directed by Jan Svankmajer.

AMELIE (2001)
Directed by Jean-Pierre Jeunet. Written by Guillaume Laurant and Jean-Pierre Jeunet..

THE BIZARRO ENCYCLOPEDIA OF FILM

THE AMERICAN FRIEND (1977)
Directed by Wim Wenders. Written by Wim Wenders and Patricia Highsmith (book).

ANOMALISA (2015)
Directed by Duke Johnson, Charlie Kaufman. Written by Charlie Kaufman, from his play (as Frances Fregoli).

ARCHANGEL (1990)
Directed by Guy Maddin. Written by John B. Harvie (story suggestion), Guy Maddin (screenplay), George Toles (screenplay).

ARIA (1987)
Written and directed by Robert Altman, Bruce Beresford, Bill Bryden, Jean-Luc Godard, Derek Jarman, Franc Roddam, Nicolas Roeg, Ken Russell, Charles Sturridge, Julien Temple.

THE BABY OF MACON (1993)
Written and directed by Peter Greenaway.

BACCHANALE (1970)
Written and directed by John and Lem Amero.

BEGOTTEN (1990)
Written and directed by E. Elias Merhige.

BEHIND CONVENT WALLS (1978)
Directed by Walerian Borowczyk, Written by Walerian Borowczyk and Stendahl (novel).

BELLY OF AN ARCHITECT (1987)
Written and directed by Peter Greenaway.

BLACK MOON (1975)
Directed by Louis Malle. Written by Louis Malle, Joyce Buñuel (additional dialogue).

BLOOD OF A POET (1932)
Written and directed by Jean Cocteau.

BYE BYE MONKEY (1978)
Directed by Marco Ferreri. Written by Marco Ferreri, Gérard Brach, and Rafael Azcona.

CAMILLE 2000 (1969)
Directed by Radley Metzger. Written by Michael DeForrest and Alexandre Dumas fils (inspired by novel)

CAT SOUP (2001)
Directed by Tatsuo Satô. Written by Nekojiru (story), Tatsuo Satô (screenplay), Masaaki Yuasa (screenplay).

CELINE AND JULIE GO BOATING (1974)

Directed by Jacques Rivette. Written by Jacques Rivette, Marie-France Pisier, Bulle Ogier, Dominique Labourier, Juliet Berto, Eduardo de Gregorio (dialogue) and Henry James (Film within a film based on the stories by).

CHELSEA GIRLS (1966)

Directed by Andy Warhol and Paul Morrissey. Written by Ronald Tavel and Andy Warhol.

THE COOK, THE THIEF, HIS WIFE, AND HER LOVER (1989)

Written and directed by Peter Greenaway.

COSMOS (2015)

Directed by Andrzej Zulawski. Written by Witold Gombrowicz (book), Andrzej Zulawski.

DAISIES (1966)

Directed by Vera Chytilová. Written by Vera Chytilová, Ester Krumbachová, and Pavel Jurácek.

THE DANCE OF REALITY (2013)

Written and directed by Alejandro Jodorowsky.

DAS BOOT (1981)

Written and directed by Wolfgang Petersen.

DEAD MAN (1995)

Written and directed by Jim Jarmusch.

JEUNET & CARO

DELICATESSEN

STUDIO CANAL

DELICATESSEN (1991)

Directed by Marc Caro and Jean-Pierre Jeunet. Written by Jean-Pierre Jeunet, Marc Caro, and Gilles Adrien.

THE DEVIL (1972)

Written and directed by Andrzej Zulawski.

DIONYSUS IN '69 (1970)

Directed by Brian De Palma and Richard Schechner. Written by William Arrowsmith, based on the play *The Bacchae* by Euripides.

THE DISCREET CHARM OF THE BOURGEOISIE (1972)

Directed by Luis Buñuel. Written by Luis Buñuel, with the collaboration of Jean-Claude Carrière.

DOGTOOTH (2009)

Directed by Yorgos Lanthimos. Written by Efthymis Filippou, Yorgos Lanthimos.

THE DRAUGHTSMAN'S CONTRACT (1982)

Written and directed by Peter Greenaway.

THE BIZARRO ENCYCLOPEDIA OF FILM

DRAWING RESTRAINT 9 (2005)
Written and directed by
Matthew Barney.

DROWNING BY NUMBERS (1988)
Written and directed by Peter
Greenaway.

EVEN DWARFS STARTED SMALL (1970)
Written and directed by
Werner Herzog.

EYES WIDE SHUT (1999)
Directed by Stanley Kubrick. Written
by Stanley Kubrick, Frederic Raphael,
from the novella *Traumnovelle* by
Arthur Schnitzler.

FANDO Y LIS (1968)
Directed by Alejandro Jodorowsky.
Written by Fernando Arrabal and
Alejandro Jodorowsky.

THE FALLS (1980)
Written and directed by
Peter Greenaway.

FELLINI'S ROMA (1972)
Directed by Frederico Fellini.
Written by Frederico Fellini and
Benardino Zapponi.

FELLINI'S SATYRICON (1969)
Directed by Frederico Fellini. Written
by Frederico Fellini, Bernardino
Zapponi, and Brunello Rondi.

A FIELD IN ENGLAND (2013)
Directed by Ben Wheatley. Written by
Amy Jump.

FITZCARRALDO (1982)
Written and directed by
Werner Herzog.

FLAMING CREATURES (1963)
Written and directed by Jack Smith.

FLICKER (1965)
Directed by Tony Conrad.

THE FORBIDDEN ROOM (2015)
Directed by Guy Maddin, Evan
Johnson (co-director). Written by
Guy Maddin (writer), Evan Johnson
(writer), Robert Kotyk (writer), John
Ashbery (additional writer), Kim
Morgan (additional writer and story
editor).

FRUITS OF PASSION (1981)
Directed by Shûji Terayama. Written
by Shûji Terayama, Rio Kishida, based
on the novel *Retour a Roissy* by Anne
Desclos, billed as Pauline Reage.

GODSPEED YOU! BLACK EMPEROR (1976)
Directed by Mitsuo Yanagimachi.

HARD TO BE A GOD (2013)
Directed by Aleksey German. Written
by Arkadiy Strugatskiy (novel), Boris
Strugatskiy (novel), Aleksey German
(adaptation), Svetlana Karmalita
(adaptation).

THE BIZARRO ENCYCLOPEDIA OF FILM

HOLY MOTORS (2012)
Written and directed by Leos Carax.

HOUR OF THE WOLF (1968)
Written and directed
by Ingmar Bergman.

THE HOURGLASS SANATORIUM (1973)
Directed by Wojciech
Has. Written by
Wojciech Has, Bruno
Schulz (story).

I WILL WALK LIKE A CRAZY HORSE (1973)
Written and directed
by Fernando Arrabal.

THE IDIOTS (1998)
Written and directed by Lars von Trier.

IF… (1968)
Directed by Lindsay Anderson.
Written by David Sherwin and
John Howlett.

THE IMAGE (1975)
Directed by Radley Metzger. Written
by Radley Metzger and Catherine
Robbe-Grillet (Novel)

IMMORAL TALES (1974)
Directed by Walerian Borowcyzk.
Written by Walerian Borowcyzk and
André Pieyre de Mandiargues (story)

INSTITUTE BENJAMENTA (THIS DREAM THAT ONE CALLS HUMAN LIFE) (1995)
Directed by Stephen and Timothy
Quay. Written by Alan
Passes, Stephen and
Timothy Quay.

INTACTO (2001)
Directed by Juan
Carlos Fresnadillo.
Written by Andrés M.
Koppel

INVOCATION OF MY DEMON BROTHER (1969)
Written and directed
by Kenneth Anger.

JULIET OF THE SPIRITS (1965)
Directed by Frederico Fellini. Written
by Frederico Fellini, Tullio Pinelli,
Ennio Flaiano, and Brunello Rondi.

LA BÊTE (1975)
Written and directed by Walerian
Borowcyzk.

LA CRAVATE (1957)
Directed Alejandro Jodorowsky.
Written by Alejandro Jodorowsky and
Thomas Mann (novel)

LA DOLCE VITA (1960)
Directed by Frederico Fellini. Written
by Frederico Fellini, Ennio Flaiano,
and Tullio Pinelli.

LAST YEAR AT MARIENBAD (1962)
Directed by Alain Resnais. Written by Alain Robbe-Grillet.

LÉOLO (1992)
Written and directed by Jean-Claude Lauzon.

THE LICKERISH QUARTET (1970)
Directed by Radley Metzger. Written by Michael DeForrest and Radley Metzger.

LIFE IS BEAUTIFUL (1997)
Directed by Roberto Benigni. Written by Vincenzo Cerami and Roberto Benigni.

LITTLE OTIK (1990)
Written and directed by Jan Svankmajer.

LUCIFER RISING (1972)
Written and directed by Kenneth Anger.

M. BUTTERFLY (1993)
Directed by David Cronenberg. Written by David Henry Hwang, from his play.

MAD DOG MORGAN (1976)
Directed by Philippe Mora. Written by Philippe Mora and Margaret Carnegie (book).

MAIDSTONE (1970)
Written and directed by Norman Mailer.

THE MAN WHO WASN'T THERE (2001)
Written and directed by Joel and Ethan Coen.

MARQUIS (1989)
Directed by Henri Xhonneux. Written by Roland Topor, Henri Xhonneux and Marquis de Sade (story).

MELANCHOLIA (2011)
Written and directed by Lars Von Trier.

MONELLA AKA FRIVOLOUS LOLA (1998)
Directed by Tinto Brass. Written by Tinto Brass, Carla Cipriani and Barbara Alberti.

O LUCKY MAN! (1973)
Directed by Lindsay Anderson. Written by David Sherwin, based on an original idea by Malcolm McDowell.

ON THE SILVER GLOBE (1988)
Directed by Andrzej Zulawski. Written by Andrzej Zulawski and Jerzy Zulawski.

ONIBABA (1964)
Written and directed by
Kaneto Shindô.

OUT 1 (1971)
Directed by Jacques Rivette and
Suzanne Schiffman.

A PAGE OF MADNESS (1926)
Directed by Teinosuke Kinugasa.
Written by Yasunari Kawabata (short
story and adaptation),
Teinosuke Kinugasa
(adaptation), Minoru
Inuzuka (adaptation),
Bankô Sawada
(adaptation).

THE PIANO TUNER OF EARTHQUAKES (2005)
Directed by Stephen Quay, Timothy
Quay. Written by Alan Passes,
Stephen Quay, Timothy Quay. (1965)
Written and directed by Jean-Luc
Godard.

PIG (1998)
Written and directed by Nico B. and
Rozz Williams.

THE PIG FUCKING MOVIE (1974)
Directed by Thierry Zéno. Written by
Dominique Garny (screenplay), John
Kupferschmidt, Thierry Zéno.

THE PILLOW BOOK (1996)
Directed by Peter Greenaway. Written
by Peter Greenaway and Sei Shonagon,
from his book.

POISON (1991)
Directed by Todd Haynes. Written by
Jean Genet and Todd Haynes.

PORCILE (1969)
Written and directed by Pier
Paolo Pasolini.

POST TENEBRAS LUX (2012)
Written and directed by Carlos
Reygadas.

POUND (1970)
Written and directed by
Robert Downey Sr.

PROSPERO'S BOOKS (1991)
Directed by Peter
Greenaway. Written by
Peter Greenaway, based on the play
The Tempest by William Shakespeare.

QUERELLE (1982)
Directed by Rainer Werner Fassbinder.
Written by Rainer Werner Fassbinder,
Burkhard Driest and Jean Genet
(novel).

RASHOMON (1950)
Directed by Akira Kurosawa. Written
by Akira Kurosawa, Shinobu
Hashimoto, and Ryûnosuke
Akutagawa (stories).

RIDICULE (1996)
Directed by Patrice Leconte. Written
by Rémi Waterhouse, Michel Fessler,
and Eric Vicaut.

SALÒ, OR THE 120 DAYS OF SODOM (1975)
Directed by Pier Paolo Pasolini. Written by Sergio Citti and Pier Paolo Pasolini.

SALOME'S LAST DANCE (1988)
Directed by Ken Russell. Written by Ken Russell, based on the play by Oscar Wilde. Translation by Vivian Russell.

SALON KITTY (1976)
Directed by Tinto Brass. Written by Antonio Colantuoni (story), Ennio De Concini (story), Maria Pia Fusco (story), Tinto Brass and Peter Norden (novel, uncredited)

SCORE (1974)
Directed by Radley Metzger. Written by Jerry Douglas.

SCORPIO RISING (1964)
Directed by Kenneth Anger. Written by Ernest D. Glucksman.

THE SEVENTH SEAL (1957)
Written and directed by Ingmar Bergman, based on his play.

SINGAPORE SLING (1990)
Written and directed by Nikos Nikolaidis.

THE SINGING DETECTIVE (2003)
Directed by Keith Gordon. Written by Dennis Potter, based on his Television series.

SPIDER (2002)
Directed by David Cronenberg. Written by Patrick McGrath, based on his novel.

STALKER (1979)
Directed by Andrei Tarkovsky. Written by Andrei Tarkovsky (uncredited), Arkadiy and Boris Strugatskiy, based on their novel *Roadside Picnic*.

THE STUNT MAN (1980)
Directed by Richard Rush. Written by Lawrence B. Marcus, adapted by Richard Rush from a novel by Paul Brodeur.

SURVIVE STYLE +5 (2004)
Directed by Gen Sekiguchi. Written by Taku Tada.

SWEET MOVIE (1974)
Directed by Dusan Makavejev. Written by France Gallagher (collaboration), Dusan Makavejev, Martin Malina (collaboration).

TALES OF ORDINARY MADNESS (1981)
Directed by Marco Ferreri. Written by Marco Ferreri, Sergio Amidei, Anthony Foutz, and Charles Bukowski (book).

TAMPOPO (1985)
Written and directed by Jûzô Itami.

THE BIZARRO ENCYCLOPEDIA OF FILM

TAXIDERMIA (2006)
Directed by György Pálfi. Written by Lajos Parti Nagy, György Pálfi, and Zsófia Ruttkay.

TELEPHONE BOOK (1971)
Written and directed by Nelson Lyon.

TEOREMA (1968)
Written and directed by Pier Paolo Pasolini.

THAT OBSCURE OBJECT OF DESIRE (1977)
Directed by Luis Buñuel. Written by Luis Buñuel, Jean-Claude Carrière, inspired by the novel *Le femme et la pantin* by Pierre Louÿs.

THEY EAT SCUM (1979)
Written and directed by Nick Zedd.

TIE ME UP TIE ME DOWN! (1989)
Written and directed by Pedro Almodóvar.

THE TIN DRUM (1979)
Directed by Volker Schlöndorff. Written by Jean-Claude Carrière, Volker Schlöndorff, Franz Seitz, and Günter Grass (novel and additional material).

UNCLE BOONMEE WHO CAN RECALL HIS PAST LIVES (2010)
Directed by Apichatpong Weerasethakul. Written by Phra Sripariyattiweti and Apichatpong Weerasethakul.

VALERIE AND HER WEEK OF WONDERS (1970)
Directed by Jaromil Jires. Written by Vítezslav Nezval, Jaromil Jires, Ester Krumbachová, and Jirí Musil.

A VERY LONG ENGAGEMENT (2004)
Directed by Jean-Pierre Jeunet. Written by Jean-Pierre Jeunet and Guillaume Laurant, from the novel by Sébastien Japrisot.

VISITOR Q (2001)
Directed by Takashi Miike. Written by Itaru Era.

VIVA LA MUERTE (1971)
Directed by Fernando Arrabal. Written by Fernando Arrabal and Claudine Lagrive (co-scenario writer).

VIY (1967)
Directed by Konstantin Ershov and Georgiy Kropachyov. Written by Konstantin Ershov, Georgiy Kropachyov, Aleksandr Ptushko, based on the story by Nikolay Gogol.

VORTEX (1982)
Written and directed by Beth and Scott B.

WHATEVER HAPPENED TO VILENESS FATS? (1976/1984)
Directed by The Residents and Graeme Whifler. Written by The Residents.

WEEKEND (1967)
Written and directed by Jean-Luc Godard.

WERCKMEISTER HARMONIES (2000)
Directed by Béla Tarr, Ágnes Hranitzky (co-director). Written by László Krasznahorkai (novel and screenplay), Béla Tarr (scrrenplay), Péter Dobai (additional dialogue), Gyuri Dósa Kiss (additional dialogue), György Fehér (additional dialogue).

YOU KILLED ME FIRST (1985)
Written and directed by Richard Kern.

A ZED AND TWO NOUGHTS (1985)
Written and directed by Peter Greenaway.

ZOO ZERO (1979)
Written and directed by Alain Fleischer.

DOCUMENTARIES

This is a very strange category to discuss, because simply documenting life in its truest form is as Bizarro as it fucking gets. LIFE IS UNSURPASSINGLY STRANGE, no matter how many phantasmagoric angles or comic trajectories we project upon it.

That said, certain films make the extra point of amplifying the strangeness in ways that resonate uniquely and indelibly. Chronicling the actual, in mind-bending ways. And here are a few of them. (JS)

THE ACT OF KILLING (2012)
Directed by Joshua Oppenheimer.

THE ACT OF SEEING WITH ONE'S OWN EYES (1971)
Directed by Stan Brakhage.

AMERICAN DREAMER (1971)
Directed by L.M. Kit Carson and Lawrence Schiller. Written by L.M. Kit Carson, Lawrence Schiller and Dennis Hopper.

AMERICAN MOVIE (1999)
Directed by Chris Smith.

THE STAR & DIRECTOR OF EASY RIDER, HIS OWN LIFE, FILMED AS HE LIVED IT

"...an unpredictable human being in the act of living."

Dennis Hopper The American Dreamer

A FILM BY LAWRENCE SCHILLER & L.M. KIT CARSON

BOND 360   WALKER ART CENTER

THE ARISTOCRATS (2005)
Directed by Paul Provenza. Conceived by Penn Jillette and Paul Provenza.

ASYLUM (1972)
Directed by Peter Robinson.

BEST OF ENEMIES (2015)
Directed by Robert Gordon and Morgan Neville. Written by Robert Gordon, Tom Graves, and Morgan Neville.

BEST WORST MOVIE (2009)
Directed by Michael Stephenson.

CARNEY TALK (1995)
Directed by Larry Wessel.

CAT DANCERS (2007)
Directed by Harris Fishman.

CHANGES (1968)
Directed by Gerard Damiano.

THE CHARLES BUKOWSKI TAPES (1987)
Directed by Barbet Schroeder.

CIAO MANHATTAN (1972)
Directed by John Palmer and David Weisman. Written by John Palmer, David Weisman, Genevieve Charbon, Chuck Wein and Robert Bernard.

CORPSE FUCKING ART (1987)
Written and directed by Jörg Buttgereit.

CRAZY LOVE (2007)
Directed by Dan Clowes and Fisher Stevens. Written by Dan Clowes.

CRUMB (1994)
Directed by Terry Zwigoff.

THE DECLINE OF WESTERN CIVILIZATION (1981)
Directed by Penelope Spheeris.

THE DECLINE OF WESTERN CIVILIZATION PART II: THE METAL YEARS (1988)
Directed by Penelope Spheeris.

DECLINE OF WESTERN CIVILIZATION PART III (1998)
Directed by Penelope Spheeris.

DOPE (1968)
Directed by Flame Schon and Sheldon Rochlin. Written by Flame Schon and Sheldon Rochlin.

EAT THAT QUESTION: FRANK ZAPPA IN HIS OWN WORDS (2016)
Directed by Thorson Shutte.

ERIC & SHAYE (2016)
Directed by Larry Wessel.

EXIT THROUGH THE GIFT SHOP (2010)
Directed by Banksy.

F FOR FAKE (1974)
Directed by Orson Welles and (uncredited) Francois Reichenbach, Gary Graver, and Oja Kodar. Written by Orson Welles and Oja Kodar.

THE FINAL MEMBER (2012)
Directed by Jonah Bekhor and Zach Math.

FINDERS KEEPERS (2015)
Directed by Brian Carberry and Clay Tweel (as J. Clay Tweel).

GATES OF HEAVEN (1978)
Directed by Errol Morris.

GOD'S ANGRY MAN (1981)
Written and directed by Werner Herzog.

GOODBYE UNCLE TOM (1971)
Directed by Gualtiero Jacopetti and Franco Prosperi. Written by Gualtiero Jacopeti and Franco Prosperi.

GREY GARDENS (1975)
Directed by Ellen Hovde, Albert Maysles, David Maysles, and Muffie Meyer.

GRIZZLY MAN (2005)
Directed by Werner Herzog.

HATED: GG ALLIN AND THE MURDER JUNKIES (1994)
Directed by Todd Phillips.

HÄXAN (1922)
Written and directed by Benjamin Christensen.

HEAVY METAL PARKING LOT (1986)
Directed by John Heyn and Jeff Krulik.

HEAVY PETTING (1989)
Directed by Obie Benz and Joshua Waletzsky. Written by Pierce Rafferty.

I AM DIVINE (2013)
Directed by Jeffrey Schwarz.

I THINK WE'RE ALONE NOW (2008)
Directed by Sean Donnelly.

ICONOCLAST (2010)
Directed by Larry Wessel.

IDI AMIN DADA (1974)
Written and directed by Barbet Schroeder.

IN THE REALMS OF THE UNREAL (2004)
Written and directed by Jessica Yu.

JEFFTOWNE (1998)
Written and directed by Daniel Kraus.

JODOROWSKY'S DUNE (2013)
Directed by Frank Pavich.

THE KING OF KONG (2007)
Written and directed by Seth Gordon.

KUMARÉ (2011)
Directed by Vikram Gandhi.

LED ZEPPELIN PLAYED WHERE? (2014)
Directed by Jeff Krulik.

LET ME DIE A WOMAN (1977)
Directed by Doris Wishman.

LINDA/LES AND ANNIE (1992)
Directed by Annie Sprinkle, Johnny Armstrong, and Albert Jaccoma.

LOST IN LA MANCHA (2002)
Directed by Keith Fulton and Louis Pepe.

LOST SOUL: THE DOOMED JOURNEY OF RICHARD STANLEY'S ISLAND OF DR. MOREAU (2014)
Written and directed by David Gregory.

THE MAN WITH THE MOVIE CAMERA (1929)
Directed by Dziga Vertov.

MARWENCOL (2010)
Directed by Jeff Malmberg.

MONDO CANE (1962)
Written and directed by Paolo Cavara and Gualtiero Jacopetti.

MONDO TOPLESS (1966)
Directed by Russ Meyer.

MULE SKINNER BLUES (2001)
Directed by Stephen Earnhart.

MY BEST FIEND (1999)
Directed by Werner Herzog.

NEVER SLEEP AGAIN: THE ELM. ST. LEGACY (2010)
Directed by Dan Farrands and Andrew Kasch. Written by Thommy Hutson.

OVERNIGHT (2003)
Written and directed by Tony Montana and Mark Brian Smith.

PROJECT GRIZZLY (1996)
Directed by Peter Lynch.

THE QUEEN (1968)
Directed by Frank Simon.

RESURRECT DEAD: THE CASE OF THE TOYNBEE TILES (2011)
Directed by Jon Foy. Written by Jon Foy and Colin Smith.

THE BIZARRO ENCYCLOPEDIA OF FILM

SAVAGE MAN, SAVAGE BEAST (1975)
Directed by Antonio Climati and Mario Morra.

SICK: THE LIFE AND DEATH OF BOB FLANAGAN, SUPERMASOCHIST (1997)
Directed by Kirby Dick.

SHERMAN'S MARCH (1986)
Written and directed by Ross McElwee.

SHUT UP LITTLE MAN! AN AUDIO MISADVENTURE (2011)
Written and directed by Matthew Bate.

THAT GUY DICK MILLER (2014)
Written and directed by Elijah Drenner.

THUNDER & MUD (1990)
Directed by Penelope Spheeris

TICKLED (2016)
Directed by Davied Farrier and Dylan Reeve.

TITICUT FOLLIES (1967)
Directed by Frederick Wiseman.

UNTIL THE LIGHT TAKES US (2008)
Directed by Aaron Aites and Audrey Ewell.

VERNON FLORIDA (1981)
Directed by Errol Morris.

WESLEY WILLIS (2003)
Directed by Daniel Bitton.

WISCONSIN DEATH TRIP (1999)
Directed by James Marsh. Written by James Marsh, based on the book by Michael Lesy.

ZOO (2007)
Directed by Robinson Devor. Written by Chris Mudede and Robinson Devor.

ADULT

Of all the film genres out there, one of the most misunderstood is Adult. The backroom of any video store is one that was often eyed with curiosity, guffaws by others and the judgmental-side-eye by a few that really need to relax. After all, sexuality is one of the most basic building blocks of human existence. Without sex, obviously, none of us would be here. When it comes to sex and art, it ain't what you do, it's the way that you do it. So many people assume that all Adult films are horribly acted, poorly made and center around numerous puns involving turgid throbbing man-meat, plumbers and pizza delivery. This makes about much sense as assuming every Drama out there has someone squawking about losing their kid or impending relationship debacles. (Aka 98% of Oscar-bait.) Stereotypes exist for reasons, sure, but it is never the whole picture.

In so many ways, the Adult genre, especially in the 1970's and early 80's, was a spiritual sibling to the Silent-era pioneers. Explicit sex in film became legal in cinema in the late 1960's, first through documentary-style "white-coaters," but became part of narrative filmmaking with 1970's MONA: THE VIRGIN NYMPH. Coupled with the countercultural revolution, a number of filmmakers and actors mixed in bold sexuality with films ranging from arthouse to thrillers and everything in between. It was a new landscape where status quo views of what was art and what was simply porn became blurry. In a world where Lenny Bruce's observation that it is more acceptable to see a maimed breast than one that is caressed is still as true as ever, the men and women who have used sexuality as part of an ever-fascinating cinematic canvas remain the pioneers who are still awaiting their proper due. (H.D.)

9 LIVES OF A WET PUSSY (1976)
Directed by Abel Ferrara. Written by Nicholas St. John.

A FREE RIDE (1915)
Directed by A. Wise Guy. Written by Will She. (Ed. Note. Obviously real names, the lot of them!)

AMERICAN BABYLON (1985)

Written and directed by Richard Mahler aka Roger Watkins.

BABYFACE (1977)

Directed by Alex de Renzy. Written by John Mulligan.

BABYFACE 2 (1986)

Written and directed by Alex de Renzy.

BAD GIRLS (1981)

Directed by David I. Frazer and Svetlana. Written by David I. Frazer .

BARBARA BROADCAST (1977)

Written and directed by Radley Metzger.

BEETLE CUM (1989)

Directed by Paul Rusch.

BIJOU (1972)

Directed by Wakefield Poole.

BLONDE AMBITION (1981)

Directed by George and Lem Amero. Written by Larue Watts and the Amero Brothers (story.)

BOYS IN THE SAND (1971)

Written and directed by Wakefield Poole.

CAFE FLESH (1982)

Directed by Stephen Sayadian (as Rinse Dream). Written by Stephen Sayadian and Jerry Stahl.

CORNHOLE ARMAGEDDON (1999)

Written and directed by Charlie Crow.

CORRUPTION (1983)

Written and directed by Roger Watkins (as Richard Mahler).

DARK ANGEL(1983)

Directed by Pieter Vanderbilt.

DARK DREAMS (1971)

Directed by Roger Guermantes. Written by Canidia Ference.

DEEP THROAT (1972)

Written and directed by Gerard Damiano.

THE DEVIL IN MISS JONES (1973)

Written and directed by Gerard Damiano.

DEVIL IN MISS JONES 2 (1982)

Directed by Henri Pachard. Written by Ellie Howard and Henri Pachard.

DEVIL IN MISS JONES 3&4 (1986)

Directed by Gregory Dark. Written by Gregory Dark and Anthony R. Lovett.

THE BIZARRO ENCYCLOPEDIA OF FILM

DIVERSIONS (1976)
Written and directed by Derek Ford.

DOCTOR PENETRATION (1986)
Directed by Alex de Renzy. Written by Anthony R. Lovett.

DRILLER (1984)
Directed by Joyce James. Written by Dick Howard and Joyce James.

FEMMES DE SADE (1976)
Directed by Alex de Renzy.

FORCED ENTRY (1973)
Written and directed by Shaun Costello.

FRESH MEAT...A GHOST STORY (1995)
Written and directed by John Leslie.

G-STRINGS (1984)
Written and directed by Henri Pachard.

HARDGORE (1976)
Directed by Michael Hugo.

HOT & SAUCY PIZZA GIRLS (1978)
Directed by Bob Chinn. Written by John Thomas Chapman.

Fred Halsted's homosexual film

PLAYS ITSELF
For mature consenting adults.

KINKY LADIES OF BOURBON STREET (1976)
Directed by Didier Philippe-Gerard. Written by Claude Mulot.

KNEEL BEFORE ME (1983)
Written and directed by Phil Prince.

LA PLAYS ITSELF (1972)
Written and directed by Fred Halsted.

LATEX (1995)
Directed by Michael Ninn. Written by Anthony R. Lovett (as Antonio Pasolini). Story by Michael Ninn.

LET MY PUPPETS COME (1976)
Written and directed by Gerard Damiano.

MARASCHINO CHERRY (1978)
Written and directed by Radley Metzger.

MARY! MARY! (1977)
Written and directed by Bernard Morris.

MEMORIES WITHIN MISS AGGIE (1974)
Directed by Gerard Damiano. Written by Ron Wertheim.

THE BIZARRO ENCYCLOPEDIA OF FILM

MISTY BEETHOVEN THE MUSICAL (2004)
Directed by Veronica Hart. Written by John Skipp (as Maxwell Hart), from the original characters by Radley Metzger.

NAKED CAME THE STRANGER (1975)
Directed by Radley Metzger. Written by Radley Metzger and Penelope Ashe (Novel).

NIGHTDREAMS (1981)
Directed by Francis Delia and Stephen Sayadian. Written by Stephen Sayadian and Jerry Stahl.

NIGHTDREAMS 2 (1990)
Directed by Stephen Sayadian. Written by Stephen Sayadian.

NIGHTDREAMS 3 (1991)
Directed by Stephen Sayadian. Written by Stephen Sayadian.

THE OPENING OF MISTY BEETHOVEN (1976)
Written and directed by Radley Metzger.

ORIENTAL TECHNIQUES IN PAIN & PLEASURE (1983)
Written and directed by Phil Prince.

PARTY DOLL A GO-GO 1 & 2 (1991)
Directed by Stephen Sayadian. Written by Stephen Sayadian

PRETTY PEACHES (1978)
Directed by Alex de Renzy.

PRETTY PEACHES 2 (1987)
Directed by Alex de Renzy.

PRETTY PEACHES 3 (1989)
Directed by Alex de Renzy.

THE PRIVATE AFTERNOONS OF PAMELA MANN (1974)
Written and directed by Radley Metzger.

PUSSY TALK (1975)

Directed by Claude Mulot. Written by Didier Philippe-Gérard, Claude Mulot and Denis Diderot (novel).

THE SATISFIERS OF ALPHA BLUE (1980)
Written and directed by Gerard Damiano.

SCOUNDRELS (1982)
Directed by Cecil Howard. Written by Anne Wolff.

THE BIZARRO ENCYCLOPEDIA OF FILM

SENSATIONS (1975)
Directed by Lasse Braun. Written by Axel Braun, Veronique Monod and Ian Rakoff (additional dialogue).

SEX (1994)
Written and directed by Michael Ninn.

SEXTOOL (1975)
Directed by Fred Halsted.

SEX IN THE COMICS (1972)
Directed by Anthony Spinelli. Written by Paul Pervertt and Miles Muff

SEX WISH (1976)
Written and directed by Victor Milt.

SMOKER (1983)
Directed by Veronika Rocket.

SOMETIMES SWEET SUSAN (1975)
Directed by Fred Donaldson. Written by Fred Donaldson and Joel Scott.

SQUALOR MOTEL (1985)
Directed by Kim Christy. Written by Kim Christy and Stan Fernando.

THE STORY OF JOANNA (1975)
Written and directed by Gerard Damiano.

TAMING OF REBECCA (1982)
Directed by Phil Prince.

TEN LITTLE MAIDENS (1985)
Directed by John Seaman. Written by Arthur King.

TONGUE (1976)
Directed by K.B.

VISIONS OF CLAIR (1978)
Directed by Zachary Strong.

WATERPOWER (1977)
Written and directed by Shaun Costello.

WET RAINBOW (1974)
Directed by Duddy Kane. Written by Duddy Kane and Roger Wald.

PART TWO

YOUR FEATURE
ENTERTAINMENT!

YOU FOOLS! FOOLS! FOOLS!
AN AMERICAN HIPPIE IN ISRAEL
RETURNS AT LAST

JOHN SKIPP

Ladies and gentlemen? What we're about to discuss is *the single greatest motion picture ever made*.

There. I said it. It's a lie, but I said it. And having gotten that out of the way, let me attempt to prepare you for the staggeringly ridiculous yet utterly adorable pure exemplar of offbeat, all-but-forgotten Bizarro film I'm about to describe.

But first, here's an important question for the film lover in you, especially if you've got a taste for what the world dismissively calls "bad" movies:

What's the difference between a massively-flawed gem that you helplessly love and a stupid piece of shit you will never stop hating?

Everybody's different. But for me, the answer's simple.

It all comes down to sincerity.

And lemme tell ya: in the film biz, sincerity is one of the roughest gigs there is. A filmmaker with his or her heart on their sleeve is rowing uphill all the way. If it's not The Man holding you down—*and He will,* oh God, he will —it's cultural stigma: the risk of finding yourself ruthlessly exposed by your own honesty.

I mean, here you are, naked for all to see. Tellin' it like it is, baby. Lettin' it all hang out. Baring your soul, in all its contradictions. Trying to make sense of your time and place. Trying to make art out of how you feel.

This is risky business, to be sure. And the iffier your innate relationship with *actual skill or talent*, the more painfully, hilariously risky it gets.

The very real possibility that people will just laugh at you is surely the second-to-worst fear for anyone who has ever opened their mouth or taken off their pants in public. Especially when you just spent your life savings—and/or every last favor you could possibly pull—in order to attempt to express yourself through the woefully expensive medium of film.

The worst fear, of course, is to be ignored completely.

But why dicker, when you can have both?

For poor Amos Sefer—the visionary writer/director/ producer of *An American Hippie in Israel* (a.k.a. *The Hitch Hiker*, or *Ha-Trempist* in Hebrew)—both of

these nightmares would inevitably come to pass. The first, and worst, ran the length of his lifetime, as the film failed to find an audience in Israel, or anywhere else, for nearly forty years. The second-worst began several years after his death, when it was miraculously rediscovered.

There's an amazing exchange in Todd Solondz's *Happiness*, wherein a woman tells Jane Adams, "We're not laughing at you. We're laughing *with* you." And Adams replies, in perfect horror, *"But I'm not laughing!"*

I can only imagine that would be Sefer's response, if he knew how howlingly, deliriously funny this film has become to the modern eye and ear.

But if I were to somehow contact his spirit—either in this world, or the next—I would wrap him up in a great big hug, kiss his cheek, and tell him, "You know what? *I really love your fucking film.* I show it to people every chance I get. I am nearly evangelical about it. And this is not a lie.

"You know why? Because it's soooooo sincere, and such a genuine reflection of its time. And because you tried so hard. And brought such interesting people into your mix. And because your heart was so completely in the right place."

It would, of course, be harder to critique the film for him, because that would involve puncturing all of its many astonishing flaws. And that would be embarrassing.

Maybe he'd already figured that out, because he never ever made another film, and appears to have done his damndest to disappear off the face of the earth. Thereby making any authoritative account of the production next-to-impossible.

THE BIZARRO ENCYCLOPEDIA OF FILM

As for the film itself…

Hippie Mike, fresh from the Vietnam War, and flush with post-traumatic stress disorder, arrives in Israel ready to spearhead a revolution against the Machine. His rage-laden message of love resonates with a woman hungry for rebellion who takes him home, fucks him, falls under his sway, then introduces him to the groovy Israeli hippie subculture also yearning for utopia. They snuggle to folk songs in solidarity until The Man shows up in duplicate—replete with sinister masks, suits, and machine guns—and one shitload of dead hippies later, forces them to flee toward an idyllic island where they can create a new society, free of social constraint.

Which, as it turns out, is utterly doomed by the fact that *they have no idea what they're doing.* Their best-laid plans aren't plans at all. Just idealism laced with self-righteous egomania that is doomed to implode, like all such ill-conceived notions.

Seriously? This is a great idea for a movie, with a lot to say about both the need for rebellion and the perils of going off half-cocked, no matter how hard your dick is. Sefer is clearly sympathetic to the "Make Love, Not War" mood of the era, while sounding the hardest cautionary note he could envision, warning his fellow hippies not to wind up historically looking like idiots.

And as fate would have it, he wound up both exposing and *embodying* that failure to deliver on that vision. Half-baked to the core and yet utterly whole-hearted, *An American Hippie in Israel* pretty much encapsulates why that revolution never happened.

The chief culprit, as usual, is the script: full of dialogue so ripely insane that it rivals Russ Meyer and Roger Ebert at their best. What I wouldn't give to know how much of that was scripted, and how much was improvised by the actors on the spot.

But as a fable, it has a weird cohesion. *It knows what it's trying to say*, and tries to say it really hard.

Again, we come back to sincerity.

The actors all give very committed performances. I'm not saying they're good. I'm just saying they're committed. And that I love every single one of them. Studly, psychotic Asher Tzarfati nails Hippie Mike so hard that, to my mind, it's a showcase for the ages. Manson, Shmanson. *Give that boy a cult!* Lilu Abidan and Tzila Karney— as the obligatory hot, wild hippie women drawn into Mike's utopian vision, before calling it for the bullshit it is—gamely throw down with taut nipples and terrific abandon. I can't say their roles are thankless, because I thank them very much. And since everyone's nekkid front and back are on display, it's only about 78% sexist.

But I can't even tell you how much I love seeing Shmuel Wolf's weird face every time it comes onscreen. His acting is solid and fun, but just the fact that he was somehow crazily cast in this sexy bare-ass role always gives me a "WONDERFUL FEELING!"

My good friend Scott Bradley (*The Book of Lists: Horror*) nailed the film straight through the head when he affectionately said, "It's like if Ed Wood directed *Zabriskie Point*." And he's right. But not entirely fair.

For one thing, Amos Sefer is a waaaaaaay better director than Ed Wood. Not great, but waaaaaaaay better than Ed Wood. Where they most obviously meet is in the screamingly on-the-nose dialogue, at which point they could almost be Siamese twins in jaw-dropping culpability.

And frankly, *An American Hippie in Israel* is roughly 8 trillion times more entertaining than *Zabriskie Point*. If that sounds like a lot, that's because it is.

Most of the Antonioni comparisons come down to the lush cinematography of Ya'achov Kallich, who gorgeously nails every scene from the Tel Aviv Airport to the Coral Islands, where the ultimate bad news goes down. The locations are all smartly, lusciously chosen, and shot with a genuine eye.
Past that, the both wonderfully evocative and painfully redundant soundtrack by Nachum Heiman does its folk/mariachi best to make a faux Judy Collins and the

Tijuana Brass upstage Cat Stevens in *Harold and Maude* and the half-a-jillion rock stars in *Easy Rider*.

Would I slap it on my Itunes? Lord yes, I would. In my mind, it's there already.

But ultimately, it comes down to the sincerity.

And this is where my Helpless Love Gland kicks in.

Because, like Ed Wood—and so many other of the best, most embarrassing ass-barers in cinema history—there's a genuine spark inside this display. A true artist—not a good one, but a true one—trying as hard as he can to both entertain and enlighten.

I don't know how enlightened you're gonna come out of this experience.

But you sure as shit ought to be entertained.

In the end, all movies are time capsules. And Hippie Cinema—inarguably the *grooviest* cinema—holds a very special place in the time capsule canon. As enacted from the mid-1960's well into the 70's, it was an art form of rebellion—an art form actively in rebellion—conceived as a revolutionary act against both the studio status quo and the prevailing culture at large.

THE BIZARRO ENCYCLOPEDIA OF FILM

Films like *Easy Rider, Woodstock, Medium Cool, The Trip, Zabriskie Point, Gimme Shelter, Getting Straight, Breaker's Palace, El Topo, Wild in the Streets, We Love You, Alice B. Toklas, Putney Swope, The Magic Christian, Joe, Jesus Christ Superstar, Harold and Maude*, and *Beyond the Valley of the Dolls* are all indelible markers of the time, at wildly varying degrees of quality.

Horror films at the margins like *The Texas Chainsaw Massacre, Tender Flesh, Messiah of Evil, Let's Scare Jessica to Death*, and *Living Dead at the Manchester Morgue* (the first hippie-flavored response to the hippie-free but entirely countercultural *Night of the Living Dead*) played their respective parts in weirdening the debate.

And *I Am Curious (Yellow), The Opening of Misty Beethoven, Behind the Green Door, The Devil In Miss Jones*, and the early San Francisco works of freewheeling radical gonzo pioneer Alex de Renzy took care of the pornographic wild frontier, where fucking onscreen was the ultimate revolutionary act.

Dozens upon dozens of shitty copycat films were also released in that era, with God-only-knows how many others that never saw the light of day, much less a drive-in movie screen.

So where does *An American Hippie in Israel* fit into all this?

Well, it's worse than the best of them, and way better than the worst. As a barometer of naivete and ultimate doom, it's actually pretty par for the course, delivering all the highs and lows with a preposterously unflinching eye.

Time has not been kind to it, unless you measure kindness in howling laughter. But if you *do* measure it in howling laughter, time has been very kind indeed.

When I first saw this glorious disaster—at the Steve Allen Theater, in shell-shocked L.A.—the audience was giddily primed for excitement. We'd seen Bob Murawski's stunning trailer for years, like a tickle in our hindbrain, begging orgasmically for release and fulfillment.

I have to tell you: I have never had more fun in a theater, or laughed so hard and often in a crowded place. It's almost as if Sefer precognitively designed his film for MST3K-style audience mockery, putting all the ripe pauses precisely where they belonged. You can laugh at it, or laugh with it. Either choice is entirely okay.

Me, I laugh with it. Clocking its heart all the way. Giving everyone involved the warm hug they so richly deserve.

Did I mention I dearly love this film? If you ask me, I will tell you that it's *the single greatest motion picture ever made*.

It's a lie.

But I mean it with all my heart.

I'LL SHOW YOU THE LIFE
OF THE MIND
ON BEING A TOURIST WITH A TYPEWRITER,
IN THE LAND OF *BARTON FINK*

JOHN SKIPP

Writer's block. Two of the scariest words in the English language, if you're a writer in the English language who believes in such things. And also one of the most boring subjects for a piece of art-o-tainment imaginable. ("I know! Let's make a creative work about the inability to make a creative work!")

Unless, of course, you're Joel and Ethan Coen. In which case, you hit a logjam in your script for the soon-to-be-legendary *Miller's Crossing*, and—as opposed of freaking out—take a little time off and write *Barton Fink* in three fucking weeks instead. Return to finish the first one. And then shoot them both back-to-back.

Amongst the reams and reams of speculative critical analysis regarding *Barton Fink* (1991)—by far the most-picked apart of their protean ouvre, with the possible exception of 2009's *A Serious Man*—I can't think of any that focused on how hilarious it is that they channeled their own "writer's block" into a story about the nightmarish absurdity of the condition, in a world full of sooooo many rich possibilities to explore.

Indeed, if you were to ask me to give a one-sentence pocket synopsis, it might be this:

"*Barton Fink* is the story of an earnest. deeply committed young writer soooo deeply up his own ass that he can't even begin to understand the world he's trying soooo hard to explain to others, until it bites him on that very same ass."

Now before I go pissing off every writer in the world that I haven't pissed off already, lemme remind you that, HEY! I'm a writer, too! Every bit as determined to tell deep truths. And every bit as ridiculous in the face of the obstacles we all confront. Most particularly, the ones we create for ourselves, in response to this cruel world.

So it is not without enormous sympathy that I ride along, gleefully, with the brothers Coen as they systematically dismantle both artistic self-importance *and* the brutal machineries facing every genuine artist who ever slammed face-to-face against "The System".

And with all that said, let's talk about our nice story!

It's 1941, and young playwright Barton (John Turturro) is the toast of Broadway. His new play, *Bare Ruined Choir*, is considered emblematic of the "new theater of the common man". (Think Clifford Odets' 1939 hit *Awake and Sing!*) And his work is too important to be saddled with commercial concerns. However, there ain't much money in it.

Striking while the iron is hot, his agent (David Warrilow, in one of the first of the film's many indelible bit parts) swings a plush deal for Barton: $1,000 a week to churn out scripts under contract for Capitol Pictures. Barton clearly has contempt for the industry, and fears being torn from his revolutionary purpose. But it's a crazy amount of money.

So Barton flies out to Los Angeles, and ensconces himself in the Hotel Earle, a seedy Art Deco relic falling to ruin he chooses because he doesn't want to be "too Hollywood". In terms of creepy desperation, it out-Overlooks the Overlook from *The Shining* (incidentally, the only other story about writer's block I ever loved), in that it never for a second pretends to be anything but haunted. Not by ghosts, necessarily, but by the lost and barely-living (for example Pete, the cadaverous elevator operator played by Harry Bugin).

Once checked into his shitty little room—a desk, a bed, two windows with no view, and a picture of a willowy brunette in a swimsuit on the beach, shielding her eyes from the sun with her back to us forever—Barton shows up at the office of Jack Lipnick (Michael Lerner), the larger-than-life head of Capitol Pictures. Lipnick assures him—in the most grandiose ballyhoo manner—that "The writer is KING at Capitol Pictures!", and that all he wants is to be given "that Barton Fink feeling. Only not too fruity. Well, all right, maybe a little for the critics."

Barton's promptly assigned a wrestling picture, to star Wallace Beery. And completely lost as to how to proceed, he asks for help from producer Ben Geisler (Tony Shaloub), a man so tightly wound and in hate with his life that when asked how to meet other writers, he says, "Oh, Jesus. You throw a rock in here, you'll hit one. Do me a favor, Fink. Throw it hard."

This leads to a chance bathroom encounter with celebrated novelist-turned-studio-indentured-slave H.P. Mayhew (John Maloney, clearly modeled on William Faulkner), who takes time off from puking then drinking some more to discuss "wrasslin' pictures, and other things literary". This drags in Mayhew's faithful right hand Audrey Taylor (Judy Davis), who feels sympathy both for the impassioned, out-of-his-depth Barton and Mayhew, despite the former's obtuseness and the latter's drunken, abusive behavior both emotional and physical. Not to mention creative.

Back at the Hotel Earle, Barton can't write. It just won't come. And on top of the alienation, there's the guy next door, who won't stop crying, or laughing, or both. Calling the gnome-like Chet (Steve Buscemi) at the front desk to complain, he is promptly rewarded by a visit by the sobbing man himself. This is Charley Meadows (John Goodman), a traveling insurance salesman who apologizes like hell for the disturbance. Offers to "buy him a drink" (pulling a pint from his pocket). And proceeds to become his best friend on the outside of the Hollywood system. You know. A common man.

THE BIZARRO ENCYCLOPEDIA OF FILM

Now I could spend another ten pages meticulously spelling out every dense layer of symbology that follows. The deaths. The betrayals. That pesky mosquito. The whole nightmarish plunge into flaming massacre chaos, designed to SHOW YOU THE LIFE OF THE MIND.

But you can find a better recitation of *Barton Fink*'s plot points and minutiae on Wikipedia (it's the longest page for any film I've ever personally investigated), and a billion other places. Better yet, *just watch the film*, and then I won't have to tell you what happens.

What I really wanna talk about is how fucking Bizarro this film is, and the deep well of strangeness from which it compels you to drink.

For starters, it's an entirely genre-resistant film, from beginning to end, kind of daring you to figure out what kind of movie it is. It's a period Hollywood satire, drenched in both noir and screwball comedy (itself a heightened reality so intense that, to my mind, it qualifies as Bizarro right there). Equal parts Raymond Chandler and Preston Sturges (more about whom in a minute).

But then there's the clear, acknowledged debt to Roman Polanski's *Cul-de-Sac*, *Repulsion*, and *The Tenant*, in their masterly depictions of psyches claustrophobically caving from within. All at the dark end of the Bizarro spectrum. It's the beauty and the artfulness with which it's all depicted that makes critics climb all over themselves, trying to decipher the secret meanings of...well...everything!

For example, I could suggest that the woman on the beach at the end symbolizes Barton's entry into authentic Real Life: a thing he couldn't begin to see with the marveling eyes of a child until forcibly wrenched from the sunken depths of his own anus. And I could make a pretty good case for it, too!

On the other hand, as the Coens like to say, sometimes a guy on the beach with a head in a box is just a guy on the beach with a head in a box. And furthermore, it's kind of comical to insist upon what "really" happened in a story that's entirely confabulated out of thin air in the first place. (Which is to say: *fiction*.)

One of the things that makes *Barton Fink* so confounding is the fact that, if the brothers are to be believed, their philosophy is that of the drunken M.P. Mayhew, who muses, "Hmm. Well, me, I just enjoy making things up." So they sit down to tell a story; and every time they think of something that gets them interested, excited, or intrigued, they play with it. And if it works, they use it.

This is creating from the unconscious: less concerned with what it means than how it plays, and how it intuitively feels. And because they're so smart, and so skillful, and so determined to amuse and engage themselves in every single thing they do, the results are right there on the screen. Soooo good that we stare at it, going, "That was incredible. WHAT'S ITS SECRET?"

Well, one of their secrets is meticulous planning on the production end. They may write from the unconscious, but their grasp of the mechanics of physical filmmaking is uncanny. There are no lazy shots of basic coverage to slog through, like so many directors who jack out a ton of footage and then let the editor sort it out in post. They *are* the editors—under the *nom de plume* Roderick Jaynes—and therefore know that they only need what they need. And go directly for that, in every single moment of every speck of every single scene.

This legendary rigor extends to the quality of the people they align themselves with, both behind and in front of the camera. *Barton Fink* was their first collaboration with cinematographer Roger Deakins (having just lost Barry Sonnenfeld to *The Addams Family*, and his own directing career). But it clearly clicked, because they've worked with him on every film since. Becoming a righteous legend of his own in the process.

Likewise with Carter Burwell, who's brilliantly scored every every one of their films since their 1984 debut,

Blood Simple. And many other skilled technicians have taken the long ride with them. Building a resilient, unstoppable film family along the way.

Which brings us to the influence of the astonishing Preston Sturges: a clear hero of the Coens (and mine as well). Not only was he the guy who broke the writer/director barrier in 1939 with *The Great McGinty*—offering the soon-to-be Oscar-winning script to Paramount for one dollar, in exchange for the chance to direct it, thereby opening the door for everyone from Billy Wilder to the Coen Bros. themselves—but he also had a ferocious loyalty to his ensemble cast of players.

The thing I immediately adored about Sturges' films is that *every character matters*, no matter how small their part. If it's worth putting them onscreen for even a second, then they should be genuinely interesting. If they have a line, it should be a great one. And even if they're just standing there, they should have a somehow-compelling face, full of period-defining personality. Even the extras need to bring a little extra something to make it make sense that they're there, bringing an unmistakable aliveness to the proceedings.

This has been a constant through every Coen Brothers film as well. And that shit is not accidental. Have you ever seen a bad performance in a Coen Brothers film? No, you haven't. You know why? I JUST TOLD YOU!

Then we come to the leads. And oh my god. Between the words on the page, the scrupulous precision of the camerawork and production design, the sheer fun implied by being part of it, and the alchemy of brilliant actors doing what they do best, some of the best actors in the world are routinely drawn back in the Coen web of wowness.

Barton Fink is not unique in this—is just part of the pattern—but you wanna talk about singular performances that, across the board, rank as "ones for the ages"?

Let's start with Turturro, as Barton Fink. He's the twitchy centerpiece, his *Eraserhead*-flavored "jewfro" and weird round Elvis Costello intellectual eyeglasses instantly singling him out from any normal person in the world of 1941. He's pre-punk/New Wave in that he doesn't fit in, and doesn't want to. This aloneness—and the self-righteous up-his-own-assness that comes with it—

appear to be his defining characteristics. If we didn't know this guy was some kind of genius, we'd think he was just another pompous art-hole. But evidently he's gifted, so we're along for the ride. (Incredibly talented losers are a Coen staple, as witness 2013's *Inside Llewyn Davis*. Which is to say: just because you're good at something doesn't mean that you're not sort of a jerk.)

But just because you're some sort of a jerk, that doesn't mean that you don't have human feelings, or a rich interior life. And Turturro reveals the insecurity, the self-deprecating haunted humility, and indeed the compassion and genuine sweetness of this very sincere young man who just wants to contribute something of value to the world. As such, he anchors himself precisely at every juncture of the "Hero's Journey" *and* the "Zero's Journey", equally befuddled by either choice. And we are with him, every step of the way.

To say that it's a performance for the ages is just stating the obvious. But it's far from the only one. Both Lerner's Lipkin and Mahoney's Mayhew are tornado-like forces of nature, dominating every scene they're in so shockingly that, were we in poor Barton's shoes, we'd be just as freaked out as he is. And Judy Davis is equally staggering as the thin-eyed Audrey, who understands what's going on better than any of the above, both cunningly and empathically. And pays for that more unfairly and harshly (at least to my mind) than the rest of the cast combined.

And much as Jon Polito's 180 turn as Lipkin's groveling yes-man Lou (after his crime lord role in *Miller's Crossing*) needs to be noted for its excellence, I'd be hideously remiss were I not to mention Richard Portnow and Christopher Murney as Detectives Mastrionotti and Deutch, respectively. They bring the hardboiled noir to such a blisteringly hilarious cynical pitch that I suspect Chandler and Dashiell Hammett may have high-fived each other from beyond the grave, wishing they'd *ever* gotten away with a throwaway line like, "You're a sick fuck, Fink."

But push come to shove, the man who takes the cake, sets it on fire, then eats it, is John Goodman. As the layers of Charley Meadows peel back to Mad Man Mundt—and beyond that, to some sort of inconceivable avenging angel from the sixth floor of Hell—the deftness with which he swings his formidable 300 pound bulk between genuinely lovable and authentically terrifying bespeaks a level of seismic grace and power I can't even begin to sum up.

He is, in fact, the deepest enigma in a movie made entirely of deep enigmas. Forced to pick a better one in the entire history of film, I'm coming up a blank.

And so, in conclusion:

The thing that kills me most about the Coen Bros. — in this film, and everything else they ever did — is how alive they make each moment. How every line of dialogue glistens like a pearl. How every face that speaks them is precisely the right face. How every camera angle and every object seen is just the right one, telling you exactly what you need to know, without telling you the secret. Which is sitting right in front of you.
For all its glorious contrivance, there's something so engaged and *excited* about their filmmaking that I feel it in every fucking frame. Such precision. Such unspeakable attention to tiny detail. SUCH JOY, no matter how dark the passage. All parlayed in a nonstop rush of silence and mayhem as alternating currents. To me, that electricity is staggering.

When I think about the art-o-tainment that I genuinely care about, it's all about the dance between rigor and chaos. Not just unleashing some astonishing vision, but meticulously capturing it in all its glory.

From the rotting mausoleum of the Hotel Earle to the ostentatious grandeur of Broadway on the east coast and Hollywood on the west, I am inside their world. It's *our world*, with the protective anti-weirdness filter turned off, and all its teeth exposed.

You can't get more fucking Bizarro than that.

BORN OF A DREAM
PANOS COSMATOS'
BEYOND THE BLACK RAINBOW

HEATHER DRAIN

*"Unmasking identity/In search of a memory/Of how it used to be/
Anonymous"*
-SSQ "Anonymous"

"I had the dream but the dream died. Hey Hey Kiss it Goodbye."
-The Fallen Angels "Kiss it Goodbye"

I always had an issue with the old proverb of "the road to Hell is paved with good intentions." The biblical unforgivingness of it disturbed me as a child and irks me as an adult. However, it took me watching Panos Cosmatos' incredible 2010 sci-fi arthouse masterwork, *Beyond the Black Rainbow*, to understand the root of such a fear-driven statement. This film is dreamlike in its pacing, lighting, artificial design and nightmare-like in its tonal shadows and implications. It mixes sci-fi and horror elements with the scariest—and truest—quotient of them all: human nature.

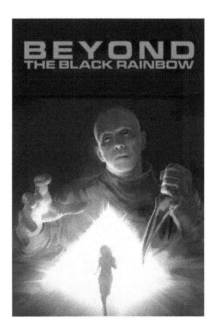

THE BIZARRO ENCYCLOPEDIA OF FILM

A promotional film for the Arboria Institute dating back to 1966 is screened. Graphics promise us, "A state of mind. A way of being." Pastoral imagery and scenes of the universe are inter-cut with a man bathed in red light talking to the camera. His rich, soothing voice is matched by a friendly face. Our narrator is the institute's founder, one Dr. Mercurio Arboria (Scott Hylands). The Arboria Institute was inspired by his dream of "finding a way for people to achieve supreme happiness...and inner peace." The fatherly voice assures us that they have found a way to secure such a Utopian state, via "neuropsychology," "new therapeutic technologies," as well as their team of "herbalists, naturopaths and healers," and the absolute kicker, their "unique blend of benign pharmacology, sensory and energy sculpting." Even promising "award winning gardens," the Arboria Institute of the 1960's, not unlike a lot of new age movements of the time, emphasizes the basic dreams of rising above the human condition while implementing metaphysical creeping into psychobabble terminology. The reel ends with Arboria inviting us to join, while a shot appears of his white-clad form, still bathed in red light but now holding a glowing pyramid.

The sweet promise of a new dawn fades to 1983. Dr Barry Nyle (Michael Rogers), a sharp looking man, once Arboria's right hand assistant and student though now all but in charge, goes to his daily meetings with a mute young woman wrapped in melancholy fragility, Elena (Eva Bourne). It is pretty quickly apparent that Elena possesses some potent psychic abilities that Barry is clearly trying to tap into. He is willfully blind to her mental plea to see her father, feeding off of her like a razor-cheeked psychic vampire.

Barry further manipulates Elena via operating a device tied to three glowing pyramids that emits a sensory wave that triggers her powers. Not content with just that, he ends up framing up a situation where after planting a picture of Elena's long-dead mother in her room, he then informs the one employee of the Institute that we see other than Barry and Mercurio, Margo (Rondel Reynoldson), that Elena has contraband in her room that needs to be confiscated. The latter, who carries the heavy shouldered damage of a low-totem pole worker needing to lord their wee power over the lowest of tiers, tries to take the picture away, triggering Elena's powers, which inadvertently kill Margo.

THE BIZARRO ENCYCLOPEDIA OF FILM

Barry soon goes to visit the now aged Arboria, who is withered, junked out and watching his old films with a sick-eyed nostalgia laced with the once bright-hearted promises of "a new, better, happier you." An absolutely brain-melting flashback begins with grainy black & white visuals, where we see Barry and Mercurio together, along with Arboria's wife, Anna (Sara Stockstad), back in the 1960's. Arboria doses him, then sends him into a circle of oil-like fluid, telling him to "Bring home the motherload, Barry." What ensues is like the most glorious fiery psychedelic spike right into the firm meat of your brain array of images. Delirious color swirls around fluids, skull-type objects and Heaven & Hell frenching and retching all at once in a Kenneth Anger-esque ode. Barry emerges from the fluid, now altered forever, both physically and mentally. He murders Anna, a woman he clearly had some sweet and possibly untoward affection for. Mercurio's reaction is to take his infant daughter and telling her right before he plunges her into the same fluid that has helped righteously fuck Barry's world forever, "Your mother's re-absorption into the life cycle won't be for nothing, my darling Elena. You will be the dawning of a new era of the human race...let the new age of enlightenment begin." Back from the past, Barry injects Mercurio in between his toes, presumably due to his main veins collapsing over the years, and intentionally overdoses his once mentor and pseudo-father figure.

Barry goes home to his wife, Rosemary (Marilyn Norry), a middle-aged Earth momma who tries to dote on him, which is akin to a flower child trying to discuss chakras and chanting with an ill-socialized monitor lizard. He enters their bathroom and takes a massive litany of prescription pills, courtesy of Benway's Pharmacy, a cute nod towards the recurring character used throughout a number of William S. Burroughs novels. Removing his contacts and wig, Barry's revealed himself to be more alien looking, all of which is part of his scars from that fateful day with Mercurio, Anna and Elena so many years ago. Greeting his wife, who comments that he has removed all of his "appliances," Barry ends up killing Rosemary and goes on the full hunt for Elena. The latter has figured out how to escape the Institute and is on the run. What results is a climactic meeting that will feel anti-climactic for some, but for a film that is less interested in black vs white dynamics and more interested in the many layers of pollution of the self, it rings more true. It is a total "give the people what they deserve" move versus "give the people what they want" on Cosmatos' end and bless him for that. A charlatan will bullshit and give you what they think you want. A true love-hearted individual will give you the real deal.

Beyond the Black Rainbow is a pure beauty that challenges you. Its languid pacing felt like a drugged dream-mare for me but for viewers wanting the quick-cut scare-machine of modern-day genre mainstream pep and pap, it will get itchy. There's an honest morality to the film. Barry is a villain, undoubtedly, between his bizarre psycho-sexual fixation and control of Elena, even threatening some stoner kids he runs into while chasing her with the question, "Did you fuck her?!?," to his cold blooded killing of Margo and his own wife. There is an emotional divide there but monsters are made and rarely, if ever, born. Barry is no exception to this, thanks in part to both Cosmatos' smart writing and an absolutely charismatic and intuitive performance by Michael Rogers.

It's all in the power of Barry's flashback. Getting that glimpse of the point-of-no-return for both Barry and Arboria is what gives us a viewpoint into the death of Barry's idealism but also Mercurio's misplaced ego. Barry's trust with both Arboria and their journey is palpable, with the two men clearly hoping for a major breakthrough utilizing some surreal sensory deprivation-type techniques and psychedelics. But the original intention of human improvement becomes mutated, with Barry being transformed into a monster and Arborio putting his own infant daughter at high risk by dipping her into that same dark cosmic sludge. Such a decision screams murky arrogance. He clearly loves his daughter, but is willing to endanger little Elena, whose mother was just murdered in front of him a minute before, in a blind stab to make this experiment work. Mercurio is the father figure surrounded by martyrs at his own hand: Anna, Barry, and even poor Elena, who ends up being robbed of a mother, not to mention a good chunk of her young life that has found her trapped in the Institute and sleeping alone in a spartan room with only a TV monitor playing old, black & white cartoons of the cute-creepy Max Fleischer variety. The death of Arboria's dream is also the mirror image of the death of the counterculture's Utopian goals of the 1960's. New age good intentions were whomped by human nature, though instead of anything supernatural, it was Altamont. It was Vietnam. It was Watergate. It was all of these things. Bringing home the motherlode is hard to do when the worst part of our humanity becomes a weapon, both to others but especially to ourselves.

The film is engineered in such a way where watching it alone feels like you're possibly going through one of Arboria's sensory-related experiments. The bulk of the film is set inside the Institute, with a set design that is one part mid 1960's bleeding into the 70's faux-futurism, part techno-Jodorowsky circa *The Holy Mountain* and some Kenneth Anger, in particular *Invocation of My Demon Brother* and *Lucifer Rising* during Barry's flashbacks. Much noise online has been made about there being a strong Kubrick influence, which I can marginally kind of see, but the strongest visual tie between *Beyond the Black Rainbow* is something far more esoteric and unexpected: the 1982 music video for Canadian new wave band Spoons and their song "Nova Heart." Directed by Robert Quartly, the video features the male members of the band clad in white, futuristic looking suits, looking onward at Sandy Horne, the band's female bassist, who is partially secluded in a neon framed bedroom. The true clincher are the shots of the three men bathed in red light with the central figure holding a glowing white pyramid, a total mirror image of not only the pyramid that Arboria holds in the promo film at the beginning, but also the larger scale ones that Barry uses to manipulate Elena's powers. It may seem a little unlikely, especially since I have not had the chance to personally bend Cosmatos' ear about it, but given that he is Canadian, in his late 30's at the time of me writing this sentence and the fact that the video got decent airplay on the Great White North's equivalent to MTV, MuchMusic, it feels like a razor tight fit.

The film's soundtrack is an electronic landscape punctuated with an atmosphere that is somehow spartan and rich, pulsating with cold beauty, warm menace and a pregnant dread. Courtesy of Sinoia Caves, a side project from Jeremy Schmidt, a member of the Canadian psyche-rock band Black Mountain, it is a fantastic sequence of musical pieces. Everything fits the imagery and tone like a sleek black leather glove, not unlike the designer outfit Barry slips on once he fully embraces his full transformed, monstrous self. (Leave it to a corrupted former hippie turned yuppie to have a secret leather designer outfit for his full-blown transgression spree.)

Beyond the Black Rainbow is a challenging work that rewards the ones who can tune in to it. It is a throbbing piece of transformative cinema, meaning that once you have watched it and fully received it, there is at least part of yourself that is forever changed. It is the kind of art that can alter your DNA and organ cells, if you let it. It is cynical, exquisite and a total tone poem for the death knell of when optimism becomes corroded from within. This is the motherlode.

VARLOTS, HARLOTS & CHURLS
RUSS MEYER'S *BEYOND THE VALLEY OF THE DOLLS*

HEATHER DRAIN

There is a contingent of Stuffy McStuffersons who are of the belief that high art and camp cannot the twain meet. This is, of course, high inanity and the end result of not allowing any light into one's rusty old soul. I have near-scientific proof for this in the form of one auteur that is more American than apple pie, baseball and a Hank Williams turkey leg and more breast obsessed than the entire 1980's Sunset Strip hairband scene. If the name Russ Meyer has not graced your lexicon yet, then you are in for a real treat. Even if you're reading the man's name right now and nodding "Ah yes," then you're still in for a sweet ride.

20. CENTURY-FOX presents **BEYOND THE VALLEY OF THE DOLLS** Color by DE LUXE® PANAVISION.® 70/179

A veteran of World War II who shot film down in the trenches, a highly successful cheesecake photographer and the director who helped usher in the nudie cutie subgenre with his film, *The Immoral Mr. Teas* (1959), Meyer was a man and a director with brass balls. But unlike other meat and potatoes workmen, Meyer's directorial resume, whether it is the gritty Flannery O'Connor-on-Spanish-Fly-like *Mudhoney* (1965) or his Technicolor blood, brutes and brazen breasty babes 1970's works like *Supervixens* (1975), all of them are unified by the unmistakable Russ Meyer thumbprint. These films often contain both a beautiful absurdity and a rich, visual flair that could only belong to a brilliant man obsessed with great camerawork, kinetic editing and uber-women with big personalities matched only by their even bigger and magnetically humongous breasts.

Another talent of Meyer's was making a significant profit while remaining fully independent, culminating with 1968's *Vixen*, which despite (or due to) being famously banned in Cincinnati, reaped some huge box office. Big enough to lure in Hollywood, in particular, 20th Century Fox, to go sniffing around Meyer. What would result from this unlikely union would not only be financially successful for a then-shaky studio but also help create one of the most stupendous cult films to emerge out of the strange brew times of the late 1960's and early 1970's. *Beyond the Valley of the Dolls*, while originally scripted to be a sequel-of-sorts to the famed mainstream cult film that you could probably watch with your parents, *Valley of the Dolls* (1967), ended up being its entirely own creature.

Scripted by a then-unknown Roger Ebert, who would go on to also pen Meyers' *Up!* (1976) and *Beneath the Valley of the Ultra-Vixens* (1979), *Beyond the Valley of the Dolls* combines soap opera dramatics, humor that is always teetering on the edge of slap-happy delirium, rock & roll, drugs and the swinging counter culture of late 60's era Los Angeles. Take all of the above mentioned and put it through the unlikely but strangely oh-so-perfect combination filter of Meyer and Ebert, who were the two least likely guys to be turned on to anything actually edgy and hip about youth culture of the 1960's. Yet, they helped create one of the ultimate cult classics. Hollywood tackling similar issues always ended up more of a miss than a hit, so it truly took two independent misfits to make a film like *Beyond the Valley of the Dolls*.

The film opens with a night scene outside of a lush looking West Coast mansion. Dramatic orchestral old school Hollywood music swells as a lurking figure, gun in hand approaches a beautiful sleeping woman. Suggestively placing the barrel of the gun in her mouth, she comes to and starts to scream, with a quick cut bleeding into a powerful female belt from one Kelly MacNamara (the super-adorable Dolly Read), lead singer of the rock trio, The Kelly Affair. Playing a school dance, Kelly is backed up by her bassist, the gorgeous and haunted Casey Anderson (Cynthia Myers) and the fun and exquisitely pretty Petronella "Pet" Danforth (Marcia McBroom) on drums. The band plays while Kelly's boyfriend and the band's manager, Harris Allsworth (David Gurian), spins a color wheel to give off that extra-groovy psychedelic lighting. Their song, "Find It," is a hard rocking swinger of a tune that does not impress the adult chaperones at all, leading one of the men to make an aside to a buddy, "I'd like to cut their-", with the film itself cutting the man off before we find out his full bad-time intent.

THE BIZARRO ENCYCLOPEDIA OF FILM

Leaving their Anywhere, America town, The Kelly Affair road trek it to the golden land of sweet dreams and dirty deals, Los Angeles, in one of the most breathtaking examples of stellar editing committed to celluloid. Meyer's films, in general, are some of the best edited in modern American cinema, but this sequence was his equivalent to the famous Odessa Steps scene in Sergei Eisenstein's *Battleship Potemkin* (1925). Instead of bloodshed, terror and a baby carriage in taut imposing danger, you have city scenes, a voluminous breasted woman running in slow motion in a sheer diaphanous lavender garment, a close-up of a man's shoe stepping on a raw egg, couples making love and various fast scenes from later on in the film. The snappy patter edited precisely to the fast array of various images all results in what I will term as "the cinematic sweet spot." It's sexy in its perfection and fueled with some NASCAR-level gun fuel. The aforementioned back and forth dialogue plays out like the wet-limbs-entwined-coupling of the "Green Acres" theme song and the spoken word jazz-poetics of Ken Nordine.

In LA, Kelly looks up her long-lost rich aunt, Susan Lake (Phyllis Davis), a hip fashion photographer. Despite the immediate weariness of Susan's lawyer and financial adviser, the squarer-than-Dick-Nixon-at-a-New-Christy-Minstrels-Convention Porter Hall (the divinely sleazy Duncan McLeod), who is instantly suspicious of Kelly, Susan is more than happy to be united with her niece. Being a rare angel in this universe, the luminescent and kindly Susan makes a point to invite Kelly, Casey, Pet and Harris that night to one of the most amazing parties in film history, hosted by Rock & Roll impresario, producer and the man with the golden ear to the teen culture ground itself, Ronnie "Z-Man" Barzell (John Lazar).

Z-Man and the actor behind him, the eternally underrated John Lazar, is so glorious that in another time, his mere presence would have warranted sonnets, vestal virgins being tossed to Pele (the goddess, not the Soccer player, though I'm sure he probably wouldn't mind!), amyl-fueled orgiastic bacchanals and, last but never least, black velvet macaroni art. If Count Dracula, Oscar Wilde, and Tim Curry all mated to a soundtrack by The Fugs, their love child could very much be Z-Man. With brilliant Shakespearean-tinged dialogue handled with satin-safe aplomb by Lazar, Z-Man gloms on to Kelly immediately and gives her a personal tour of both his home and the various party-goers shaking some action.

A fabulous creature like Z-Man is going to naturally have some of the most colorful cats and kittens at his party, including supermodelesque bodyguard Vanessa (Lavelle Roby, who was also in Meyers 1968 film *Finders Keepers Lovers Weepers*), the luscious lioness Ashley St. Ives (Edy Williams, who devours the screen with nary a crumb left in sight) whose main profession is starring in "prettily pornographic pictures," flaxen-haired, blue-eyed pretty boy gigolo, Lance Rock (Michael Blodgett), Emerson Thorne (Harrison Page), part-time waiter and full time law student, Ronnie's German bartender Otto (Henry Rowland) who could be the infamous real-life Nazi Martin Bormann in disguise, and Roxanne (Erica Gavin, who was the sexually insatiable lead in Meyer's blockbuster *Vixen*), a designer whose tastes lean on the Sapphic side. To top all of that off, the Strawberry Alarm Clock, a true life successful rock band who had a massive hit in 1967 with their song "Incense & Peppermints," is Z-Man's house band.

The party also features two characters that are minor but magnificent in their mutated peacock glory. There's an orange haired groovy grandma, billed simply as "Matron" (Meyer semi-regular Princess Livingston, like there could be a cooler name for an equally wild lady) and her dance partner, a middle-aged guru type with thinning dark hair and a tendency to wag his tongue like an Indian demi-god. These two are so good. Wait until you see the latter talk with Ashley about her experience of going to a man's house who has a wading pool full of MAYO-NAYSE!

Harris, Pet, and Casey soon arrive at the party. Casey catches the attention of Roxanne, while Pet immediately sparks with Emerson and Harris finds Z-Man giving Kelly a tour of his palatial estate. Or as Z-Man describes it, just a little meeting "...between Mary Wollstonecraft Shelley and Count Dracula." The vibe between the two is chilly, to say the least, with Z-Man mocking the name "The Kelly Affair" as very 1950's, like "...The Haircuts...", not helping matters between the men. He re-christens the band The Carrie Nations and has them play a song, which goes over like a bottle of Thunderbird in your drunk great-uncle's gullet. In short, they are a hit and

are soon on the road to mainstream success and fame, with Z-Man usurping Harris' role as manager.

The darker side of such gilded delights appears, with Kelly getting swooped up by the handsome prince of looking-out-for-number-one Lance, Casey becoming a loner comforted only by pills and liquor and Harris succumbing to the over the top carnal delights of one Ms. Ashley St. Ives. Their lovemaking in her Rolls Royce is so great. Not so much the sex itself, which is fairly tame, but her lascivious crowing about how "..nothing's better than a Rolls..not even a Bentley....a Bentley....nothing's better than a ROLLS!" is some glory glory.

The Carrie Nations continue to storm through the charts and record shops, while Kelly gets more and more wrapped around Lance's gold-digging pinky. Some of their post-coital talk includes Kelly gleefully telling Lance, "You've made me into a whore," with his golden boy response being "And you dig it, you little freak!" That scent in the air? It's not romance. Meanwhile, Harris has been hitting the pills and booze a little harder. Ashley tries to make love with him on the beach and when that mission doesn't launch, she gets frustrated, calls him a "lousy lay" and then tells him it might not be too late for him to find a '...nice, tender BOY." She gives a leonine smile, salutes him and then literally seduces the first man she encounters. There are girls and there are women and there is Ashley St. Ives. Edy Williams is the best kind of over-sexed comic book character in this film.

He ends up crashing Z-Man's party. Spotting Lance and Kelly making out hot and heavy, Harris decides to find his former girlfriend's current squeeze. Egged on by heavyweight champion boxer and Lance's "soul brother" Randy Black (James Iglehart), Harris tries and fails to kick Lance's ass. Kelly freaks out and dumps Lance, Pet is upset at seeing both Kelly torn and Harris beaten to a pulp and she ends up being comforted by the almost always shirtless Randy. Meanwhile, Z-Man flirts with Lance, telling him that maybe he should try "switch-hitting." Lance, being the evolved soul that he is, responds by punching Ronnie and leaving. Pet ends up sleeping with Randy and almost loses Emerson after the two men have a nasty confrontation. Harris goes over to Casey's apartment and the two bond over drinks and pills.

THE BIZARRO ENCYCLOPEDIA OF FILM

What unfurls after that is some over-the-top soap opera-type series of events that are, yes, even more insane than what I have just detailed. In the mix, there's a happy twist with Susan reuniting with the one true love of her life, the square-jawed eagle-heart of a man, Baxter Wolfe (Charles "Uber-mensch" Napier).

Everything culminates at a private party at Z-Man's that only has Casey, Roxanne, and Lance on the guest list. Otto brings the costumes, with Roxanne and Casey dressing up as a sexy Batman and Robin and Lance as "Jungle Boy." The latter is clearly not happy but after resorting to seducing some octogenarians, is happy to get some bread. And Z-Man? Emerges with a red cape as a "Super Woman!" Like I couldn't love him/her any more than I already do. This leads up to one of the best sequences in the film, featuring some gorgeous primary color lighting, the best use of the "Sorcerer's Apprentice" outside of FANTASIA (1940) with the four of them imbibing a potion that features some "peyote and other benign goodies" and going on a sexy-weird and intense trip.

After a really beautiful and tender love scene between Roxanne and Casey, things are not as serene between Superwoman and Lance. The latter completely rejects the former, giving us what could possibly be the best dialogue ever with the line "You will drink the black sperm of my vengeance!" What results is a climax that is ultra-violent, inspired by the then still very recent Tate-Labianca murders by the Manson Family, bonkers and ultimately heart-warming in a deliciously brain-damaged way.

Beyond the Valley of the Dolls is many things. Ridiculous? Absolutely and thank god, because it takes the phony-over-the-top dramatics of soap operas, emotional dramas and yes, the original *Valley of the Dolls* (1967) and makes them actually fun and non-stop compelling. But it is not just the intentional camp that makes this film such a multi-colored gem. What truly cinches it is how perfectly made *Beyond the Valley of the Dolls* is. The framing, the cinematography, and that superbly lively editing all hit the ace notes. Fully fleshing out the rest of it is the roundhouse kick combination of the cast and music.

Every human being that pops up in this film is fascinating, great to look at for a myriad of reasons and are an authentic part of such a high-dramatic, sex, drugs and rock & roll universe. The main cast is especially fantastic. Dolly Read is so charming and feisty as Kelly. Even when her actual British accent occasionally floats to the surface of her American accent, it actually works and just makes her even more appealing. Marcia McBroom is crazy-pretty as the sweet Pet and has some great chemistry with Harrison Page, who is always a welcome sight to see. Page would later on pop up as the gruff Captain on the brilliant cult comedy TV show, *Sledge Hammer!* (1986-88).

As the beautiful to the point of ethereal and yet quite haunted Casey, Cynthia Myers is incredibly prime. There are enough hints throughout that explains Casey's loneliness, including being the estranged daughter of a powerful Senator, that actually give the character a little bit of depth. Despite this being Myers' first major acting role, she makes such a strong impression. Her sensitivity is a great reflector to Erica Gavin's more predatory Roxanne. The narrator at the end even describes the two of them as "light and shadow," which is an on the nose comparison.

David Gurian is likable as the cute and long-suffering Harris. His interactions with Edy Williams' Ashley St. Ives are so great. He's like a denim boy getting swallowed whole by a Lovecraftian sex goddess. Michael Blodgett, an actor who is quite a bit underrated, is absolutely hilarious as Lance Rock. It's a performance that initially blends in with the rest of the film, but on repeat viewings, his nuance and above-it-all two-bit lover boy attitude really make such a thin character really crackle. And of course, we have to talk about the true star of the show here, the one and only Mr. John Lazar.

Talk about an undervalued actor. Why this man did not have a massively huge career after this film is a testament that the Hollywood machine is one that runs on the fuel of money fear and top grade horseshit. Playing

20th CENTURY FOX presents **BEYOND THE VALLEY OF THE DOLLS** Color by DE LUXE® PANAVISION.®

70/179

a gender-fluid and more than likely pansexual character like Z-Man was not and probably still would not, make a mainstream superstar out of anyone but goddammit, it should. Lazar inhabits this role like a pure charismatic. Once he appears, he will be the one your eyes will land on, which given the bevy of strange characters and half naked beauties that litter every frame here, that is no mean feat! He's my kind of dynamite. Lazar would, later on, appear in Russ' 1975 film SUPERVIXENS in a small but stand out creepy role.

Speaking of men who are godlike in their presence in both *Supervixens* and *Beyond the Valley of the Dolls*, seeing Charles Napier pop up in a film is a positive reaffirmation of pure spirituality. Napier had previously appeared in Meyer's *Cherry, Harry & Raquel!* (1970) and would have a long and successful career as one of THE character actors. He sadly passed away back in 2011 but will live forever in the hearts for those of us who like our artists with some testicular gravitas and strong-footed swagger.

Then there's the music, which ranges from the dramatic and occasionally comedic instrumental interludes to the rocking, hook-laden tunes of The Carrie Nations. The film's killer soundtrack was a result of legendary film and TV music composer Stu Phillips and actress/singer Lynn Carey, who provided the throaty-blues-rock vocals for The Carrie Nations. (Though Dolly does do a helluva job miming to Carey's unbelievable voice.) Given that Carey was a gorgeous blonde with a cornfed-dame-pinup figure, it's a bit strange that she isn't in the actual film.

The two brains behind this wonderment of cult cinema have both since crossed the rainbow bridge, with Meyer passing away in 2004 and Ebert in 2013 but what they created here still lives and breathes in a world that is always in dire need of color and fun that borders on phantasmagorical

STAY POSITIVE:
A FILM IN THE KEY OF THE COOL
STEPHEN SAYADIAN'S *CAFE FLESH*

HEATHER DRAIN

Good evening mutants and mutettes and welcome to Cafe Flesh.

Humanity pays for its sins every single day. It is the devastating effects of
terrorism or the daft judgments of the folks in charge who have the luxury of
never being the ones that have to get their hands *really* dirty. Atomic threats,
while technically still laying there in a sleeping snake formation, may feel a
bit retro for some, with the danger of the "Nuclear Kiss" feeling its most dark
and ominous from the late 40's till the post Reagan-era. In the early 1980's,
a generation that was raised with wildly misleading 1950's "Duck & Cover"
Atomic "education" films were entering a new "Cold War" between the US and
the Soviet Union. (Of course, none of it was actually new at all.) Out of this
political and pop culture melee of old fear and forward thinking vision emerged
Stephen Sayadian's, under the nom de porn Rinse Dream, wholly one-of-a-kind
sci-fi-surrealistic opus, *Cafe Flesh*.

The melancholy jazz-funk stylings of Mitchell Froom's "Thrill Factor" begins
the title card, coinciding with the introduction about a post-nuclear world where
99% of the populace is "sex negatives." People who can function to experience
everything "but pleasure." This leaves the one percent of "sex positives," who
are able to make physical love without getting severely physically ill, unlike
their less lucky counterparts. Their special status ensures that they get drafted
(which, remember, kids, is a sweeter way of saying forced) into performing live
sex shows for the reverent sex negatives. Once the film itself begins, you will

soon start to wonder who are the lucky ones and if a quotient like luck can live at all in such a world.

In *Cafe Flesh, we* the audience are the sex negatives. Voyeurs led to the damaged razzmatazz show by the club's emcee, one dark haired and darker-hearted Max Melodramatic (the absolutely incomparable Andrew Nichols, who really should have had a far bigger career than he ever received). If Joel Grey's Master of Ceremonies from Bob Fosse's *Cabaret* was merged into the most bitter Borscht Belt Vaudevillian reject/local television horror host, then you would be skating right near the county of the figure that is Max. Uttering the film's first line with reptilian ooze and genuine disdain, he greets us with "Good evening, mutants and mutettes and welcome to Cafe Flesh." The opening shot, with Max's white tux, black pompadour, lit cigarette and his weirdly handsome mug framed by pitch shadows is noir-perfect and framed in an extreme close-up style to make sure that you don't even stand a chance to feel warm, comfortable and most definitely aroused.

Leading up to the first act, Max continues to taunt the audience, who are all a wan crew of stylish but lost souls that could have emerged out of the very waters of *Carnival of Souls*, Herk Harvey style. "I love those little tears of hunger in your eyes," he gleams, before miming a junkie getting their IV hit as he describes their need as *his* fix. Finally getting to the actual show, Max tells us that this is a return to "the old days" with a "tableau of desire in decline." And before the industrial-wasteland/dance mix of Froom's "Fruito Prohibito" can kick in, our MC adds one last word with simply, "MAX KNOWS."

The show begins with a 1950's styled housewife knitting as her babies cry in the background. Both she and the furniture are lit and stylized like a Norman Rockwell painting by way of Edward Hopper. That is until the music comes in and her "babies" are revealed to be three grown men in the background, wearing bibs, wielding giant femur-type bones to the beat of the music and sporting fangs and faces that only Dr. Moreau could love. Each beast-man-baby is lit in a bright neon light, giving an amazing and gloriously queasy contrast the earthy-loveliness of their Mom. Who is quite lonely until the milkman shows up, which may sound like the oldest porn cliché in the world until you immediately realize that this man is part rat, complete with large tail, nose, and whiskers. If only one could travel back in the early days of this film's release on video and see the look on any unsuspecting soul hoping to have a swingtastic night with his or her hand and whatever lubed up luscious apparatus that was handy who rented *this*. Within the first ten minutes, it is a given that any plans for "amour," were not only killed but doused with gasoline and promptly firebombed. Keep in mind that while *Cafe Flesh* rightly gained heat as a cult film on the midnight movie circuit in the 1980's, it was and still is put in the "porn" category, right down to being distributed by adult film Titans VCA (who have released titles ranging from *Ass Vamps* to the nightmare inducing 1973 film, *Sex In The Comics*). Hopefully, by the time this tome is in your hot little hands, this wrong will be righted and it will be taken out of the back rooms and put next to its art-house brethren where it rightfully belongs.

Anyways.

The explicit coupling of suburban hausfrau and the world's most multitasking half-rat/half-human milkman finishes up, leading us to being introduced to Nick (Paul McGibboney) and Lana (famed "scream queen" Michelle Bauer, acting under the nom-de-erotica, Pia Snow), a couple sarcastically described by Max as "the Dagwood and Blondie of Cafe Flesh." Nick is straight out of the most anguished 40's noir film. A ruggedly handsome hero who has experienced too much and whose heart hasn't seen the sunshine in a long, long time. The closest thing he's got is Lana, a stunning brunette who views the Cafe as a creative respite from their reality, as opposed to Nick's masochistic fly-to-the-spider draw. They are the "beloved regulars" of Cafe Flesh, despite Max's especially hostile attitude towards "Dagwood."

It is here, that Sayadian and his co-writer, Jerry Stahl's (under the pseudonym of Herbert W. Day, a name cherry picked as a personal fuck you to an old high school teacher of Stahl's), dialogue starts to shine more and more, with Nick's comments about the interpersonal spelunking between Hausfrau and Ratman being the tip of the iceberg.

"Class act. Next time we come, remind me to set a trap."

Fresh meat enters the club in the form of leggy and straight-outta-Wyoming Angel (Marie Sharp), arm in arm with super-sex-positive agent Silky. Her wide-eyed naivete and Silky's sleazy-used-car-salesman-mustachioed charm are a great contrast with each other, especially when she spots Nick and Lana and asks her new friend if they are negatives or "can they do it?" With a rodent-like squint, he replies, "Negatives. All the best cake is."

Knowing how this machine runs, he warns her to "hold tight" as Max approaches the stage. Smart move since Max is shown sitting on an old fashioned rope swing and dressed like a ghoulish white-faced, rosy-cheeked version of Holly Hobbie while murmuring monk-like chants by way of Curly Howard. This is simply an act of surrealistic love on Sayadian's part. If ever there is a moment that you can almost hear the artist in question whisper, "You're welcome," it is this.

He looks up from his doll-from-Hell reverie, saying "Hi little peepers!" giving the audience the literal middle finger while doing so and then asks "How are things in the carnal charnel house?" A perma-stunned audience holds no reaction as Max zeroes in on Angel, noting "Look at the innocence on her.... there's something to make Uncle Foamy stand up and tap dance!"

Before he can make things even more borderline-Artaud like for the poor "halo" of a girl, he gets back on stage and switches into an Elvis impersonation to intro the next act. Black cutouts of oil rigs flank a rich blue sky, as industrial noises pipe in right before Froom's appropriately named "We Don't Dream" kicks in. A sexy business woman sits on a desk while a well-suited man with a giant pencil for a head comes out, staggering to the beat. In the background, a bespectacled secretary, clad only in pasties and the aforementioned glasses, mechanically types as she drones, "Do...you...want...me...to...type...out...a...memo?"

The businesswoman and Pencil man get down, eliciting reactions from the audience ranging from perplexed to angry to the most haunting of all, one beleaguered man whose face whispers internal fatigue as a tear slides down his cheek. Are we having fun yet?

Angel, who was undoubtedly sheltered in more ways than one, inquires if all of that was "real?" It is all too much for Nick, who leaves with Lana, as the doorman, appropriately named Mr. Joy (Paul Berthell), possessing all the charm of a mortician with the wrong kind of twinkle in his eye, says to Nick, "Leaving so soon friends? Feeling a little...*queasy?*"

Back at home, Nick confronts his emotions of emasculation with Lana, revealing the main reason of why he can't help returning to the Cafe with the line, "... torture is the one thing left I can feel." Trying to comfort him, they attempt to make love, only to end up violently ill and loudly retching. With sheer perfect timing, the film cuts to Max, bedecked in a Bolero jacket (that looks like it made love to a 1970's love seat) and propped up against a coffin. His voice dripping with Lugosi splendor, he implores "Good evening ladies & gents and velcome to Cafe Flesh!" Two topless women wearing daisy head pieces emerge from behind the coffin, flanking Count Maxula. "Pleasure is a widow maker, brothers," then his voice dips down to somber and adds "Just look at Maxy." Pulling out a trumpet, he starts miming to the music, as men wearing long black coats and white, blank-faced masks come inside, moving rhythmically to the music. Jazz from Hell? You'd better believe it.

An anemic man tries to get in the club, almost felled by Mr. Joy until he shows him a live bird, brought as a gift to the club's owner, Moms (Tantala Ray), who is known for her love of all things avian. This gets him in, with Nick and Lana right behind, with the diseased-mojo of a doorman leering at Nick, grinning. "Kind of a habit, eh?" That said, Nick gets in for free since he is Moms' favorite and is enlisted to bring her the living bird in person, which he does, much to her delight.

Now given that up to this point, you have already witnessed grown, mutant baby-men wearing bibs with the word "BRAT" on them wielding bones and Pencil-Man getting biblical with a pretty business lady, it may be hard to believe that things can get topped. But topped they do, both stylistically and even better, intellectually. (Just think of Murray Head in the musical *Chess* intoning, "I get my kicks above the waistline, Sunshine.")

With shades of Tod Browning's shot of John Gilbert's disembodied head in 1927's *The Show*, we see Max's head, sans body, in a cage, with a nude woman sitting astride the top of it, her taut back facing us. Painted up in ghoul-makeup, Max play acts trying to lick the top of the cage as air sirens play on in the background before acknowledging his audience.

"Uh oh! Civilization's foaming at the mouth again. Keep it in the cage, brother. He who makes a beast of himself gets rid of the pain of being a man."

His "Skull in the Cage" monologue is one of the most brilliant and brain piercingly great pieces of film dialogue to have emerged post 1970's. Utilizing a line originally scribed by British 1700's writer Samuel Johnson that was made massively popular by Hunter S. Thompson, it is fleshed out to deceptively irreverent lengths and made all the more powerful by Nichols. He delivers it with theatrically-trained and taut aplomb. The scene leads to two women making love to each other, as the air sirens continue, adding a strong discordant air to the glistening sapphic visuals. (Note that one of them is sporting an American flag bikini, an image that Sayadian had invoked during his days working at Hustler magazine in the 1970's)

Coitus interruptus is bound to happen, which it does with Max in the cage popping back up, halfway barking, "Hey hey! Show's over. Hold the applause, folks. This ain't Vegas." The camera pans up with the nude girl on top of the cage, finally peers her face over to reveal a monocle and a Hitler-type mustache.

Fascism wears many faces, with one of them being The Enforcer (Dennis Edwards, who was also featured in the music videos for both The Ramones "Psycho Therapy" and "Howling at the Moon") arrives to flush out the club of any sex positives who aren't doing their duty and "performing." He zones in on Angel, whom despite being protected by Nick and friends, gets dragged off, but not before revealing the real reason why she was hiding: her virginity.

After a heady conversation between Lana and Moms about Angel's fate, our heroine is left behind to lock up the joint. Finally having some alone time, Lana begins to caress herself on the floor, revealing the fact that like the recently absconded Angel, she too is a sex positive. Much like her sex negative friends, her face is less aroused and more sad-eyed acquiescing, though she is lost enough in her self-pleasure reverie to not notice the wing tip sporting, smirking but silent figure of Max in the doorway. (A taxidermied vulture is placed near his head, mirroring what post-nuke life can make an already bitter heart become.)

The next night, Max intros the main act and not so subtly tries to bait Lana, even at one point telling her to "be positive." Nick ruffles immediately, only making Max switch into a series of impersonations ranging from Brando to Russkie to finally the Big Bopper.

"Hello, Baybbbeeeeaah!"

A set in Art Deco black & white and German Expressionist shapes, Angel is there to make her live sex act debut, which includes her being slid up, down and around on top of a horizontal old-style phone booth, complete with a trapped, semi-nude woman underneath her. (A motif that pops up again and again in this film, as the club is decorated with an assortment of nude women in Plexiglas boxes, echoing the "desire in chains" ethos.) Disembodied arms jut through the side of the stage, snapping in time to Froom's "The Key of Cool." Sweet, naive Angel is a girl no more.

Heading to the bar, Nick gets to hear a wonderfully insane story from the world's coolest bartender, Bosco, about giving his old pet hamster a "Chicago overcoat," before getting cornered by Max. The reasons for our emcee's vitriol is revealed two-

fold, with the first reveal being that pre-Nuclear war, Max was a failed stand-up comic whose career impotence has quixotically targeted Nick as the aim of his deep-seeded rage. The bigger reveal, however, comes via the dominant insistence from Moms, who is more than pissed to see her favorite customer being badgered by the emcee and forces Max to recite "the poem."

I'm little Maxy, the star of the show.
But down in my boxers,
nothing will grow.
There are posies & neggies,
but I'm between.
Cause I lost my weapon in World War III.

On his knees and loudly sobbing, everyone laughs at Max's humiliation save for Nick. The end of the line grows more and more near as live sex performing legend Johnny Rico (Kevin James), who is described by Bosco as looking "like a young Mitchum," arrives. The buzz for Rico is rivaled only by the King himself on the Ed Sullivan show, with Lana barely able to contain her excitement, which is all too noticed by both Nick and Max.

Back in his white tux glory, Max intros the biggest star to have graced Cafe Flesh while simultaneously commenting on the absurdist nature of pornography, noting that, "Well, kind of exciting, huh? Hey, not too pathetic that the biggest night of your life is watching some strange palooka get his hog washed by some bimbo you don't even know." It's not pretty but the truth is rarely jewel-like, with Max capping it all with the descriptor, "The bitter terrific end."

The seeds are sown and as Rico, who looks like a 1950's heartthrob as drawn by Patrick Nagel, begins the show with one of the in-house lovelies, set in a bedroom suite placed in a neon-German-woodcut swamp. Lana's libido, having been suppressed in the name of love for too long, is unleashed with Max summoning her to the stage like a blood-starved vampire. Staggering up front in a hypnotized, juiced-up somnambulist-manner, Lana's real life status is revealed to a bleak-faced Nick and a guffawing Max, who has transformed into full hyena-mode. Nick is eventually dragged out of there by his friend Spike, while Lana is penetrated by Rico, looking smacked out and joyless. Cut to black and a reprise of Mitchell Froom's haunting "Thrill Factor."

Cafe Flesh is a science-fiction art film like no other. The mix of snappy, Raymond Chandler meets Dr. Gonzo dialogue, fever-dream sexual imagery rich with color, anti-eroticism, stand-out characters who have all seen the big ugly, an eerie yet jazzy score courtesy of Mitchell Froom and a tonality that will ink itself into your own personal film psyche like a tattoo that you can never laser off. It is a film that over the years has garnered either massive love or strong distaste, which is always the sign of something worth investigating. (After all, indifference is far more of an offensive reaction for an artist than abject hate. At least the latter is a vibrant emotion.)

Sayadian's art director background with both experimental theatre, as well as his layout work with Hustler, shines fiercely here. What worked fantastically in 1980's *Nightdreams* (a film he co-directed with his then often partner-in-crime, Francis Delia), works thrice-fold in *Cafe Flesh*. The visual set-pieces are pure post-Cold War American Expressionism and could and should be featured in any art-film book dealing with themes of surrealism and Dada. Lining up each scene with perfect skill, with some help from his own creative consultant, Mark S. Esposito (who did not co-direct the film, despite what some internet sources may claim, though he did create a meticulous storyboard for CAFE FLESH), there is nary a false move or filler here.

The players who help bring Sayadian and Stahl's bent-neon visions to life are all great. Paul McGibboney has the all-American good looks combo'ed with this old Hollywood anti-hero gravitas that makes Nick both compelling and an empathetic character. Michelle Bauer as Lana is equally good as a woman with great intentions but is as damned as the rest of the crew. The real star of the show, however, is, without a question, Andrew Nichols as Max. Charismatic, nasty and even, at times, sympathetic, it is a performance that obliterates barriers and dares you, the audience, to simultaneously love and hate him. Nichols, who had worked previously with Sayadian in a diametrically different role in *Nightdreams,* was a character actor who brought 110% powder keg talent and "it" factor to everything he did. His turn as Max is absolutely the crown jewel in his all too short filmography.

Cafe Flesh is a perfect example of when every single ingredient in a film can stand on its own two legs, then comes together to form one roundhouse kick of an experience. There is love, biting truth, black humor, the rarest of visions and a firm commitment to a polluted tonality that makes this film the masterwork it truly is. The end of the line, indeed.

THE WRONG KIND OF LOVING
MICHAEL FINDLAY'S *THE FLESH TRILOGY*

HEATHER DRAIN

If good film making has a pulse, then great film making has its own rhythm and when the great explodes into full tilt auteur theory, then the rhythm has a 12 piece horn section, three electric guitars and at least one unpronounceable musical instrument. This was never more true than when the underground, arthouse and overground all got in a fist fight in the 1960's and begat us the one and only Michael Findlay. Every true blue artist has a magnum opus to claim and with Findlay, it is *The Flesh Trilogy*. A trilogy that is one part black & white noir, a liberal dash of Hubert Selby Jr. and a tonal heart beat that could only be described as "batshit acid jazz." We're talking John Coltrane processed

through a stack of blood and semen stained pulp novels and a Masters degree in English literature level good.

Along with his wife, Roberta Findlay (who would later go on to make her own mark as a director in both the adult and horror genres), Michael forged a path that was wholly his own. Combining cinematography (often the naturally skilled handiwork of Roberta) worthy of a Blue Note album cover, dialogue that is insane and at times, strangely poetic and a worldview bleaker than a child's toy covered in filth in the gutter, Michael Findlay is an artist who should have been heralded much more than he is. But hey? That's why we are here.

Prior to the first installment of the *Flesh Trilogy*, Findlay had directed a small handful of features, including the now-lost *Body of a Female* (1964), as well as the incredible, *Take Me Naked* (1966). Whatever loose boundaries of his creative sanity were in play with his earlier efforts were set on fire and tossed to the winds with the *Flesh Trilogy*,

Without further ado, are you, dear reader, brave enough to enter an exquisitely crafted, sordid world of heartbreak exploding into super villain madness amidst doomed fleshy dames? If you think this intro is pure hullabaloo, then you ain't seen nothing yet.

Now, step right inside and ignore the sticky floors.

TOUCH OF HER FLESH

With the crude introductory credits projected on various parts of a nude woman's body, the film begins. A striking tall man with a voice of a debauched English professor and dark, wavy hair that's a little too messy tells his napping wife, Claudia (Angelique), that he has to leave for a work trip. This man, Richard Jennings (Michael Findlay himself, billed as Robert West), is about to have his life changed forever. While Richard heads to the train station, Claudia's clean cut looking lover, Steve (Ron Skideri), stops by the apartment for some daytime delights. When Steve asks her when her husband, who is working on a book about weapons, is getting back home, Claudia says not for another week and then adds that he has "nothing to fool around with" anyway. Not exactly the paragon of feminine sensitivity, that one.

Little does she know that Richard has to come back home, which he does, catching Claudia and Steve inflagrante delicto. Face riddled with betrayal, he dashes out of the apartment and into the streets. An emotional wreck, Jennings ends up getting hit full on by a car, causing temporary paralysis from the waist down and enough ocular damage to lose his right eye. (Male emasculation metaphors and commentary abound throughout this series.) Jennings, now living in a micro-apartment littered with a whole lot of nothing, a shitty bed, and the best product placement Old Crow ever had, states "I have no home." (Giving us some echoes of Bela Lugosi's speech in Ed Wood's equally insane 1955 film BRIDE OF THE MONSTER.) He does have a small flower vase and a pet cat, which indicates some shreds of love still left in the broken man. However, brokenness will soon flourish into a brand of homicidal intention that is unhinged and brilliantly pre-meditated.

The dulcet tones of Jennings opine, "Claudia, you have done this to me, but you are not alone. Strip any girl naked and you will find a filthy slut like you. Bare breasts and bare stomach waiting for a man's caress...once a man is locked into the hot vice of love that is their thighs, he can never escape." (A weapons expert with sexual hangups and female issues turns out to be a pretty volatile combo!) Every woman that has Claudia-type actions is now the real deal in Jennings' eyes, with his fervent mission to be pure eradication.

"There is only one escape. To destroy her and all that act like her...I will slash open the very core of your perversion."

His one-man mission of murder begins when he kills a gorgeous, sweet faced stripper by sending her a rose with a poisoned thorn, which slowly works until she literally dies on stage. (Note that during her dance sequence, we get to hear what is the unofficial theme song for the entire FLESH cycle, a really terrific rock/R&B number called "The Right Kind of Loving." The irony of using such a happy, hip shaker tune about the joys of love with this sex and murder show is prime beauty.) Meanwhile, we meet Janet (Suzanne Marre), a moneyed looking lovely whose industrial looking studio space, neatly tucked away in the woods, is harboring Claudia. The former Mrs. Jennings plays piano and tells her friend that she fears that Richard knows where they are and that he will come for her.

Cut to Richard wheeling himself in a glorious looking fleapit that is advertising the big sleazy "Burlesk!" There's some fabulously greasy-bom-bomb-bom music while a buxotic bumps and grinds on stage, only to have her light snuffed out by a poisoned blow dart (!) administered by the man himself. He then spots Janet outside, chatting up a pretty brunette sex worker. (Or in the words of Jennings, "...there's that pig that poses nude for Claudia and one of her hooker friends..." Lord of the Sensitive he is not!) Janet leaves, giving the man the perfect chance to approach the working girl for a good time.

A good time ends up involving some mild groping, overdubbed moaning and Richard threatening the girl for information regarding Janet's whereabouts. Afraid, she reveals that it's a woodworking studio in Oyster Bay. He still kills her and the film races towards its inevitable confrontation between Richard, Janet, and Claudia. (Or as Findlay deliciously drawls out in his inimitable New England meets New York educated voice, "Clawwwdeeyaw.") Also, I would be remiss if I did not mention that the climax has Janet running around topless with a bow and arrow.

If *Touch* is a slice of demented, lurid fun, *Curse of Her Flesh* (1968) is a powder keg of a film that truly must be seen to believed. The second installment opens with one of the most striking strippers in film history. Sporting a dark bouffant, sparkly underwear and radiating the kind of insanity that spells sexy for some, but the kind of sexy where someone is going to wake up and be missing their dick. Literally. The jazz from Hell music, that has a loud "YEAH" punctuating the beat, is equally amazing. Cut to one spectacularly nasty looking men's room. While a man hears nature calling and relieves himself, the title credits are revealed via graffiti. This is a brilliant touch, by the way, seeing it all scrawled on a wall that has witnessed many a body fluid atrocity. The intermittent shots of the young man, looking dubiously at the credits and curious obscene drawings and phrases (including "Up Your Bucket!"), are framed at a tilted Expressionist angle and all in beautifully shot black and white. It is Caligari Noir at its best.

We soon see our man Richard, who survived apparently the final act in *Touch* and is in front of a stage mirror, applying spirit gum and fake facial hair. A female VO kicks in, updating and informing that "police are looking for him all over New York!" Our heartbroken misogynist has become a master of disguise and is seen mopping up a grindhouse floor. A familiar looking man asks for the men's room, giving a chance for Jennings to tell him about the "real show" that goes on in the latrine. Even telling him about the time, "...there were four men in one stall during a show...with their pants down!" The man walks away and it becomes apparent that he is Steve, the lover of Claudia. Jennings pulls a sword out of his cane, stating "I could stick you like a pig while you sit in there, you cancerous worm! That would be too easy."

RUGGED and ROUGH!

FAST PACED THRILLS!

THE TOUCH of HER FLESH

ADULTS ONLY

Steve is safe, at least for now, though soon he is alone, looking messed up and getting soused on Four Roses bourbon while noting that "There's nothing new in the news anymore...just different people." That is some good wisdom. This is intercut with two pretty (and pretty half-naked) girls, wearing matching skimpy bottoms with cash money covering their pubic area. They dance to the "Right Kind of Loving" in a dark room lit up only by flashing lights. In one of the more surreal scenes, one of the dancers clutches a pillow ominously over the other, who is lying supine and silently screaming. It is not in slow motion but the pacing of it is near syrupy.

We then get some kicking spy-jazz music and see Richard, now clean faced and looking near dapper, picking up a dancer at the bar. The girl, Adele (Jane Bond), is the same girl we saw screaming just a few beats ago. This indicates that the

The power-packed sequel to the daring, lusty 'TOUCH OF HER FLESH'

THE *CURSE* OF HER FLESH

dreamlike murder was either a vision of Steve's or even a fantasy of Richard's. (It feels like just his speed.) They go back to her place, neck a little bit and engage in some flirty banter that takes the innuendo to a Bazooka Joe wrapper level. Commenting on her pet cat, Richard notes, "That's a nice little pussy you have there." Adele responds with, "Thanks. Everyone who sees my pussy likes it." You get the picture.

Things quickly grow sinister and Jennings ends up murdering her by poisoning her cat's claws and ensuring that she gets scratched. Death by kitty maybe one of the more dignified ways of leaving this plane in the *Flesh Trilogy* universe. A stage show entitled "Red Hot Scandals of 1968" is displayed, featuring a tough then tender S&M tinged sequence starring a fierce brunette, Stella (Linda Boyce) and her comely blonde victim/lover (Uta Erickson, who will come more into play in the next film). Jennings approaches Stella post-show. Presenting himself as "Joe Davison," the owner of the theater, the two make out on a couch and he then enlists her to seduce a particular woman. Leering, he asks her if she knows what a dildo is. Not missing a beat, she beams and retorts, "Oh yes! A girl's best friend."

Arriving at her targets door, under the auspices of needing to use the phone after locking herself out of her apartment, the Woman is agreeable and goes to take a bath. Stella uses this chance to make them both a drink and gets in the tub, where she gets to experience the woman's "educated toes." (Take a pause and soak in that last phrase. Very good.) Post-bath, while we never see the dildo in question, the implication is strong, with Stella playing the aggressor, purring "You can take it." Take it she does, with a scream ringing fatal. Confusion becomes disgust with her pulling out and an extreme close up of the blade that popped out of the phallus, dripping with viscous blood.

Freaked and disgusted, she tries to hassle "Joe" for payoff money. He'll take care of it but after the show. Stella performs, only to meet her inevitable end after getting poisoned by the ropes she and her partner are entwined in. It is explained by an officer to the husband of one of the newly dead, that the poison on the ropes mixed with the "secretions" of the dancers. Then the lawman actually quips to the widower that "You might say that they died from something they ate." What the hell?

The bereaved, Terrence (played by legendary adult filmmaker and frequent partner-in-crime with both Findlays, John Amero), recognizes one of the girls as one of Claudia's lovers and suggests that the killer is Jennings. The latter, later on, approaches the officer like he's motherfucking Godzilla and before he kills him, tells him, "You don't know how filthy those girls are!" The film returns to our crazy eyed stripper from the beginning of the film, whose act has escalated to humping a pillow. True story, but a late friend of mine once told me that he literally ejaculated blood while watching this scene. If you needed further proof of a darker force at hand behind this big titted revenant than that, I cannot help you.

Richard goes on to murder Terrence, making Steve the sole heir for an inheritance. What follows is one of the most nutzoid double crosses. Steve courts and eventually marries Paula (Eve Bork), but only due to the assumption that she is a virgin when they marry. After they consummate their marriage, a mysterious package arrives, featuring an 8mm film that not only shows Paula in a stag reel entitled "Squash Crazy" featuring implied use most lurid of a butternut squash and then her at a doctor's office that looks like a back alley version of *Dead Ringers*, where she receives a re-virginization surgery.

Steve doesn't handle this reveal too well, calling her "a filthy pig" and confesses that he knows that Jennings is behind all of this, but then adds "Some women deserve to die!" and murders her with a HARPOON GUN. Who is the real villain at this point? As if he just heard me say that out loud, Jennings pops out behind a screen in the motel room, lets out a war cry and the chase is on! It is a crisscross of limbs kicking and punching, all in a moving truck bed and can be pristinely defined as awesome.

Curse was a tough act to follow but given the serial style cards at the end of the film asking the audience "Will this end the bloody career of Richard Jennings?," he was bound to return for one and final installment, resulting in 1968's *Kiss Of Her Flesh*. By far the bleakest of the three, the film opens with a pretty girl walking by herself near a snow covered beach. A man in a black ski mask runs up and strikes her with a tire iron. He ends up taking her to a dirty mattress in a shadowy room and mauls her while we hear Richard's voice intone in a VO, "All you pigs are the same! Just like my wife Claudia." Offbeat jazz plays while the visuals cut to an incredibly stark and arty shot of an underpass at night, with the credits are then revealed via scraps of paper placed on a nude female body.

Cut back to Richard, who is still wearing the mask but partially removes it so he can munch on some lobster while this poor girl is tied up in front of him. Being a utilitarian kind of man, he ends up torturing her a bit with one of the lobster claws (!) and then ends up electrocuting her using a few wires, tongs and a cheap generator.

We are soon introduced to the closest thing the entire series has to a hero, in the form of the ever-so-lovely and plucky Maria (Uta Erickson returning.) She greets her amour Don (Earl Hindman) for a touching love scene involving brief full frontal nudity from both parties (the first in the *Flesh Trilogy* and still not quite a common sight for late 60's cinema) and implied anal bead usage. (For those of you wondering, yes Virginia, Santa's not real and anal beads existed in the 1960's.) Post-coitus, she talks about the most recent victim, who was best friends with her sister and that she basically knows that it was Jennings. "Who else would electrocute a girl?" Maria soon hatches a plan to trap Jennings.

Maria leaves to go visit her sister and former lover Mona (Janet Banzet), giving us such inappropriate sweet words like, "I forgot what it was like to lie in my sister's arms." After the two get way too friendly, she leaves while Mona's doctor comes for a visit. While Maria's sister receives a bedside visit, Mona's

194

other lover, Doris (Suzzan Landau), sneaks and watches the doctor-patient exchange through a secret peephole. Her "Doctor," who ends up being, of course, Jennings, provides some sensual massage and then gives her a douche to help "clean her out" first thing in the morning. Doris ends up meeting him in another part of the house and they make out in front of a fireplace to some swinging music. He then pushes her head down and intones "Keep on sucking!" in a pretty racy though clearly staged scene. They finish with her smiling, licking her freshly used lips and asking "How'd you like that?" Richard responds

with a hearty laugh and informs Doris as she begins to writhe in pain, "My poisoned semen should take care of you well enough! So long, sucker!" I don't even know if poisoning one's seed is even humanly possible but there are James Bond villains (on angel dust) that may want to jot down some notes.

The next morning, Mona goes to shower and douches, only to yell in pain and collapse in the tub, with blood pooling next to her. As Richard goes on the hunt for yet another victim, stating "I'll kill every last woman on Earth if I have to!" Maria becomes absolute hell bent on revenge. Another girl dies by fire, but in the meantime, Maria enlists Don as backup and visits her sister's "Doctor." The two end up finally capturing the elusive madman and mildly torture him before Jennings manages to free himself. The resulting climax on the beach finds our ultimate anti-hero meeting a grisly and justly ironic end. The last title card informs us that it is "Positively the end of Richard Jennings."

The *Flesh Trilogy* is a beast that is nearly as potent now as it was when it first screened in the less respectable grindhouses back in the day. One can only imagine the dropped jaw of any poor man that paid for a ticket with money and the hope of spanking at least one out underneath a heavy coat or hat as they were greeted with so much art and nihilism, but with just enough skin show to keep the producers happy. It's a nasty yet glorious body of work that predated the slasher film concept of not only killers reacting out of psycho-sexual hang-ups and fears but also being indestructible to a nearly supernatural extent. (In the 80's, they, of course, went full on into the supernatural realm, but that was still a little over a decade away from Michael Findlay's vision.) The worldview we are given is one where the villain is clear but everyone else is, save for Maria in the final act, is a variation of either a hustler (Stella in *Curse*, whose moral guilt can be wiped away with some hush money) or those only marginally less damaged than Richard himself (the harpoon gun wielding Steve.) The fact that Maria is our only true hero and is sexually liberated to the extent of being transgressive with her incestuous relationship with her sister actually puts *Kiss* above a lot of future slasher films. The latter, while not always, usually tended to favor "good girl" virginal types who have bought their safety by not threatening any societal expectations of what a woman should be. Maria is the kind of woman Richard fears the most, so it is absolute in its essentialness that she be rooted to his ultimate downfall and end.

At the end of the day, Michael Findlay was and forever is, a true artist, whose creative thumbprint vibrated so clearly on much of his work. It's not for everyone but anything worth your time should never be so homogenized that it pleases the whole room. This is not some quaint butter cookie served at a church social and I am beyond grateful for that.

WHERE NOBODY'S DREAMS COME TRUE (WELL, MINE DO!)
GOING DOWN, DOWN TO THE *FORBIDDEN ZONE*

JOHN SKIPP

Lemme tell you about a little place I know. It's called the Sixth Dimension. You enter it through a cartoon intestinal tract, looping through the guts till you land with a splut on some brown throw pillows, beneath a crudely-painted set of enormous splayed buttocks. And from there, you follow the checkerboard pattern of pre-rolled dice to the heart of a zone so forbidden you wouldn't even *believe* what they call it down there.

And how do I know these terrible truths? Only because I've gone there at least twice a year for most of the last three decades. Often alone, but as often as possible with someone who's never before made the journey, if not a whole crowd. Initiating people has been one of my life's great joys.

To that end: there's a secret society of Sixth Dimension enthusiasts, to which I now invite you. WANNA BE A MEMBER? I'm thinking you do. But might just like a little history.

As legend has it, it all started like this...

197

Once upon a time, there were a couple of weird fucking brothers named Richard and Danny Elfman. Along with their deranged childhood pal Matthew Bright, they formed a musical theatre troupe called The Mystic Knights of the Oingo Boingo, where they performed crazy-ass shows all over Southern California throughout the 1970s. Inspired equally by burlesque and avant-garde theater, Betty Boop cartoons and The Three Stooges, they specialized in mutating early jazz and traditional klezmer with the goofiness of Spike Jones and the dangerously anarchic precision mayhem of Frank Zappa and his Mothers of Invention.

Richard the Elder founded the Mystic Knights, but brought in little brother Danny as musical director. And with Danny's front man prowess growing — performing stunning versions of Cab Calloway numbers dressed as Satan, just for starters — and Richard's visionary ambitions overflowing, they reached a turning point from which there was no coming back.

Danny was tired of lugging a tractor trailer's worth of sets and props and equipment to every gig. And Richard wanted to make movies. Thus was born *Forbidden Zone* (1980): a last hurrah for the Mystic Knights, and an attempt to distill everything amazing about their live happenings into one brain-boggling cinematic assault of gloriously tacky hand-painted sets, against which an absurdist confabulation of freakish characters sing and dance and dry-hump each other in between bouts of hilarious dialogue and set pieces that defy description.

Forbidden Zone is the touching saga of the Hercules family, freshly moved into the tiny home formerly owned by drug dealer/pimp/slum lord Huckleberry T. Jones (Ugh-Fudge Bwana, also known as producer Gene Cunningham). While stashing some heroin in the basement, Jones discovered the door to the Zone, saw just enough to say, "Feets, do yo

stuff!", retrieved his junk, and unloaded the unsavory estate on Pa Hercules (also played by Bwana) and his clan.

But when precocious and totally hot daughter Susan B. "Frenchy" Hercules (Marie-Pascal Elfman) is warned never to enter the Forbidden Zone in their basement, her overwhelming curiosity gets the best of her. Next thing you know, she's provocatively dancing front-and-center in the madness, where she catches the attention of the swaggering, diminutive King Fausto, Ruler of the Sixth Dimension (Herve Villechaize, fresh off of shouting "De plane! De plane!" on TV's *Fantasy Island*).

Smitten by a lust so pure it can only be love ("You're French!" he declares. "And therefore of the Master Race!"), he has Frenchy sent to Cell 63, where he imprisons all his favorite concubines. This enrages his wife, the hypersexual psychotic Queen Doris (Susan Tyrrell, in her favorite from a lifetime of outrageous performances), whose frenzy of revenge propels the rest of the madcap antics.

Frenchy's elderly Boy Scout brother Flash Hercules (Phil Gordon) comes to the rescue, with his deranged ex-wrestling grampa, Gramps Hercules (Hyman Diamond, Richard's attorney, and clearly far younger than Gordon). For reinforcements, they call in poor Squeezit Henderson (Matthew Bright), a.k.a.

"Chicken Boy": the only remotely intelligent person in this film, unfortunately suffering from crippling self-esteem stemming from his abusive, alcoholic whore of a mom (also played wickedly by Tyrrell).

Ultimately, all of them are almost completely useless, none more so than Pa Hercules when he finally shows up. In the end, it takes Ma Hercules (Virginia Rose) to put a stop to this nonsense with one single well-placed bullet to the boob. Leading us to our preposterous grand finale, as the entire cast comes out for what's essentially a final curtain call for The Mystic Knights of the Oingo Boingo. All singing. All dancing. All exploding as one.

This brisk plot encapsulation does almost nothing to capture *how fucking insane* every speck of this motion picture is. It's inarguably one of those films for which no description is remotely sufficient: a nonstop flurry of manic bizarro invention, where frog-headed men and human chandeliers bear witness to shit far stranger than themselves. Cult icon cameos include Joe Spinell as Squeezit's monstrous sailor dad, Warhol superstar Viva as the Ex-Queen, and the Kipper Kids as the Kipper Kids, all every bit as nutsoid as you'd hope.

To me, one of the biggest innovations *Forbidden Zone* brings to the game is the collision of the entertainment the Elfman boys grew up on and the emerging punk culture that swept the 70s clean of peace-and-love hope or sentimentality. The most controversial aspects—using blackface as part of racial caricature, for example—is straight out of the Fleischer Bros. and Warner Bros. cartoons of the 30s and 40s, and a staple of vaudeville. It's the same stuff Robert Crumb riffed off of in 60s underground comix like *Zap*, in which artists of the time grappled their asses off with the vividly-stunted images they'd been raised with.

One can certainly argue that the big-lipped Negros in everything described here are racist as fuck. But I would argue, conversely, that everyone from the Fleischers and Robert Clampett to Crumb to the Elfmans fucking LOVE their black characters. Certainly do not see them as any less than the ridiculous white or non-human characters also being relentlessly made fun of. (Special note must be made of the Black Demon who helps escort Squeezit to Hell. *He's a black man wearing blackface makeup.* Which, to me, pretty much says it all.)

Forbidden Zone is not remotely a political film. It's a sheer mindfuck party, with no agenda beyond outrageously delighting. Its unbridled wantonness is its super-strength. And for me, few films have gone there so successfully and freely.

Matthew Bright joined Richard, co-producer/editor Nick L. Martinson, and associate producer/editor Nicholas James in sculpting the script, as well as portraying Squeezit Henderson and his transsexual sister, Rene. Richard, of course, produced and directed. Danny provided his first musical score (intercutting with vintage Josephine Baker, Felix Figueroa and his Orchestra's

1947 classic "Pico and Sepulveda", and Tyrrell's musical showcase, "Witch's Egg"), as well as delivering Calloway's "Minnie the Moocher" in deliciously-modified Satan-based terms.

Monte Hellman/DePalma veteran Gregory Sandor came on as Director of Photography, bringing crisp filmic energy to the set-bound proceedings. John Muto brought the juicy animation that bridges the gaps between cartoon-like reality and full-on cartoon, with plenty of swell optical effects and Terry Gilliam-style cut-up stills to meld the animation and live action.

But I can't say enough about Marie-Pascal Elfman's production design, which brings the Sixth Dimension cartoonily to life in ways no realistic sets possibly could. Certain bits (like the "room full of doors" sequence from Dave Fleischer's 1931 classic "Bimbo's Initiation") are lovingly lifted almost straight from the animated cells. The fact that she was married to Richard at the time is one of the movie's luckiest strokes; between her astonishing tableaus, her uncredited producing, and her star turn as Frenchy, she puts her unmistakable stamp upon this film as much as anyone else.

Forbidden Zone took three years to make, from its humble 16mm beginnings to its final 35mm black-and-white glory. When it premiered at last, the critical reception was not warm. (Again, the racial element, and charges of insensitivity to women, gays, Jews, little people, large people, frog-headed people, and everybody else who shows up onscreen.) Not to mention the fact that, as Zappa would say, it was weird down to its toenails.

From there, Danny and guitarist/arranger Steve Bartok stripped the band down and called it Oingo Boingo, then unleashed their alarmingly-complex ska-based new wave progressive punk upon the masses, with remarkable success. As

fate would have it, their biggest hit to date ("Dead Man's Party") came out in 1985, the same year that *Pee-Wee's Big Adventure* took Danny (and Bartok, still arranging) to the Hollywood big leagues of motion picture scoring. The band lasted almost 10 more years before Danny hung it up, devoting the rest of his life to being one of the most influential film composers of the late 20th century and beyond.

Richard has had a much harder time cracking the showbiz hierarchy, making only two more features under his own name: 1994's *Shrunken Heads*, from a script by Bright, for Full Moon Entertainment; and 1998's *Modern Vampires*, also written by Bright, with a cast including Casper Van Dien, Natasha Gregson Wagner, Rod Steiger, Kim Cattrall, Craig Ferguson, and Udo Kier.

The former is a completely off-kilter riff on the kids-fighting-monsters craze (*The Monster Squad*, *The Goonies*) on a super-low budget. I'm not a huge fan of that sub-genre, which makes it hard for me to love this film, but have to deeply admire the way it ruthlessly kills its heroes. And making Meg Foster a mobster dyke in man-drag is totally inspired.

Modern Vampires, on the other hand, is flat-out amazing, and demands to be written about at length (I PROMISE! I WILL!), then seen repeatedly. There's something about watching ancient vampires at cocktail parties, trading real estate tips, that cracks me up big-time. The mechanics of routine urban body disposal, and the complications that ensue when your pregnancy goes into its 10,000th trimester, are all hilariously addressed here. The performances are priceless, across the board. And for *Forbidden Zone* completists, there's a feeding sequence in the vampire bar that's utterly worth the price of admission. I absolutely love this criminally underseen film.

Bright went on to write and/or direct several stunning features of his own, including *Guncrazy* (1992), *Freeway* (1996), *Freeway II: Confessions of a Trick Baby* (1999), *Ted Bundy* (2002), and *Tiptoes* (2003). Every single one of them unutterably crawling with weird brilliance.

As for *Forbidden Zone*? Time has been extraordinarily kind to it, the cult growing and growing with each passing year. And I'm proud to have done my part, personally screening it in my living room for easily 500+ people. Often throwing parties around the event. Because that's how much I care.

Up until this week, however, I have stuck strictly to the original black and white, being a purist at heart. But I must admit that the colorized version Richard unleashed in 2008 is a surpassing beauty. Turns out that he'd *always* wanted it colorized, along very specific specs that took twenty-eight years to happen. And damned if it wasn't worth the wait.

Speaking of waiting: as of this writing, *Forbidden Zone 2* is in the works, with an Indiegogo crowdfunding campaign bringing it well within reach. Or so we all hope. Richard himself is clearly on fire with love and determination. And every little peek looks more promising.

In the end, however, I've got to say that even if he never shoots another fucking frame, Richard the Elder has already earned a righteous place at the tippy-top of bizarro film history. Without he and his faithful compatriots, there would be no Sixth Dimension. And you can enter any time.

WANNA BE A MEMBER? I think you do!

And wholeheartedly welcome you in.

AGONY IN ANGORA
ED WOOD PULLS THE HEARTSTRINGS
ON *GLEN OR GLENDA*

JOHN SKIPP

"The world is a comedy to those that think;
a tragedy to those that feel."
– Horace Walpole

As I begin this piece, it is July 14th, 2016, and my friend Nathan Carson is live DJ-ing a rooftop party in Portland, OR. But the headlining act for the night's scheduled fun is a screening of Ed Wood's legendary cinematic bad-sterpiece, *Plan 9 From Outer Space*. Made in 1959 for probably half as much money as Eddie's annual drinking budget, its raw combination of jaw-droppingly guffaw-able cheapness and earnest, lofty sincerity has made him both the pride and the laughing stock of the cult movie kingdom, for nearly sixty years.

Edward D. Wood, Jr. — as his every work proudly proclaimed in the opening credits — was a writer/director/producer/auteur in the truest sense. With the soul of an artist, the gung-ho spirit of a post-WWII American go-getter (indeed, he was a multi-decorated war hero), and the mind of a bright, horny, pulp-loving, 12-year-old transsexual boy who never grew up, but just kept getting older, he most emphatically carved a unique and distinctive swath through the no-budget landscape of 1950s outsider film history. This left him with only *twenty more years* of wounding anonymity and crushing defeat before he finally died, broke and homeless, in 1978.

For those of you who know him only for his ambitiously bottom-of-the-barrel science fiction (*Plan 9*), horror (*Bride Of The Monster*, *Night of the Ghouls*),

and crime thrillers (*Jail Bait*, *The Violent Years*, *The Sinister Urge*), it's easy to laugh at the increasingly-careless production values, loopily-remedial dime-store narratives, stunted performances, and stunningly delirious stream-of-consciousness soliloquies that are, in fact, the heart and soul of his charm to this day.

Indeed, I walked into this book wanting dearly to write about 1965'S *Orgy of the Dead*: one of my all-time favorite bizarro movies, because it gets *every single thing so wrong* that it begs your mind to laugh out loud, if only in self-defense. (And for those who argue that Ed Wood is the world's worst director, please allow me to assure you that Stephen C. Apostolof directs Wood's insane script nearly *twice* as badly as Wood would have, had he been sober enough to do so.)

But then I remembered his debut feature, 1953's groundbreaking *Glen Or Glenda*. A film I hadn't seen in nearly thirty years, when his post-death 1980s cult eruption made checking out the entirety of his oeuvre imperative. I remembered laughing my ass off at the time at the storytelling techniques, and shaking my head incredulously, but also being deeply moved by the story he was telling.

So I watched it again, three nights ago.

And damned if Ed Wood didn't break my heart in two.

Glen Or Glenda was originally conceived by intrepid sleaze producer George Weiss as an exploitative faux-documentary cash-in on the then-sensational story of Christine Jorgensen: the first American to surgically undergo a full-on sex change operation in Europe. (Such things were not yet allowed, or even considered, in the States.)

But when Christine declined to be involved, Ed salvaged the production by pouring his own autobiographical soul into every single word and frame. This story was *his* story, and he knew how to tell it, down to actually performing both titular roles with an honesty and courage that far outshines his modest acting ability.

Wood writes, directs, and (under the stage name "Daniel Davis") stars as Glen, a handsome heterosexual man so deeply in love with women (and their sweet angora sweaters) that he's only really happy when dressing as, and thereby becoming, a woman himself.

Here in the 21st century, trans-formative stories like this are roughly a dime a dozen. But this was the fucking 1950s, where sex-transitioning WAS far-future science fiction, and cross-dressing was burlesque comedy at best, hooking in the shadows and/or getting beaten to death in the parking lot at worst. (In other words, tragically not all that far from here.)

As such, Glen is deeply tormented by both personal shame and the terror that he'll be discovered and disgraced. This comes to a head when he falls in love with toothsome, blonde, angora-sporting Dorothy Fuller (who would later, in real life, write a dozen hit songs for Elvis Presley and others). He wants to marry her. But can she possibly accept his shameful secret? CAN THEIR LOVE SURVIVE?

By itself, this is all juicily melodramatic as shit. But playing it straight wasn't on Eddie's agenda.

So he built the movie as an ambitious layer cake, opening with a darkly phantasmagoric set (aka somebody's living room) replete with a spooky skeleton and skulls aplenty. But centered in frame, as the camera slowly pulled back—elegant and commanding, in a plush and comfy checker-print chair straight from the J.C. Penney catalog—was none other than *Bela Lugosi himself*: the legendary star of *Dracula*, *White Zombie*, and innumerable horror classics from the 30s and early 40s.

The once-celebrated actor had been thoroughly kicked to the curb by Hollywood in the ensuing ten years, his star tarnished by both changing times and a sciatica-driven opiate addiction that landed him on the no-hire list. But he was Eddie's hero (the first film Wood remembered seeing as a child was *Dracula*); and the opportunity to enlist Bela in his dawning crusade was so exciting that he managed to raise the extra $1,000 it would take to get a one-day shoot out of him. STAR POWER, BABY! Tarnished or not.

From said comfy chair, the mysteriously supernatural cosmic puppeteer Lord
Lugosi (hilariously credited as "Scientist", with a homemade laboratory full
of mad scientist beakers, attempting to replicate Dr, Frankenstein's lair)
delivered the God's-eye view of the human race, with all its flaws and foibles,
his incantations scripted by Wood so lovingly that many of us can recite that
dialogue verbatim, even today.

Cut into this, as it recurs throughout the film, is an abundance of stock footage:
L.A. freeway traffic and busy downtown pedestrian thoroughfares (meant to
give the Big Picture of a lost and meandering humanity); a buffalo stampede (to
signify the turmoil in his soul); impoverished industrial landscapes (exposing
the grim pointlessness of our labor); and, most of all, *lightning*, used almost
as liberally as his exclamation points, as segues to punctuate every moment of
shock and horrific implication.

The next layer of his cake was the one that George Weiss originally employed

him to do: the faux-documentary, with official-sounding "White Male Authority Figure" narration. It begins with cops and detectives descending on a suicide scene: a dead transvestite, prone on her death bed. This discovery so disturbs the chief detective that he seeks consultation with a psychiatrist who attempts to explain—with breathtaking open-mindedness and generosity of spirit—how such a thing might come to be.

This is where the story of Glen and Glenda emerges, as an anecdotal case study. And we proceed to see it enacted before us, with the psychiatrist's voice-over walking us through that central melodrama as straightforwardly as any conventional audience member might possibly hope.

And then, at the 35-minute mark. shit gets hallucinatory as fuck for a full ten minutes that symbolically lays out—in genuine surrealist form—*a kaleidoscopic expiation of Glen's soul*, including:

- Barbara (Ms. Fuller) responding in horror to Glenda's entreaties for love and understanding;
- Barbara trapped under a tree (in their living room), which Glenda is unable to lift, but *Glen can,* as she responds with grateful and unreserved love for him;
- Glen and Barbara marrying in a church, which would be great if the priest didn't invite The Devil up to condone it, Satan nodding and smiling and staring holes of baleful triumph through Glen as the happy couple is bound in unholy matrimony;
- Lugosi going off on a crazy riff, warning Glen to beware the big green dragon that eats little boys, puppy dog tails, and big fat snails;

- fever dream close-ups of Glen, as he's confronted with his inner fantasies, involving...
- kinky s&m shit with a woman getting whipped,
- a sultry minx, luring him toward her open doorway,
- a woman so overwhelmed by her own hotness that she tears her dress off, unleashing herself as he recoils in terror and she luxuriates in her freed undie-clad body, urging him to join her, and offering him her heart, then sadly taking it back as he rejects it,
- a Marilyn Monroe-esque beauty undulating on a couch until she's tied up and gagged by a spiteful other woman, and
- yet another beauty at the makeup mirror, perfecting herself, then restlessly undulating (on the very same couch) just in time to get banged by The Devil (and it turns out, SHE LOVES IT!).

This all culminates with tortured Glen in his living room again, while a little girl's disembodied voice says, "I'm a girl, and you're not!" Suddenly, he's surrounded by the ghosts of all those who would judge him. The Devil leads the charge as they descend upon him, a mob behind which he vanishes.

Only to reappear, as they recede, as Glenda Triumphant. *She is who she is.* Afraid no longer. And when Barbara walks in, with open arms, that triumph seems complete...

...until she turns into The Devil, then a beckoning Barbara who just laughs at him, as the clutching hands of this cruel world super-imposingly paw at and mock him.

Leaving Glenda to face herself in the mirror. Tear off the wig. And confront Glen's made-up face, eye-to-eye.

211

Ladies and gentlemen (and all those flowing fluidly between), let me tell you flat out: if I wasn't in love with this movie already, I sure as shit fell in love with it there. It is SUCH a deep and personal unspooling of all his doubts, dreads, demons, and ghosts—such an applaudable unburdening through creative expression– that while I can't quite call it a masterpiece (because that would suggest *mastery*, a quality Eddie lacked in spades), I can without a doubt call it his finest achievement.

And, yes, an authentic work of art.

However much I am culpable in joining the ranks inclined to make raucous fun of poor Ed Wood, *Glen Or Glenda* is the exception to the rule. His gleaming spirit shines here at its brightest and most unmitigated, flaws and all. And, for me, all his cut-rate techniques wildly succeed at their aims. The one place where he actually did it right.

It makes me ache at all his lesser achievements, hilarious as we might find them. For the rest of his life, he tried and failed to make the kinds of popular, exciting movies he loved, in the hope others would love them, too. Roughly eight trillion bottles of Imperial whiskey and bad business/life decisions later, that hope finally died in a flurry of delusional late-night ranting phone calls, wife-beating, and screaming at the tenement walls that imprisoned him, flailing at the injustice of this world. One of the unhappiest endings I could possibly imagine.

Whatever else you can say about Tim Burton—a truly gifted bizarro artist who achieved all the success Wood craved, even as Hollywood proceeded to swallow him whole—the fact that Burton used his showbiz clout to pay high-end homage to this lowliest of noble failures gives him all the infinite street cred he needs to make up for all those big-budget atrocities every bit as ridiculous as *Plan 9 From Outer Space*. (I'm looking at *you, Planet of the Apes!*)

The extraordinary script for Burton's 1994 Academy Award-winning love letter *Ed Wood* (by Scott Alexander and Larry Karaszewski, inspired by the painstaking, heartbreaking Wood bio *Nightmare of Ecstacy*, by Rudolph Gray) wisely and beautifully focuses on and celebrates Eddie in his ascendance, such as it was. A little boy who shot backyard movies with his friends from the age of 11. A young man who thought fighting and killing in WWII had prepared him for the horrors of Hollywood. A soul so utterly in love with movies that he devoted his entire life to them, win or lose, with an inspiring optimism and sincerity I frankly wish I saw more often.

Glen Or Glenda is, at its core, an urgent and unadulterated appeal for understanding. And while the bulk of the world laughed dismissively in 1953, and every year since, I have no doubt that it has inspired (and quite possibly saved) innumerable lives. An outreach of solidarity for people struggling with their sexual identities, easily a decade before any such movements existed. A wish-fulfilling message of hope whose messenger died nearly 30 years before gay marriage became U.S. law, and questions of sexual identity took the forefront of modern discourse. Planting seeds that would pay off beyond his wildest dreams.

If there's a Heaven, and Ed Wood ain't in it, I have no interest in going there either. As one art-intoxicated acolyte to another, drunk with dreams we'd rather die than leave unexpressed, Eddie's the little brother I'd hope to hug beyond those pearly gates. Making fun of him is just my way of telling him, "Dude, THINK YOUR SHIT THROUGH BETTER! I love you, and I want you to win. Better luck next life, okay?"

"If I were you, I'd always aim as high as *Glen Or Glenda*. That's the one, lover." (He loved to call people "lover".)

That said: all the people enjoying the shit out of *Plan 9* on that Portland rooftop tonight would have been utterly robbed, had he listened to my advice.

So thank you, Eddie. You did not get the life you wanted.

But you'd be stunned by how hard you still reverberate today.

AND ON THE SEVENTH DAY, GOD FUCKED THE WHOLE THING UP
DUKE MITCHELL'S MYTHIC *GONE WITH THE POPE*, REVEALED AT LAST!

JOHN SKIPP

It's funny, the way legends spread. You hear a whisper of something that sounds too good to be true. You laugh and go, "Really?" And wait for proof. But while you're waiting, you can't help but pass the story along. Hoping to God that it's real.

Then some evidence rolls in, and you're hooked. Like Bigfoot footage, or Christ on a tamale, your heart leaps even as your eyes helplessly roll. Faith and common sense battle for primacy. Wanting to believe, but not wanting to be a chump.

This is how I've felt, for years, about the rumors regarding Duke Mitchell's *Gone With the Pope*: a movie whose tangled history and central premise are so insane—so rife with fun, pathos, and crazed profundity—that I didn't dare give in to the longing of my heart.

It just sounded like one of those dream-movie ideas so ridiculously cool that it had to be thrown out there as absurdist "high concept" hilarity at a party, laughed about by hammered people until the tears squirted, and then spread as a prank. A dis-informational meme, designed to fuck with the unwitting. A motion picture Shangri-La that could not possibly be.

THANK GOD I WAS WRONG!

THE BIZARRO ENCYCLOPEDIA OF FILM

As you may have gathered, the hook here is that Duke (playing "Paul") and a couple of old prison buddies named Peter, Luke, and John set out to kidnap the Pope, then charge a buck ransom to every Catholic on Earth. And as hooks go, it's so completely insane that I'm automatically in.

But here's the secret scoop: *Gone With the Pope* is an incredibly ambitious no-budget Italian-American 1976 crime film/spirit journey/wickedly funny and sporadically brutal no-bullshit meditation on friendship, love, faith, corruption, and doom, replete with some shockingly matter-of-fact racism (more on this in a minute), and a deeply heartfelt but entirely conflicted foxhole Catholicism that made my short hairs both dance and stand on end.

It was made by the afore-mentioned Duke Mitchell, in the last years of his extraordinarily colorful life as lounge-singing "King of Palm Springs", close friend of Sinatra (though not so much Mia Farrow) and numerous other showbiz luminaries, and notorious career-detonating self-saboteur turned true renegade indie filmmaker.

For those who only know him from his ill-fated one-off with Jerry Lewis copycat Sammy Petrillo in the 1952 throwaway *Bela Lugosi Meets A Brooklyn Gorilla*, you're in for several layers of revelation. The suavely watered-down Dean Martin-esque Duke on display there is barely a whisper of what we get here.

Duke's a *genuine character*, a for-real indelible charismatic, as you'll witness every second he's onscreen. It's like he's barely acting, cuz just being himself is more than enough. Whether impishly grinning in antic prankery, expressing soul-deep compassion, or killing in cold blood, there's a rich and resonant warts-and-all humanity to his performance that anticipates *The Sopranos* as it riffs off The *Godfather*. And would have felt at home in either.

This extends to the filmmaking itself. And as a director, Duke is strikingly astute, his sensibilities infused into every shot, edit, and music cue. He and cinematographer Peter Santoro pull off a stunning range of styles for such a no-budget film, from tense cross-cut murder sequences to haunting, atmospheric God moments to loopy comedy bits (particularly one juvenile dick-move involving a very large woman that Benny Hill would have surely envied). And

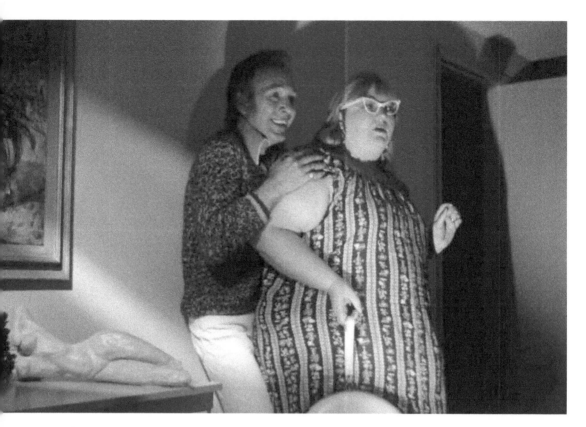

there's a Rube Goldberg bit of pure visual storytelling—a little lost object, pinballing toward destiny—that knocks me out every time.

He also made cunning use of his friends and connections, both as "talent" (most of the cast are non-actors, giving *Pope* a weirdly naturalistic, almost Cassavetes groove) and resources (a staggering range of locations, from L.A. to Palm Springs to Vegas to Rome, contributing to the movie's epic feel). From the Vatican reflected on Duke's sunglasses to a tall, gawky woman shredding on electric guitar in a weirdly-garish club scene that makes my jaw drop to the floor, *there's a lot going on* in this picture. It's incredibly alive.

For all the sprawl, though, there's a singular pulse and vision here: the sense that no one else in the world could ever have made this film, this way. Or put this much love into it.

Which brings us to Duke's flagrant, unabashed racism, here revealed in a scene with a lovely black prostitute who fascinatingly goes uncredited. (Maybe

because she was a real prostitute, not wanting the unwanted publicity? Wouldn't surprise me a bit.)

It's a moment that threatens to stop the film dead—a what-the-fuck, out-of-nowhere note of total wrongness—that is miraculously redeemed (at least to my mind) by the fact that they seem to *genuinely like each other.* Which is Duke's way of saying "Yeah, I'm an asshole. That's how I was raised. But I actually know better." (A notion reinforced by his mind-blowing speech to the Pope, at the film's centerpiece.)

This speaks to what a complicated, authentically deep and human film this is. It's the story of a violent man with a crazily warm heart, coming face to face with his contradictions as his time runs out. And in its Face Of God moment, it eerily echoes Timothy Carey's equally outsider film *The World's Greatest Sinner,* but with a lot more polish.

Duke's Paul *is* the world's greatest sinner. (He abducts the Pope, fer Christ's sake!) But he's still just a soul on a journey. And if this work of art doesn't

qualify as confession, I don't know what the hell to tell you.

Flat out: this is one of those movies that no committee in the world would ever approve. It's too personal, too idiosyncratic, too-everything-I-love-about-movies. You can almost hear Duke saying "Go fuck yourself!" every time the plot twists in ways that sway from conformity. Fists raised. Soul grinning. Fighting every step of the way.

Gone With the Pope is a sheer labor of love. And I can't thank Bob Murawski, Sage Stallone, and Jeffrey Mitchell (Duke's son) enough for rescuing it from oblivion. (Bob spent 15 years painstakingly restoring it, cutting it from Duke's notes, promoting it, and finally presenting it to you in the glorious in-depth BluRay release, from his Grindhouse label, which is its first and only home.)

Some legends are worth every minute of waiting.

That's why they're fucking legends.

NO FREE DRINKS IN HELL
DISCO, DEATH, A REALLY BIG DICK,
AND THE DAWN OF *THE GREASY STRANGLER*

JOHN SKIPP

It's hard to know where to start with *The Greasy Strangler*, Jim Hosking's 2016 unrelentingly ooze-droozling and utterly fucked-up feature film debut. So let me just tell you the first thing that fell out of my mouth—muttering, dumbstruck—as the closing credits unspooled at the Horrible Imaginings Film Festival in San Diego (where Cody Goodfellow and I had spent the entire running time laughing so hard that we looked like a couple of bearded anacondas, jaws unhinged, eyes periodically rolling back in our heads in self-defense):

"It's like Tim and Eric remade *Napoleon Dynamite* as a horror film, in Jersey or something, with John Waters as Executive Producer of bad taste and total wrongness." To which I added, "JESUS CHRIST, that was funny!"

I could pretty much leave the analysis right there. But having just watched it for the second time—in my room, horribly alone, and helplessly cackling nonstop —I'm forced to admit that there is more to say about this terrible, terrible, absolutely wonderful film.

As directed by Hosking, from a script co-written by Toby Hovard (who one can only assume is *also* completely insane), *The Greasy Strangler* takes place in a universe so thoroughly stunted and degraded that it makes *Forbidden Zone*'s Sixth Dimension look like a nice place to raise your kids up. (I don't know why I guessed Jersey, since it's actually just some of the shabbiest parts of southern California.)

Sky Elobar plays Big Braydon—a gawky, baldingly long-haired and bifocaled lump of simple, innocent self-loathing—who lives to serve his sinewy, grease-loving father, Big Ronnie (Michael St. Michaels). Big Ronnie has nothing but contempt for his half-wit son; he's not a deep thinker, either, but at least he has a little hair on his chest. And that ain't but the half of it.

Together, they conduct "Disco Tours" of their godforsaken neighborhood, dressed in matching pink short-shorts and turtleneck sweaters. "Well, who likes The Bees Gees?" Big Ronnie asks their first tour group, standing in front of an ugly little gray one-story concrete building with bars on the windows and trash cans out front. "Well, here is where they came up with that fabulous, funky song, 'Night Fever'". And when the Indian Tourist (the unspeakably lafftastic Sam Dissanayake) asks for confirmation on this, an irritated Big Ronnie spins a ridiculous story about them writing the lyrics in the doorway while waiting for a friend to pick them up for Chinese food on his birthday, and concludes by saying, "Trust me. I know disco."

Shit goes downhill from there, ends in authentically bare-assed confrontation. But it is on this tour that Big Braydon meets Janet (Elizabeth De Razzo), a teensy round bundle of pure sassy flirtation. They connect at once, at the most

remedial possible level; and when he tells his dad excitedly that he's going on a date tonight, Big Ronnie is infuriated, immediately berating his son on every possible self-esteem-bashing level. Big Ronnie is, it seems, a very angry and spiteful old man.

So it should be no surprise that the three remaining tourists are hideously murdered that night by—you guessed it—THE GREASY STRANGLER! And please allow me to assure you: in the long history of human strangulation, there has never been a strangler even REMOTELY this greasy. He's a lumbering, pus-colored, humanoid monster, made entirely out of coagulated grease. But with a terrifyingly familiar face.

And for anyone on the slow end, the secret identity of The Greasy Strangler is revealed when he walks into Big Paul's Car Wash, slips some coins in the slot for "Full Body Wash", and gets himself cleaned up by standing between the giant whirling brushes as he screams...

...and is revealed as Big Ronnie, being dried by the industrial fans, with his ENORMOUS COCK waggling. And just to be clear: even limp, it perambulates halfway to his knees. Where it will hilariously, visibly remain, throughout much of the rest of this film. (You will never see this much full-frontal outsized cock outside of porn, I can fucking guarantee you. And never to so much comedic effect.)

What follows is the world's stupidest murder mystery, as Big Braydon and Janet gradually come to suspect Big Ronnie's secret identity. There's more greasy strangulation. Some crotchless disco dancing. Some severe double-crossing emotional betrayal.

Bottom line, *it's like film noir on elephant tranquilizer*: every plot twist so logic-smearingly absurd, every verbal square-off conducted on such a arrestedly-developed 10-year-old level that it drags you screaming back into your hindbrain, where every intelligent thought and sensitive feeling you ever thought or felt were reduced to single-celled drooling...

...before catapulting you back with whiplash strength into SubGenius-like brutally cheerful self-mockery. Wherein you remember that yes, we're stupid. People are stupid.

LIFE IS SOOOOO STUPID.

That's where the helpless laughter comes in, and steers this film to much-deserved infamy. In a world with any justice whatsoever, *The Greasy Strangler* would be playing the counterculture midnight circuit, doing for the 21st century what *Pink Flamingos* did for the 1970s in terms of building a mass cult audience. But trust me, it's not too late. If Tommy Wiseau's staggeringly malformed 2003 bizarro classic *The Room* can sell out midnight shows, how far behind can *The Greasy Strangler* be?

Speaking of injustice, I boycotted the Oscars when they snubbed Michael St. Michaels for Best Actor, because this is certainly the finest performance ever committed to film by anyone, ever, for any reason. Whether pouring on the charm as a wanger-dangling disco "smoothie", blowtorching his son's ego with a ruthless snarl, or literally strangling the greasy shit out of a hapless hot dog vendor (yes, this happens), St. Michaels doesn't just chew every speck of the scenery. He greases it first, so that it shimmers in the light of his raw, undeniable power. Which is to say, he is genuinely fantastic. (And if you don't believe that, *you're a bullshit artist!*)

On the flip side of the acting scale, Sky Elobar's self-proclaimed "cheesy old cornball" Big Braydon sucks the life from every moment, through sheer force of lameness. This is not a criticism. It's what the role requires.

Very few fine professional actors can successfully flense themselves of every proven performance technique they ever learned and deliver *first-rate terrible acting.* This is usually the province of amateurs, who do it naturally, because they have no skill.

But much in the same way that people say, "You can't deliberately create a 'bad cult film'; it's either genuinely shitty and awesome, or it's faking it", *The Greasy Strangler* belies that logic. And that's never clearer than in Elobar's

performance, which is so deliberately, spectacularly stunted that it transcends itself into bad-movie greatness. It's so far beyond camp that camp becomes quainter than the 50s potboiler plots it mocks. As such, it's pretty fucking brilliant work.

The rest of the cast is completely adorable in its wrongness, as well, trumping most of early Waters and Troma in that there's secret skill behind their performances. Which is, in fact, a secret fact behind why this movie works so well.

While most of the nascent iconic Waters and Lloyd Kaufman was populated entirely by non-acting friends, and whatever fabulous weirdos they could pull in off the streets, Hosking and his producers (including Ant Timpson, Elijah Wood, and exec Ben Wheatley) cast actual *trained* actor/weirdos, who brought actual skills like, for instance, comic timing. No well-vetted names attached—totally pulling from the vast pool of the unknown—but far wider than the neighborhood reach.

The same goes for the production at large, which delivers all the anarchic thrills without feeling like the director was just guessing on set. For a movie so unutterably foolish, there's an incredible discipline to it. It's not a series of lucky accidents that happened, stitching together an eternally half-baked, ever-shifting plot with however many seconds they had left before getting kicked out of their location.

Jim Hosking is an authentic weirdo, so there's no faking it at all; and this is an authentically insane gutter film that was miraculously allowed to bake in that gutter until it could be cooked to perfection. A rare and wondrous thing, indeed.

So to wrap up: I fucking love *The Greasy Strangler*. Could talk about it all day, to anyone who brings it up. Find myself bringing it up frequently. Laugh out loud, every time I even think about it.

If that ain't love, I don't know what is.

HOOTIE-TOOTIE, DISCO CUTIE!!!

MELANCHOLY MAN
ON THE URGE TO NOT KILL IN *HE NEVER DIED*

JOHN SKIPP

If you ask most people what they fear more than anything, odds are pretty good that the answer is "Death". We may point at innumerable possible triggers for it: cancer, terrorists, drinking and driving, casual or intimate sex gone wrong, guns, thugs, police, addiction, heart attacks, random violence, military siege, global warming, psychopaths. You name it, we fear it.

Very few of us will include "living forever" at the top of our terror chart. In fact, that's *the hope* most people carry. That somehow our eternal spirit will eternally survive, whether through a) heavenly beneficence, b) reincarnation, c) some high-tech download of our essential nanobits into forever-replicable digital sentience, or d) an infinite series of transplants and age/disease eliminators that keep us happily immersed in our never-to-be-carcasses *ad infinitum*.

But what if you don't *want* to live forever? If living forever is the worst possible curse that could be visited upon you? Suddenly, infinity doesn't look so great. This is why some people fear Hell even more than death.

And for those of us who suspect that life on Earth is already Hell? Horror is the notion that we'll be stuck here forever. With the same ugly shit, sucked down over and over.

As the title implies, Jason Krawczyk's 2015 debut feature *He Never Died* deals with precisely this existential conundrum. The result is a blackly comic, demonic punk rock horror noir fable that mirrors and echoes the dark side of Alex Cox's 1984 punkstravaganza *Repo Man* in ways I've been awaiting for roughly 30 years. Telling a very old story. In a very new way.

We open with Jack (Henry Rollins), asleep in his shithole Toronto efficiency apartment, while the wails of the damned and doomed ring all around him. It's interrupted by a persistent knocking on his door, which he ultimately has to answer. And as he reluctantly rises, we can't help but note the twin scars on his shirtless shoulder blades. Did he get stabbed twice in the back, symmetrically? Or did somebody clip his wings?

Whatever the case, Jack couldn't be less interested in the parade of knockers who interrupt his slumber. His landlady? He hands her a couple $100 bills from a trunk with a seemingly endless stash, then shuts the door. A strange young woman he's never seen before, who gapes at him before retreating? He shuts the door. A couple of thugs who try to muscle him? He shuts the door.

When said thugs kick the door in, he sighs resignedly, lets them punch him in the face just long enough to decide he's tired of it before nut-crunching and otherwise fucking them up, despite a gunshot through the hand that should have hurt, and mace in the eyes that just makes him beat them harder. At which point, it becomes pretty clear that nothing anyone does or says is gonna make much of an impact on this guy.

But Jack's don't-give-a-shit-about-anything attitude gets put to the test when Gillian, an ex-girlfriend from some twenty years back, informs him that the strange girl who knocked and ran is the daughter he never knew he had. His deadpan response is, "Why are you calling me? I remember hating you. Abortions cost about $300. You could afford it."

"Fuck you, Jack," she fires back. "Just don't let her drive home drunk as shit. She's got a habit of doing that. She's had her license suspended..."

And next thing you know, Jack finds himself the central character in a low-rent 21st century punk noir, with himself as the reluctant Sam Spade. Hitting a dive bar called Crackles where his daughter was getting loaded, but split with a shiftless postman named Tim; tracking Tim to his own shithole apartment; and getting formally introduced to Andrea (Jordan Todosey), a drunk, lost, willful Wild Child who just wants to get to know him. And maybe, like, crash at his place for a couple of days.

It should be noted, at this point, that Jack doesn't *want* anyone to know him. His whole life is dialed around disengaged anonymity and mundane distraction. He eats oatmeal and drinks warm tea at the same diner every morning, where waitress Cara (Kate Greenhouse) clearly dotes on him, but knows better than to pry too hard. Then he goes to daily Bingo sessions at a church filled with barely-sentient elderlies. Then he picks up a mysterious package from a young hospital intern named Jeremy (*Twilight* werewolf heartthrob BooBoo Phillips). Goes home. And sleeps as long as he can.

What we don't know, till later—and THIS IS YOUR SPOILER ALERT—is that Jeremy's bringing Jack big packets of blood. Which are his methadone. For which he pays dearly. Because drinking that blood is the only thing keeping him from *ravenously killing, then consuming human flesh.*

Jack doesn't know why. He just knows that he has to. It's the only thing that makes him feel remotely level and sane. Which he is desperately trying to be. Avoiding all temptation.

And it's all good until the thugs who tried to muscle him earlier kidnap Jeremy, and take Jack's paid-for blood-stash with them. And it only gets worse when Andrea gets kidnapped as well.

At which point, all Jack wants to do is kill kill kill. Looking for any excuse to do it.

THE BIZARRO ENCYCLOPEDIA OF FILM

This is where *He Never Dies* launches into its gorgeous defining centerpiece: a haunting montage draped with the choral mellotron psychedelia of hippie heroes The Moody Blues, and Mike Pinder's "Melancholy Man" (from their 1970 album *A Question of Balance*), wherein Jack goes off the slaughter wagon and *dares* someone to do wrong. Faux-carelessly dropping a wad of money in front of a group of street punks, only to have one of them tap him on the shoulder and say, "Hey, man. You dropped something." Then hand the money back, like any decent human should.

Next batch of pedestrian punks he meets, he does the passing shoulder-slam to the biggest guy, daring him to fight. But when the big guy says, "Whoa, man. Sorry about that," and grins, then moves on, Jack has nothing to feed on. Nobody worth killing. WHY DO THESE PEOPLE HAVE TO BE SO NICE?

Jack's kill-addiction leads him to a chain link fence on the outskirts of town, where he just happens to puke on the boots of a trio of assholes who aspired to jack him up. Because, lo and behold, there's always *someone* who richly deserves killing.

Now Jack has fallen fully off the wagon. But also fully remembers that not everybody deserves to live in a Hell like his.

Case in point is waitress Cara, who evidently also had a thing with Postman Tim. Jack steps in on a fight between them outside the diner, takes a couple more punches—severely hurting Tim's fist with his face—before Tim takes off with "their" car. And in the resultant walk to their respective shithole apartments, Cara manages to pry more information out of Jack than he's told anyone in years. (His litany of previous jobs includes bodyguard, antique dealer, history teacher, potter, blacksmith, construction worker, business manager, fisherman, bootlegger, wreck diver, stunt man, nurse, and professional gambler, not to mention long stints in both the military and prison. In other words, far more than any ordinary lifespan would allow.)

The genuine potential for intimacy is here. And when she hugs him, he surprises himself by hugging her back. But when she pulls back for the kiss that would rightly follow, *he just can't do it*: leaving her hanging as he walks away just as fast as he fucking can. Back to his apartment, where he licks the last of his blood stash off the floor.

And goes looking—albeit most likely too late—for his daughter.

At which point, we meet Alex (Steven Ogg), a smug and oily club owner in a bath robe with deep ties to organized crime he clearly inherited from his late father, very recently deceased. Jack suspects him of involvement with Andrea's abduction and death-threat. Alex denies any knowledge, but Jack extra-naturally hears a woman crying from behind the book-shelved walls. Says, "You'll never see me again." And departs.

But the game is on. And when bingo no longer works, Jack goes back to the cafe, where a bunch of sinister goons lie in wait. Terrified Cara's still in charge of waiting tables, but the rest of the staff are either cowering at the back table or already dead on the floor.

In the resulting bloodbath—one icepick in the kidneys and bullet hole in the forehead later—Jack saves the innocent, and offers one very freaked-out Cara $1,000,000 to give him a ride home, with the last surviving thug (David Richmond-Peck) in her trunk. At which point, she realizes she's in way over her head.

It is at precisely this point that I'm gonna stop spelling out the plot. Not just because I still want you to be continually surprised as you watch (and you wouldn't BELIEVE how much cool shit I've deliberately avoided mentioning already), but because those of you who've already seen it already know.

So let's cut to the chase.

WHO IS JACK? He is Cain. As in Cain and Abel. The son of the biblical Adam and Eve. And the man who *invented* murder, when he killed his brother, at the dawn of mythic human time. Forever cursed for this misdeed (when, as he says, "We were barely even men yet!") by being forced to walk the earth through all the thousands and thousand of years that ensued. Civilization by civilization. Nightmare by nightmare. Human crime by human crime. With this terrible hunger for flesh inescapably at his core.

Thereby making him the first and *only* vampire. And as such, the basis of all our legends, no matter how wrong we've gotten them. When he invokes Wallachia, it's a nod to Vlad the Impaler. And when Cara asks, "How come you don't you have the...teeth?", his response is, "Why would I need them?"

Which brings us, at last, to the Goateed Man: a cryptic and ominous figure who periodically shows up throughout, and who *only Jack can see* until it turns out that Andrea can see him, too. And, as it turns out, the only character more unreadable than Jack himself.

Is he God? No. *Is he the Devil?* Maybe, but that doesn't quite explain it. *Is he Death?* That's the most popular speculation, but I don't quite buy that, either. He's *some other kind of demon*: one creepy enough to hurt *Jack's* hand when punched in the face, much as Tim's was when punching Jack.

I was prepared to think this was some inscrutable matter I'd have to dig through Biblical texts for, until I learned that *He Never Died* is (as of this writing) in full pre-production as a mini-series. So I guess I'll wait for the facts to unfold before venturing further guesses. Must admit that I never for a second suspected that this full-blown indie wonder was a pilot for a series. But can totally see it in retrospect. And, without a doubt, would watch it like crazy.

Which is where, at last, I give fucking enormous props to first-time leading man Henry Rollins, who carries the full weight of human guilt, rage, and shame upon his shoulders in this spectacularly nuanced performance-for-the-ages. And who would totally *own* this show, should it come to fruition.

As a life-long punk rock star, incendiary spoken word performer, relentless advocate of outsider music, social critic, and volcanic force of nature, the last thing *anyone* would expect from him is the near-miraculous level of restraint he exhibits here as Jack. But in dialing back every last speck of affect, he becomes the straight man for an insane world spiraling all around him. The Melancholy Man, doing what he can.

And the secret ingredient behind the beauty and craft at the heart of writer/director Krawczyk's film is that Rollins is *really funny*, without even trying. The more he reins it in, the funnier it gets. And his supporting cast is more than up to the task, hilariously reacting like regular screwed-up humans on the fringe, who are used to weird stuff, but in no way ready for *this* fucking guy.

And I gotta say: even if the series turns into regular showbiz pablum, we will always have this wonderful film. Which I recommend with all my heart.

As a spirit inclined to suspect that we *all* live forever—with infinite chances to someday get it right, amidst a trillion opportunities to forever get it wrong—I adore this soulful deadpan peek into the poignant soul of the damned we are.

And the better angels of our nature, whose wings we've yet to find.

But know, every time we truly see.

BUSBY BERKELEY BARNUM'S MAD WORLD
RAY DENNIS STECKLER'S *THE INCREDIBLY STRANGE CREATURES WHO STOPPED LIVING AND BECAME MIXED UP ZOMBIES*

HEATHER DRAIN

Carnivals are one of the most thrilling and occasionally terrifying creations on God's green planet. Candy colored rides, the scent of sweat mixed in with funnel cakes and corn dogs and all manners of what I like to call "the human sketch" are just some of the flavors of the carnival experience. It's the whimsy of childhood and the seediness of adulthood all wrapped up in one lurid cotton candy swirl. Carny cinema is a small but mighty sub-genre and glowing with number one atomic power is Ray Dennis Steckler's delirious full tilt boogie of a film, *The Incredibly Strange Creatures Who Stopped Living and Became Mixed Up Zombies*. That's right. I didn't stutter. This film is called *The Incredibly Strange Creatures Who Stopped Living and Became Mixed Up Zombies*. Let me take you aside right now and assure you that the film does the impossible and actually lives up to that lengthy and insanity love letter of a title.

Incredibly Strange is a horn o'plenty, brimming and winning with evil carnies, sexy ladies, musical numbers, murder, more musical numbers and a slothful young hoodlum with a roving eye as our hero, played by the one and only Cash Flagg aka our auteur at the weird helm himself, Ray Dennis Steckler.

The smoky ambiance of the rube jungle is established by the first frame, when carnival fortune teller, Madame Estrella (a former stand-in for Susan Hayward, Brett O'Hara) is rebuked by a drunk hobo (Titus Moede) who tells her to go

239

paw at one of the local sideshow freaks. Angering a volatile carny with powers of hypnosis and a mumbling henchman named Ortega (Don Russell) who aids in turning people into man-made freaks is high on the bad ideas list, so off goes Captain Sauce. Also, I like to think if someone made a film about Ortega, it would be called *Dances With Fleas*.

Meanwhile, at the carnival, we see the leggy Marge (Carolyn Brandt) and her dance partner Bill Ward (William Turner) do a little dance number for a cocktail swilling audience. It's a Percy Faiths-ville scene, making this particular Midway truly one of the strangest, if not goddamned swankiest, in the history of carny employment. After the show, Marge knocks back a drink in her dressing room, looking darkly contemplative until a black cat enters the room. There are cat lovers, the indifferent, the superstitious and then there is a fourth category: the Marge category. The Marge category basically involves losing your shit and freaking out like the feline in question has evolved opposable thumbs and is wielding a chainsaw with "This means you!" written on the rotating blade.

Her stage manager walks in and tries to comfort her, kind of, with Marge revealing the reason behind her deep fright of cats, telling him that every time a cat comes upon her path, something really bad soon happens. We are then introduced to one of the greatest flawed heroes in cult film history, Jerry, played by the inimitable Mr. Flagg himself. Jerry's

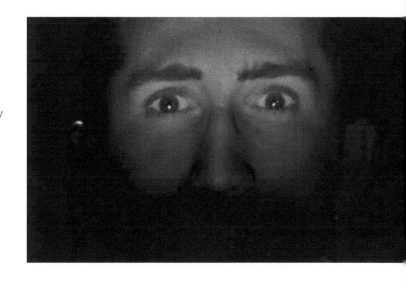

a man's man. Well, if the man in question lives in a cramped apartment that borders on Bukowski-levels of depressing and treats the word "job" like it's a four-letter obscenity, then yes. He hangs out with his sweetheart of a best-friend, Harold (Atlas King), who may not have the best handle on the English language,

but makes up for it with warmth, likability and a fantastic pompadour.

They drive off to pick up Jerry's clean-cut cutie of a girlfriend, Angela (Sharon Walsh), who is having to defend dating him to her very WASP-ish but well-meaning mother. Angela explains that Jerry's exciting and that with him, she get's to do things she never even imagined, which has to be one of the most blood-chilling things a parent has to hear from their teenage daughter, along with "I'm on heroin," "I'm pregnant" and "Daddy's taking me to a Purity Ball." Her knight-in-dirty-sneakers arrives and off they go to the carnival!

After a fun afternoon of roller coasters and merriment, night falls. Marge visits Estrella, who predicts an early demise for the troubled young dancer. Running out of the booth, Marge almost bumps into Jerry, Harold, and Angela. The young trio, apparently nonplussed by the distressed goddess running out of there like a bat out of the inferno, decide that a fortune teller visit would be quite groovy. Estrella seems annoyed but makes a prediction that a person near and dear to Angela will die in a place close to a body of water. Hey, give it to Estrella, she is clearly not of the Madame Cleo school of "...you will meet a handsome and mysterious stranger abroad..." soothsaying.

The dark mystical cloud laid upon them does not ruin Jerry's good mood, especially when a girlie show starring Estrella's fetching sister, Carmelita (Erina Enyo), catches his eye. Angela, for some strange reason, does not want to spend part of her date night watching her boyfriend eye a carnival stripper and gives him an ultimatum. Classing it up, Jerry chooses to go to the show over his now very angry girlfriend. Enjoying Carmelita's performance, he receives a note during her act that summons him backstage after the show. Will Jerry do the honorable thing and immediately leave to make amends with Angela or meet the sexy half naked dancer with the queer stare? If you guessed the latter, then you are more correct than a Miles Davis album.

This move ends up being Jerry's undoing, leading him to get unwittingly hypnotized under the control of Estrella, who urges him to successfully murder poor Marge and her dancing partner. The next morning, he wakes up having no memory of anything past the show. Visiting Angela, he ends up trying to strangle her after she accidentally triggers his hypnosis when she starts flippantly twirling her umbrella. Coming to, Jerry runs off, scared and confused. From there on, we have multiple musical numbers featuring festooned scat singers, sensitive folk musicians, jazzy and snazzy dancers and more sequins and feathers than an international drag convention, as well as startling and brain-searingly crazy nightmare sequences and a tragic ocean-side end for our mal-intented but likable hero.

Incredibly Strange Creatures is an entertainment buffet for the hardy, intrepid, bright-loving soul. It's fitting that this film is a horror-musical with a carnie theme because the whole experience is akin to dropping acid with your goony friends with a rap sheet and entering a carnival style amusement park that was created by Robert Goulet, Anthony Newley and an evil clown named Scritches. Steckler's background in both cinematography, including lensing Timothy Carey's directorial debut, *The World's Greatest Sinner*, as well as creating a lot of the early Scopitones (a precursor to what we now call music videos), is used to an absolute high-caliber degree.

The use of color throughout, especially during the large scale dance and nightmare sequences pulsates with tones and vibrance, even when watching the less than ideal prints of the film that are currently available. (Please, for the love of all that is sacred and great, someone do a proper restoration and release of this mighty beast.) Steckler was truly a man that lived and breathed film making, even reportedly living in his car at one point, just to save up money to make his next film. That is hale and hearty, not to mention committed by metaphorical blood, dedication. His passion for the form and commitment to making truly wild-card cinema is absolutely moving. This man was no hack or phony. Ray Dennis Steckler was the real deal who had the type of brazenness that only pioneers, madmen, and lovers display.

The cast is ten tons of fun, with Steckler aka Cash Flagg displaying a beautiful sort of charismatic loutishness as Jerry. Right up there is Brett O'Hara as the barking mad Estrella. She chews up the scenery and yet, leaves you wanting more bread sticks and by bread sticks, we're talking her hypnotizing and calling men "feeelthy peegs!" Carolyn Brandt, who was married to Ray Dennis at the time, is really effective in her small but important role as the haunted Marge. Then there is Atlas King, with his affable manner, Greek accent and pompadour of swag, who makes such a marked impression. Sadly, he only had one other screen appearance, though it was in Steckler's black and white crime-thriller from around the same era, *The Thrill Killers*. At least he got to be in two equally great and completely separate beasts of film.

Over the years, *Incredibly Strange Creatures* has taken a lot of flack, including being riffed on an episode of "Mystery Science Theater 3000" back in the late 90's and was later listed as one of the "worst films of all time." I've been trying to think of a classy, even eloquent way to say "this is bullshit." Fuck it, let's lay the cards out and just call a duck a duck and bullshit *bullshit*. Like other maligned films, *Incredibly Strange* is not "the worst film" on any properly researched list. Labeling films that are created, written and directed outside of the strict parameters of what is considered classically "good" is a cheap and inherently lazy move. To quote The Tubes, "don't you got no vision?" I hate to think of what these mentally boring and heart starved critics would have written about people like Frank Zappa, Willem DeKooning, and

Antonin Artaud. You know what a truly horrible film is? One that is boring and plays it so safe that you can barely remember scraps about it as soon as you're exiting the theater. The worst film in the world is one that is created with dry emotions, barren loins, rusty souls and a greed muscular with cynicism. Steckler was a director that knew exactly what he was doing, executed it fantastically and was a sheer auteur.

Speaking of critics, one of the few that nailed some of the real charms of this film was the one and only Lester Bangs, in a rare movie article for the famed music critic. As someone who considers Lester one of her spirit writing gods, I can truthfully say that the man could be cranky with his opinions, including slagging bands I would get in a bare-fisted bar fight for. Yet, much like Steckler, Bangs had heart, balls, and brains and absolutely loved this film. Lester was right and if you go into *The Incredibly Strange Creatures Who Stopped Living and Became Mixed Up Zombies*, you could be too. Ray Dennis Steckler, wherever you are, know that you are loved, honored and missed by the right ones who feel it and get it.

NEVER KNOW WHEN, NEVER KNOW WHY
FEAR OF FUCKING, AND THE DREAM IN WHICH *IT FOLLOWS*

JOHN SKIPP

Many of the best movies I've ever seen played for an audience of one, in the Cinerama Dome of my slumbering skull. That's where my little waking brain gives way to the arcane projections of the collective unconscious, shining strange light on the contents of my psychology and soul.

Of course, being dreams, they don't entirely make sense. In fact, they funhouse-mirror the living shit out of "sense". That's what's so amazing and befuddling about them. Dreams have their own rules, if they have rules at all. And though

they're often ripe for interpretation, they seem to take strange delight in defying analysis. As if to say, "Yeah, your logic is all good and well. But you're on MY TURF NOW, BABY!"

As such, they paint a world that would be entirely unfamiliar to us, if it weren't for the fact that we spend at least a third of our lives there, whether we remember it or not. (Some people are more tuned into the other side than others.)

And given how insane waking life is, I'd go so far as to say that the *only* thing weirder than waking life is dream life (although they run close); and the ways in which these worlds intersect is the foundation of bizarro art, in all its forms.

So it should be no surprise that many of my favorite movies are stitched from the fabric of dreams: every detail just slightly off-kilter, so that even the most mundane acts take on slippery meaning as reality shifts beneath our feet, and behind our frontal lobes. And then—should they choose to go FULL DREAM—literally anything can happen.

Which brings us to writer/director David Robert Mitchell's *It Follows*, perhaps my favorite horror film of the 21st century to date. Definitely the one that has creeped me out the hardest, getting under my skin in ways I'd need a professional dream analyst to ruin for me, were I remotely interested in doing such a horrible thing.

It Follows (featured at Cannes in 2014, hitting mainstream screens in 2015) is also perhaps the most divisive in a string of indie art-house horror hits from this century's second decade, including Jennifer Kent's *The Babadook* (2015), and Robert Eggers' *The Vvitch* (2016). Other extraordinary, attention-grabbing wonders were released around this time, including Ana Lily Amirpour's *A Girl Walks Home Alone At Night*, Nicolas Winding Refn's *The Neon Demon*, Anna Biller's *The Love Witch* (2016), and Jim Hosking's *The Greasy Strangler* (2016), but none of them made the same kind of box office splash, or got nearly the same kind of bloodletting love-hate reactions from both critics and fans, largely taking shit for the very same gushing industry hoopla that brought them to our attention in the first place.

THE BIZARRO ENCYCLOPEDIA OF FILM

I love every single one of these films, and delight in their dreamy illogic. But of all of them, *It Follows* is the one whose controversy runs closest to my heart, and which I feel most compelled to defend.

It's the story of Jay (Maika Monroe), a lovely, sassy teenage blonde on the verge of dispensing with her virginal status. Unfortunately, the first guy she does the deed with gives her something far worse than herpes. Because he's not passing along a venereal disease; he's passing along a curse he inherited from the last person *he* slept with. If he doesn't, it will kill him, then go back and kill the person who gave it to him, then the person who gave it to *them*, and so on, ad infinitum. (It is, I suspect, *a very old curse*.)

To make matters worse, the curse comes in human form. The titular "It" can, in fact, take ANY human form: strangers, loved ones, *naked* strangers or loved ones. You will know It only by Its blank, soulless stare, and the way It walks toward you slowly, purposefully. You are the only thing It sees. And It will not stop until It gets you. And fucks you in the very worst way.

Yes, you can jump in your car, put miles between you, buy yourself hours or days. But eventually, It will catch up. It is on your trail. It follows wherever you go. And the only thing you can possibly do is pass It on to someone else. Warn them of what's coming. Hope they pass that baton a couple hundred hapless people ahead. Because otherwise, It will come back for you eventually.

And you'll never know when.

And you will never ever ever know why.

This is Jay's predicament through the rest of the film, resulting in a relentless paranoia that alternately rustles and hammers through every fierce frame of Mitchell's slow-burning nightmare dynamo. Jay goes to school, and It follows her down the hall. She hides in her room, and It breaks in the kitchen window, makes it way past her houseful of sister and friends completely unseen (while her drunk mother sleeps, forever uselessly offscreen). They all drive at least twenty miles to a lakeside cabin, chill out long enough to pretend it's a vacation... and suddenly, It is upon her once again.

THE BIZARRO ENCYCLOPEDIA OF FILM

How this all resolves is deliberately ambiguous, and I'm more than happy to leave it that way. But I do want to address the central criticisms lobbed at this film: not in an attempt to prove them wrong (cuz that ain't never gonna happen), but to clarify my reasons for loving it so completely, in the hope that it adds worthwhile dimensions to the debate.

1) IT'S JUST ANOTHER STUPID ANTI-SEX TEENAGE MOVIE.

The premise here being that because she gets "the curse" from her first sex act, the message of the film is "sex is bad". And indeed, this is the dumb, reactionary notion that resonates through most teenage horror cinema. Every *Halloween* or *Friday the 13th* knock-off (not to mention the originals) for the last forty years has made bank on slaughtering sluts, establishing the tradition of the virginal "Final Girl" who somehow kills the unkillable Daddy figure. HOORAY!

It Follows, however, strikes me as playing a very different game. Just for starters, by making our heroine someone who just got laid—for what she thought were very good reasons (intimacy, pleasure, growth into adulthood, freedom)—and then sticking with her, as if she still mattered even after her hymen got popped. Her shame isn't that she got laid—EVERYBODY wants to get laid—but that she picked the wrong cute guy, with a secret he couldn't divulge until she'd made the same mistake he did.

I never felt, in watching *It Follows*, that the message was "sex is bad". Far more tragically, the message for me was: *there is a force out there that wants to take THE MOST BEAUTIFUL ACT YOU CAN PERFORM and corrupt it, invade it, ruin it for you. It is a monster, a spoiler attached to your joy. It hates you. Hates your pleasure. Will not rest until every human connection you value has been poisoned by It. Passing that corruption along.*

The level of love—or at least caring—in Jay's subsequent onscreen encounters suggest a heroic level of life-risking courage, using sex as not a weapon, but a method of connective healing on the part of two guys who certainly have their own horny reasons for wanting that moment. But know, on some level, that they may die as a result. And are doing it more for her than for themselves.

As such, I'd like to postulate that *It Follows* is a pro-sex horror story that laments Jay's ruin, rather than gets off on it. The monster doesn't hate sex; It will fuck you to death with no remorse.

It just hates us. And this is how it is joylessly doomed to punish us forever.

2) THE MOVIE'S STUPID, AND DOESN'T MAKE ANY SENSE.

This is the notion that sticks hardest in my craw, because the fact is that this is a *very smart film*, operating on multiple levels both surface and subterranean. But where a lot of audience members get thrown is precisely at the point that nightmare logic most severely takes over, seemingly not realizing that it's been playing by those rules all along.

The main point of contention—the lightning rod, as it were –is the infamous "swimming pool" scene, wherein Jay and her ragtag team line the Olympic-sized swimming pool of some spooky abandoned community center with electrical appliances (toasters, printers, computer monitors, etc.). With Jay in the water as a lure, they hope to electrocute the monster when it jumps in after her.

One is forced to admit fairly quickly that this maybe isn't the world's greatest plan. Especially when the invisible It shows up (in the form of her father, no less) and starts lobbing appliances at her head with terrifying force. And this is precisely the point where many of my friends start jumping up and down, yelling, "THIS IS STUPID!" at the screen.

Me? I fucking love this scene. Find it completely, terrifyingly insane, rife with riveting symbolism that buries my need for logic like the craziest Dario Argento (say, the barbed-wire scene from *Suspiria*, or pretty much anything in *Inferno*). And as it winds to its glorious blood-pluming conclusion, I feel a Lynchian level of unconscious mastery at play.

It's a bravura set piece, in a film overflowing with Mitchell's inspired and uniquely nuanced indications (both sneaky and overt) that our reality is not what we thought it was. It's right there in the gobsmacking opening sequence, when our first teenage victim runs into the suburban street in a little white teddy in broad daylight, frantically looking in all directions, only to wind up hours later on a beach some miles away, with her leg snapped backwards and dangling over her own dead face. A heartbreaking work of gorgeous, gruesome art, to kick us off and drag us in.

Much has been made of the clamshell e-reader Jay's friend Yara spends the whole film engaged with, reading Dostoyevsky's *The Idiot* while the rest of them watch Peter Graves argue with a ping-pong-ball-eyed alien in the 50s sci-fi numbskuller *Killers From Space*, on a black-and-white TV. "What period is this even s'posed to BE in?", irate haters ask me.

My answer is, "Well, since that clamshell unit has never existed anywhere, *I think we might be in a dream.*"

This sense of trippiness is wildly propelled by the camera work of DP Mike Gioulakis, who periodically and without warning slowly spins into 360 degree shots centered around whoever's being hunted by It at the time. It's precision shooting that drags every speck of paranoia along with it. Because you never know where It might be coming from next.

The one thing *nobody* argues about is the phenomenal soundtrack, by video game composer Disasterpeace. It elevated the film to John Carpenter levels of sonic propulsion and atmosphere, without relying on mimicry. Like Mitchell, he evokes those levels of primal terror without imitating the source material, making something new and fiercely original for others to pilfer from for years to come. Which, of course, they will.

But what ultimately grounded me, and made *It Follows* emotionally pay off far beyond most horror films, was how much I connected with and believed the teenagers at the core of this story. How naturalistically they played it, no matter how weird it went.

Much of this has to do with the writing, of course, and Mitchell takes great care in etching them all with ordinary human charm. No superheroes here. Just a bunch of nice, well-meaning kids who like to hang out together. Completely unprepared for the shitstorm to come.

THE BIZARRO ENCYCLOPEDIA OF FILM

All that being said, casting is everything, and the entire ensemble hums. Keir Gilchrist is perfect as Paul, Jay's dorky lifelong friend who loves her more than words can say. Daniel Zovatto plays studly stoner neighbor Greg with just the right amount of tough, tender, and cool. Lili Sepe makes an excellent sister to Jay, in a million little gestures and ways. And to round out our *Scooby Doo*-like team of bumbling would-be monster fighters, Olivia Luccardi as Yara is the spitting image of TV's Velma, and is wonderful throughout.

On the monster end, every It-eration is bone-chilling to behold, from the first naked woman in the abandoned parking garage (one of the scariest scenes I've ever seen, anywhere) all the way to the bitter end. Comparisons to the haunting spirits in Herk Harvey's *Carnival of Souls* (1962) and the meat-eating zombies that changed the world in George Romero's *Night of the Living Dead* (1968) are inevitable, but these shamblers are something else again. Completely silent, dead-eyed but still utterly malevolent, *I am never not scared of them*. They get me every single time.

In the end, of course, it all circles back to Maika Monroe, who owns this shit from the second she arrives onscreen, completely holding the center. From flirty fun to abject terror and every single little beat in between, she never drops a false note, making her impossible not to care about. We are right there with her. Her feelings are ours. And God, does she ever make us feel them.

As for David Robert Mitchell, I'm insanely curious to see what he tackles next. Will this be a one-off horror outing, or is fear the foundation of the career he hopes to carve? His first feature, *The Myth of the American Sleepover* (2010) concerned teenage hopes and dreams, which beautifully prepped him for the human element of *It Follows*. At this writing, *It Follows 2* is already in production, with his name nowhere near it, God help us. The project he's attached to now, *Under the Silver Lake*, is an LA noir that transports him for the first time away from his home town, Detroit.

Last time I checked, noir equals fear. And while it lacks the supernatural, it's still all about dreams. Mostly dreams gone wrong and shattered.

THE BIZARRO ENCYCLOPEDIA OF FILM

I just hope and pray that his firm grasp on delirium remains in play. Because honestly, the mind-fucking Bizarro skills he deploys here are not frequently found at this level. He has a gift that I hope he pursues, giving us decades of previously unplumbed weirdness, as only he can.

God speed, young master Mitchell. Thanks for scaring my balls off.

I grew new ones, for next time.

GOOD LUCK!!!

WORLDS BUILT OF BLOOD, HEART, & MAGICK
THE FIRST THREE FEATURES OF ALEXANDRO JODOROWSKY

HEATHER DRAIN

Good art is fun, silly, whimsical, deep and gives you the odd inner tremor. Great art is all of those wonderful descriptors but with more vibration. But when art grows fleshy and transitory, when it wraps itself around and within your very own DNA strands, is when it becomes magick. (Note the k, since it helps separate fantastic parlor tricks from something that lies deeper outside of our typical tangential experience.) When you enter the cinematic realm of Alejandro Jodorowsky, you are in the presence of art that can shatter your heart, mind, and perception, only to help rebuild it into something more strong and rich.

Born in Tocapilla, Chile in 1929, Jodorowsky worked extensively in the theater and moved to Paris in the 1950's. After making *La Cravate*, a surrealistic

short film based on Thomas Mann's novella *The Transposed Heads* in 1957, Jodorowsky would go on to be a founder of the Panic Movement, along with artist, writer and actor Roland Topor (who was great as Renfield in Werner Herzog's 1979 *Nosferatu the Vampyre* and also wrote the novel that would become the basis for Roman Polanski's 1976 film *The Tenant*) and playwright and future filmmaker himself, Fernando Arrabal. The Panic Movement was an art collective that was the riot-inducing child of the Surrealism and Antonin Artaud. Only lasting for a few years, the seeds planted with the Panic Movement have proven to be long lasting, between Arrabal's own film masterworks, *Viva La Muerte* (1971) and *I Will Walk Like a Crazy Horse* (1973) and Jodorowsky's feature film debut, 1968's *Fando Y Lis*.

Based on Arrabal's 1958 play of the same name, Jodorowsky's *Fando Y Lis* emerged onto the film scene in a bloody scream of birth, with its debut at the 1968 Acapulco Film Festival resulting in a literal riot. (Forget standing ovations. When your art inspires people to actually revolt and pelt your getaway vehicle with rocks, then you know you have truly tapped into something really sacred.) In pure surrealist fashion, *Fando Y Lis* opens with a medium-close up of a white-haired porcelain girl-woman thoughtfully eating the petals of a rose.

From there, the brutal poetry of this Universe set after "the Great Catastrophe" is framed like a fairy tale. The intro credits roll with a narrator (Alejandro himself, his voice sounding rich with co-conspiratorial secret), who shares "Once upon a time..." and tells us that all of the cities are left in rubble save for the mystical city of Tar. A series of old German woodcut-style art appears as he talks, including imagery like a nude female body with a feminine *and* masculine head, as well as a man surrounded by flames. (Art of a similar style would also be incorporated in Arrabal's intro for *Viva La Muerte*.)

THE BIZARRO ENCYCLOPEDIA OF FILM

Two vulnerable figures, Fando (Sergio Kleiner) and Lis (Diana Mariscal), are placed in the landscape of this desolate world of dirt and rubble, trying to find the city of water and wine, Tar. (The narrator cryptically informs us that "If you know where to look for it, you will find it.") The film shows their frail journey while revealing through dream-like fragments, the similar but different inner scars Fando and Lis have earned throughout their young lives.

Their childlike nature shines through early on, with a shot of Lis surrounded by a vast array of broken dolls, dirty and cracked with neglect, while Fando plays with plastic toy soldiers, then sets a dead spider on fire. The latter image will be repeated in quick cuts with the film's use of repeated images as fast cuts used as a transition. This was pretty radical stuff, especially for 1968. A year later films like *Easy Rider* would use similar techniques, though compared to *Fando Y Lis*, that classic counter-culture biker flick looks more like *Gidget*.

The two run into a series of strange and occasionally menacing sorts, with each encounter often revealing a layer of past that explains the damage. Early on, they stumble upon a group of well-dressed society types, dancing with each other as a man plays the piano that is literally on fire. The elegant mob swarm around Lis, while a woman pulls Fando away. The flurry of boundary-pushing limbs triggers a flashback to little Lis in a theater watching a lone puppeteer (Jodorowsky). Cutting all the strings to the weak-kneed marionette, he starts to sweep the doll up with a broom. This elicits Lis to playfully jump up and try to grab the puppet. The man pulls her up to the stage, uttering to the little girl, "Let me show you my world." He pushes Lis up over a wall, where she encounters eccentric theater types. At first. Things turn nasty on a dime though when a group of men approach her, saying things like "What a cute little girl! What nice legs! Lie down with us." They swarm her down, with the screen being blunt forced with her screams and cries, while the film cuts to a shot of a hand crushing a raw egg. More potent imagery tied to childhood trauma has rarely been as used in such a disturbing and poetic way. It's intense in a way that is not exploitative but honest. It also gives some insight into possibly why Lis, who was fully mobile as a child, is paralyzed from the waist down as an adult.

While poor adult Lis is left to fend for herself, the women of the group blindfold Fando, leading and teasing him around an auto junkyard, ultimately tricking him into kissing a man. The cruel upper-crusts mock and thank him for "entertaining us." Fando finds his way back to Lis, embracing her. The two then stage a mock post-death ritual, noting "How beautiful is a funeral?" Soon they get stuck in a large ditch, only to be freed by a straggly bearded mystic, who cackles like sanity left that wheel-house a LONG time ago. The man then tries to force himself on Lis, who is lying on a pile of thorns. Fando manages to pull the man off, who then runs to his female plan B, "the beautiful child." The "child" in question is a nude pregnant woman who breastfeeds this worst kind of magical rascal, who ends up doing a little dance and jump after feeding time.

The love between Fando and Lis, while pure, is soon revealed to be fraught with an intense amount of unhealthy dynamics. Finding a large mud pit, which is littered with a multitude of writhing, languidly orgiastic bodies that border on revenant, Fando places Lis' feet in the mud and acts like he is going to leave her. He does remove her, only to drag her limp body around, then walk away as she weeps right from the gut. Fando meets his second batch of cruel ladies, a small group of old women playing as gambling, oversexed grotesques. One woman tries to lure Fando over to her with canned peaches, only to call him a "faggot" when he walks off, resulting with her squeezing the wet fruit in her fist, providing a twin image with the egg crushing hand from Lis' childhood assault.

A group of younger women arrives, hurtling bowling balls at Fando, while an especially beautiful woman emerges with a whip and lashes the business end of it upon his body. But it is the sight of a man in an open grave that makes Fando pass out, as the deceased gets out of his grave. With help from the women, he puts Fando in the now vacant spot. The man then attacks the women, with Fando coming to, yelling out "Father! Father!"
Fando has a vision of a topless Lis lying in a supine Christ-on-the-Cross pose upon a pile of cow skulls. He sees a man kissing a baby doll, only to viciously

stab it in the crotch with a blade, gauging out a large hole. As the man starts to place worms inside the cloth maw, Fando screams out "Lis" and runs to her. He licks her dirty feet as she rolls her eyes in ecstasy, echoing a fascinating permutation of Christ washing the feet of his disciples. (Obviously, that is a different type of religious ecstasy!)

A moment of lightness follows when a large group of drag queens arrive. These Amazonian ladies dance and vamp around to some great Jazz from Hell dissonance while Fando and Lis smile. Unlike almost everyone else we see that the pair encounter, there is zero malice from these friendly transvestites. In fact, they end up giving Fando and Lis a gender swamp makeover, with the former in a ratty wig and cocktail dress and the latter dressed up in Fando's clothes. The group moves on, with Lis caressing Fando aggressively until her hand lands on his breast, pulling fabric out of the cup, making the two of them erupt into childlike laughter.

One of the most fantastical scenes bursts out, showing a fever dream of Fando and Lis painting their names on each other's bodies with black paint. They then paint rhythmic repetitions of "Fando" and "Lis" all over the white room until they are almost blended in with the environment. It

all culminates with the two of them throwing paint all over the room and each other, creating a cavern of ink. Lis has full use of her legs, indicating a dream of freedom of movement.

From there, we see a blind man calling out for blood, resulting in his father taking a syringe full of Lis' and drinking it out of a small glass. An older, slightly mannish woman gluts herself, as Fando is told to "Kiss your mother, she's about to die." He flashes back to himself as a little boy at what appears to be his father's execution. A man cuts a bird out of his father's chest and then stuffs it into a laughing woman's mouth. Fando as a grown man attacks his mother, first choking her and then pulling off her false eyelashes and wiping her mouth. Ultimately they embrace, with her telling her son, "Thank you for killing me" as he walks her to an open grave. Fando grows more and more cruel to Lis, with devastating results, though by the very end, redemption and the mystical city of Tar itself take on a whole other light and meaning.

Fando Y Lis is many things but the central crux of it is that it is a tale of two people crippled by the cruelty of life and their fellow man. Lis is robbed of personal mobility by being molested as a little girl and Fando is emotionally crippled because of his oddly distant and self-focused mother and the murder of his father. Both are ailments of the mind for the two and with such things, finding a cure in a landscape riddled with so little love is beyond a thorny riddle. Lynch-pinning this are the dual lead performances of Sergio Kleiner and Diana Mariscal as the titular Fando and Lis. They are so perfectly cast, with Kleiner managing to pull off the violent duality of Fando. His savagery is not heartless but heart-scarred. He is vulnerable, sweet and boyish at times, as well as angry and vicious. You never hate him but loathe how life has truly stunted him. Mariscal is positively luminescent as the fragile and doll-like Lis. She easily projects this quality that makes anyone whose core isn't fully jaded feel instantly protective. Kleiner would go on to have a very fruitful career, especially on Mexican television. Mariscal sadly disappeared from film altogether by the mid-1970's after a premature retirement. She passed away in July of 2013 in a hit and run accident.

Like all of Jodorowsky's work, there is nothing here that is weird for weird's sake. All of the imagery has meaning and the layers have further layers underneath. Imagine a voluminous hand-stitched tapestry depicting the words of vast poetry, the dreams of man and the worlds of spirit and then your mind has understood the beginnings of Jodorowsky's cinema. If *Fando Y Lis* looked at journey and redemption through surrealist imagery, then Jodorowsky's next film, 1970's *El Topo* would take these elements, add copious religious imagery and set it all in a flammable arthouse powder keg.

El Topo, which translates to "The Mole," was Jodorowsky approximating the Western film genre and using its assorted tropes to infuse a tale about life and death in its many guises—both corporeal and metaphysical. The film opens with a man clad in black, the titular El Topo (Jodorowsky) riding a dark horse with his nude save for shoes, son (played by Jodorowsky's real life son, Brontis). They stop, with El Topo telling his son that now that he is seven

years old; he is a man. He has his son bury a picture of his mother and his first toy. Riding off into the distance, we see the portrait and toy peeking out from the sand.

Being a man means seeing the world's brutality first hand, which happens as the two enter a small village that has been massacred. Shrieks and moans of the dying merge as ambient noise, as the father and son pass by disemboweled animals and bloodied people. Bodies hang from the rafters of a church and a dying man crawls to El Topo and *Hijo*. Capping off the death show mural is El Topo handing his gun to his son to put the poor townsman out of his misery.

The bandits in this universe have a special kind of perversity. The first group we see include a man making a crude drawing of a nude woman on a rock and writhing on top of her, while one of his comrades sniffs, licks and even inserts part of a woman's shoe in his mouth. One of them sees El Topo's rings through a spyglass and launches into an attack. Placing his young son behind him, El Topo deftly kills all of them but not without getting answers about who was responsible for the village massacre. Getting his answers, he removes all of his rings and places them inside the man's now dead mouth, fulfilling a grim irony about greed.

Another group of criminals, headed by a man known as The Colonel, are staked out at a Franciscan Mission. The group of monks there are sexually degraded by the Colonel's men, one of whom is sporting three hats. The men slow dance with the monks and paints one of the monk's mouths red with blood. The sole biological female at the Mission, Mara (Mara Lorenzio), comes out of the stone tepee to get water and is greeted by the loined-up men who are riding iguanas like horses. Their words and movements shriek gang rape but they are halted when she reminds them that the Colonel will kill whoever touches her.

Speaking of The Colonel, Mara helps him get dressed and he is comically dandified, right down to glued-down hair and royal military drag. We first see him as a sad-looking middle-aged man with a bloated paunch and a hairline hanging on by a tiny handful of hairs. She helps him transform, complete with girdle, make-up, a glued-down hairpiece and a gaudy militaristic uniform. The blowhard-peacock emerges outside, as a mass of pigs sprint out behind him. His men cower and The Colonel makes them bark, referring to them as his *perros*. Apparently tired of Mara, he offers her up to his dogs, with El Topo arriving just in time to spare her a nasty gang rape. The men are shot and El Topo confronts The Colonel within a stone circle, stripping him of his clothes, shooting his toupée off and finally, murdering him by gunning him down directly in the crotch. Before his death, The Colonel asks him "Who are you to judge me?" with El Topo answering, "I am God." This castration by gunfight results with Mara and El Topo sort of dancing around each other, like two cautious animals sniffing each other out. The boy tries to get in between them, with Mara knocking him down to run towards El Topo. Forsaking his own son, he leaves him with the Monks, telling him "Destroy me. Depend on no one."

Riding off with Mara, the two find a small oasis with bitter water that he transforms to taste sweet. They find eggs in the sand and when she complains of thirst, he mentions "With my soul, I thirst for God, the living God." and then shoots a rock that bursts out water. She quickly grows bored and starts to circle him while he meditates. Erupting, he jumps up and rapes Mara, making her scream to the heavens, with the film cutting to her drinking water from a phallic rock.

She asks of love and when he says that he does love her, she tells him that she does not and that to earn her love, he has to be "the best." The best is defined by El Topo defeating the four great gun masters that live throughout the desert. He notes that the desert is a circle, so to find the masters, they must travel in a spiral.

The cycle of masters that El Topo must encounter is a step closer to a form of death. The first master is a beautiful young blind man who is protected by two men, one armless and the other legless, who are joined together in a phalanx of one. He resides in a small circular stone building that possesses no door, only a hatch on the roof to enter the interior. This Master tells him that "I don't fear killing you because there is no death." El Topo speaks of his fear of fighting this man to Mara, explaining "Even though I'll win, I'll lose." Blinded by a lust for winning, she ignores this and encourages him to cheat.

The Master's long hair is braided by the feet of his guard in preparation. El Topo ends up winning, though crumples immediately to the ground while Mara laughs and guns down the two guards, separating them. El Topo manages to get up and place the two human pieces back together as whole as they both die.

A woman in black who speaks with a man's voice, looking all the world like a glamorous reflection of El Topo, has started to follow them. El Topo soon finds the second Master and his mother, who greets them with tarot cards, stating "The deeper you fall, the higher you'll get." Her son, looking like a comic book character clad in furs and physically built like a bull, creates delicate geometric shapes out of pure copper. He tells El Topo that perfection is "...to get lost. In order to get lost, you have to love. You don't love. You destroy, you kill and no one loves you." He speaks of his deep love of his mother, whose outdoor table sports a crucified owl. He ends up shooting the second Master in the back, leaving his mother to cradle her dead son.

The Woman in Black and Mara have a whip fight, with the former being the victor and kissing the bloody wounds on the latter's back. El Topo finds a dead rabbit and a crow, which lead him to a living rabbit that is attached to a rope. This trails to the third Master, who is surrounded by a throng of rabbits. He lets El Topo know that he does not distrust him and offers to play music with him, noting his challenger's flute. Bonding over music, this Master tells El Topo that he loathes himself and notes that his presence is a black plague, killing off the surrounding rabbits. The third Master shoots him and succeeds until it is revealed that El Topo has placed a small copper disc under his clothes that deflected the bullet, giving him the chance to shoot and kill his opponent. He then buries the third Master with dead rabbits and palms Mara's bare breasts with his bloodied hands.

Lastly, there is the fourth Master, an old man who long ago traded his gun for a butterfly net. He offers a fist fight with El Topo, with the latter not able to connect his hits with the nimble old master. The old mam tells him that life does not mean anything and to prove it, shoots himself, telling El Topo, "You lost" before he dies. Screaming from the gut, he stumbles to the site of the third Master, where the pile of bunnies bursts into flames. The first Master's body is covered in honey and honeycomb.

"I have been spilled like water and my bones have been dislocated. Why has God forsaken me?"

Stumbling midway on a bridge, the Woman in Black challenges him. El Topo walks towards her as she shoots both palms of his hands and the tops of his feet, committing a forced Old West style stigmata. She looks at Mara and tells her, "It's him or me" and hands over the gun. Mara makes her decision and shoots him in the side, then leaves with the Woman in Black. A small group of people, including a little girl deformed from what looks like the results of polio, pick him up and save him.

The second section of the film begins with El Topo, now with frizzy bleached blonde hair and make-up, sitting in a large cave with his eyes closed while holding a flower. A pretty woman who is a dwarf visits him, freshening up his make-up and giving into a chaste kiss. This wakes him up and he states that "I am not a god." This woman, Mujercita (Jacqueline Luis), tells him that she has been taking care of him since she was a child. She is part of a village that has been trapped underground for years, with nary any help from the above-ground townspeople due to their deformities caused by incest. He then meets an old woman who suckles the hindquarters of a large beetle. El Topo mirrors the elder's actions and has a complete come-apart, with the old woman giving birth to him, making him now literally a reborn man. Mujercita cuts off all of his hair and beard. Donning a brown robe that is exactly similar to a monk's. He comes up with a plan to build a tunnel to help free the underground villagers. El Topo and Mujercita manage to climb out and head towards "the great town."

The great town looks almost perfectly cut out of any classic Western film. That is, save for the inhabitants who are a throng of absolute living ghouls. There are people uniformly marching with signs featuring a pyramid with an eye in the center. (An old symbol that is also called "the all-seeing eye" it is best known to Americans as being on the back of every one-dollar bill.) A black man gets chased, terrorized and branded in the middle of town, much to the smiles of some well-dressed society women. Men dressed in white are ridden like horses and when they try to escape, they get shot in the back for their troubles. This is the scene that El Topo and Mujercita are arriving to.

They decide to busk in town to help raise money for the digging project, which initially works fairly well for them. Noting the hellishness that constantly simmers over the barely polite veneer of the town, Mujercita notes to him that the town is worse than the cave, but El Topo simply responds with, "I'll keep digging." The town's Sheriff hires them to help clean the jail toilets, which he makes sure is freshly used before they start scrubbing. Meanwhile, a handsome young monk who looks a lot like a younger version of El Topo arrives to the town. He meets the local priest, who is found kneeling before a bottle of wine. He does seem legitimately happy to see the monk and has him

attend one of his sermons. The latter centers around the priest and his parish playing Russian Roulette with a blank bullet, unbeknownst to anyone save for the religious leader. Each time someone survives the game, it's proof of the glory of God. When the priest whispers his parlor trick to the Monk, the latter takes the gun and puts a real bullet inside it. A little boy grabs the gun and loses the game.

The priest declares "the circus is over," leaving the church to the monk who pulls off all the sheets painted with the "all seeing eye." The local "Decent Women League" declare a local bar "decent" and leave. (These same "decent" women are seen earlier obscenely harassing and raping their black servant, only to accuse him of trying to violate all of them.) The proprietor of this establishment beckons El Topo and Mujercita inside, offering them the chance to earn some extra money. He leads them to the bar's basement, which is where the real den of money and sin reside. They first are requested to do their kissing act, which is an innocent gag where Mujercita uses a tiny ladder to climb up and kiss El Topo. After this, by gunpoint, they are requested to do "the wedding night." In one of the most touching and yet, heartbreaking scenes in the film, Mujercita comforts him, saying "I love you. They do not exist."

Mujercita ends up getting pregnant, with El Topo rejoicing in the news and takes her to go get married. It is at the church that they meet the monk who turns out to be, of course, the son of El Topo. The latter promises to kill him but agrees to wait until the tunnel is finished. He ends up joining the two in helping out with their busking and assorted cleaning duties. When push comes to shove, his son utters "I cannot kill my master," making him more evolved than his father had previously been. As they finish the tunnel, the underground people rush out, running towards the town. The climax, which is two-fold, is devastating and will leave a stain long after the film has stopped running.

While *El Topo* might be the most accessible out of Jodorowsky's first three feature films, it is still a challenging and unforgettable experience. With an artist like Jodorowsky, you simply do not just watch his films, but are put in the passenger seat for each and every journey. It successfully marries the beautiful with the brutal. Bright blue skies and golden deserts are littered with death, splattered grue and human pain. The most beautiful of all though is El Topo's relationship with Mujercita. Their love and affection is the orchid in this charnel hothouse. Jodorowsky and Luis play off of each other exquisitely.

Out of all the ways that *El Topo* takes assorted Western film tropes on their head and vivisects them is the role of the villain itself. Typically there is a singular bad guy that the hero or antihero must face in the ultimate duel. Interestingly, El Topo begins as the man in black, which in classic Hollywood style Western cliché, usually signified the bad guy. While he does some fairly despicable things in the first half, he shows enough glimmer to make him more than a 2-D character. So he is not a villain nor are any of the Masters, obviously. As dysfunctional as Mara and even the bandits are, they can all be seen as people warped by a life of dirt to the flesh survival. Instead, the real villain is society itself. The ones who try to stuff their id and darker nature under a proper guise, which in turn only perverts everything they do and all that surrounds them. They are not seekers and are formed to be wholly incapable of basic human emotions like empathy and kindness.

Jodorowsky is absolutely captivating in the role and he accurately illustrates a changing and evolving person. Luis is charming as Mujercita, to an extent that it is too bad that she never popped up again in any notable films. It is also amazing getting to see Brontis Jodorowsky here as a little kid, especially after watching his absolutely blazing performance as his own grandfather in Jodorowsky's 2013 's *The Dance of Reality*. One of the first bandits is played by Alfonso Arau, who would have a fruitful career, including playing other western bandits including in the 1987 Hollywood comedy, *The Three Amigos*.

El Topo would become one of the earliest "midnight movies," signifying a time when films that were considered outside the parameter of mainstream were played at midnight for crowds specifically looking for something different. This is the same era where films like John Waters' *Pink Flamingos* (1972) and Jim Sharman's *The Rocky Horror Picture Show* (1975) would take bloom. (For more information on that halcyon phenomenon, please check out J. Hoberman and Jonathan Rosenbaum's *Midnight Movies*. It is required cult film reading...after this book, of course!) *El Topo* found further notoriety by being championed by John Lennon and would be distributed in America thanks to Beatles manager, Allen Klein. (Klein was also Lennon's solo manager around that time.)

THE BIZARRO ENCYCLOPEDIA OF FILM

Klein would also go on to produce and finance Jodorowsky's 1973 film, *The Holy Mountain*. Trying to dice out *The Holy Mountain* in any sort of linear way is a foolhardy enterprise. To truly bury yourself into even half of the nooks and crannies of this film would take at least a novella. *At least*. Could anyone wholly describe a psychotropic spiritual journey with a palmful of paragraphs? Because that is what *The Holy Mountain* truly is. It is Jodorowsky's *Lawrence of Arabia*.

Epic in both visual, aural and subject scope, this is the kind of gift one can receive when a real artist has the benefit of getting truly solid funding. Which is how exactly it should be. Does the world really need the next Michael Bay BJ-wank-o-rama CGI-shit fest while guys like Jodorowsky are having to crowdfund? Absolutely fucking not. So to give you an idea of this great film, regard this section as your amuse-bouche into the world of *The Holy Mountain*. (No TGIF horseshit Jack Daniels buffalo wings here!)

The film's plot is less traditional story and more like a large, taut canvas for Jodorowsky's imagination and soul to accurately explode on every single untouched fiber. But for the sake of this chapter and for those of you uninitiated, I will do my best. The opening scenes reveal Jodorowsky as The Alchemist. Clad in all black and sporting a large tall hat, he prepares for a ritual in a black and white tiled room. Two women who are styled as bobbed-blonde-Hollywood-glamor twins flank him. He ritualistically wipes the makeup off of their faces, pulls off their fake nails, strips their clothes and begins to cut and shave their heads. The stark contrast of their bodies, naked and shorn of hair, crouched next to the mysterious and entirely clad Alchemist is one of the film's most iconic images. (This scene would also be re-enacted almost wholesale in Marilyn Manson's music video for his song "No Reason.")

After that intro credits sequence, a thief (Horacio Salinas) is lying in the streets with a face full of flies and openly soiling himself. A small man missing his hands comes over and cleans the thief's face with his stumps. A horde of children, all of them naked save for some green paint covering their genitals swarm in and pick up the thief. They place him on a wooden "T" and start to throw stones at him until he comes to and steps down, looking physically like the classic Western depiction of Christ (i.e., white skin, long brown hair, blue eyes, slender frame, etc.) The armless man shares a spliff with him and the two laugh and hug. The town they are centered in is not unlike a modern-day version of the Western berg in EL TOPO. People march while holding up skinned and flayed lambs crucified on the cross, while white tourists gleefully take pictures and 8mm film of locals getting executed. (All of whom bleed blue, black and yellow hued blood.) One executioner starts raping an all too willing leggy blonde tourist, while her husband has the Thief hold a film camera so he can pose in front of his violated wife.

There's the Great Toad & Chameleon Circus which starts out adorably whimsical...at first. Several small chameleons are colorfully festooned like Aztec warriors standing very zen and regal among small replicas of the pyramids. It gets scary pretty quickly when the invading toads are introduced. The invaders are swamped in, eating, for real, some of the lizards. The ones not munching look pretty stressed and then the whole structure ends up exploding, revealing a nauseous amphibian and reptile death-a-go-go.

The Thief and his friend pass by the "Christs for Sale" stand, which features rows and rows of crucified Christ-figures, all ready and waiting for the capitalist dollar. The vendors have the Thief carry a large wooden cross for the excited tourists, then, later on, get him to chug a large bottle of alcohol. The method to their madness works, getting him good and passed out, all for the purpose of making a mold of his body for more of their life-sized Christ statues. There's a perverse nod to the Pieta, with a vendor sporting bleached facial hair, make-up and feminine religious robes and hood, cradling the Thief. The Thief wakes up completely surrounded by the Christ statues literally created in his image and freaks out. Enraged, he whips the vendors and destroys most of the statues.

A group of prostitutes, all ranging in ages from the older end of middle-age to a little girl, plus a chimpanzee, pray in a church. Walking on the streets, an old man picks out the child, kisses her tiny hand, plucks out his false eye, then puts it into her hand and kisses her hand some more. You will never unsee this.

The Thief, carrying around one of the few intact Christ intact statues, ends up eating its face off and then sends the rest of the body into the air with an array of red and blue balloons. The prostitutes follow him all the way to a sky-high skinny orange brick building. Much like the first Master's building in *El Topo*, there is no proper front door. Instead of an entrance through the roof, this building has a circle at the very top. A large hook drops down from the entrance. Seeking gold, the Thief brushes off the food originally offered on it and is drawn up the building.

Breaking through the white paper membrane greeting him, he arrives at a rainbow (or more accurately, perhaps, a chakra) hued labyrinth. At the end is the Alchemist, now clad in all white and sitting in a chair that has two white and black stuffed ram attached to it. Standing near him is a striking woman nude save for religious script written all over her body (appropriately known as The Written Woman) and a two-humped camel.

If things were strange before, they are about to get full tilt boogie, both for us and the Thief. A small blue octopus is removed from a lacerated large boil on the back of the Thief's neck and he is then bathed in a beautiful pool by the two while a baby hippo cries out. The Alchemist asks the Thief if he wants gold and he excitedly nods yes. The gold in question is created from the Thief's own excrement, showing the absolutely purest of alchemies. They enter a spinning room that has nine figures on the wall. In addition to the Thief and the Written Woman, there are seven people who will become the Thief's companions. The Alchemist tells him that they are "thieves like you" but instead of being poor common criminals, they include politicians, industrialists, etc. (The more things change, the more they stay the same.)

In a captivating array of sequences, we meet these companions. The first is Fon (Juan Ferrara) who is head of a textiles and beauty empire that was built by his father. The latter is still alive though now confined to a wheelchair. All of his major decision making is based on the dry/moist ratio in the nethers of his wife's mummified corpse. Fon makes a point to sleep with key workers in the factory, elevating them to secretaries and wives. (But only during working hours.) There's Isla (Adriana Page), a beautiful and androgynous woman who dresses like a man and is a weapons manufacturer. In addition to your standard bombs and guns, she also develops various types of biochemical weapons. There are specialized guns for the counter-culture, since "Young generations needs arms for its marches and sit-ins."There are psychedelic shotguns and grenade necklaces, as well as weapons sporting an assortment of religious iconography. Klen (Burt Kleiner) is an artist who has a literal factory for his art, right down to employing an assembly line process approach. There's his biggest project, "The Love Machine." His beautiful wife stays at home playing piano in their mansion while he and his paid for lover (Re Debris aka Re Styles, who was a dancer, singer and cover model for some of The Tubes' most seminal work) plays around and tests his sexualized yet homogenized creations.

There is Sel (Valerie Jodorowsky), whose "customers are children." She is first seen as a glittery, whimsical clown in the streets riding a large elephant. Arriving at the Sel Foundation building, she changes from a colorful yarn hair merrymaker to a severe 1940's style business-vamp. Her workers are largely sad looking old folks. Part of the Sel Foundation's activity includes manufacturing "War toys" for children, which includes some great looking propaganda-style comics book starring a hero called "Captain Captain." Their main aim? To condition children to hate their future enemy.

Berg (Nicky Nichols) is the financial adviser to the President and lives with a woman sporting turquoise hair (and a merkin) who is akin to the uber-bizarro love child of Divine circa *Female Trouble* and a two-bit burlesque dancer gone to seed. They bottle feed their pet snake and she writhes around on a large toy horse as part of their foreplay. Berg doesn't seem quite as a bad as the others, comparatively, especially next to Axon (Richard Rutowski). Axon is the chief of a large police force who operate like a cult. He publicly castrates the newest initiate who is then taken up to a blue room brimming with properly organized jars of severed testicles. It's a room full of testes. This is both horrific and amazing. Last but not least is Lut (Luis Lomeli). An architect whose money-hungry aim pushes him to come up with the idea that "Man doesn't need a home, he needs a shelter." This approach takes the working class, sets them up with no electricity or water, conditions them to eat only at the factory and then sleep single person in these coffin-like beds.

The Alchemist assembles everyone together and tells them "You have power and money but you are mortal." He speaks of seeking the secrets of the immortals and heading to the holy mountain of Lotus Island. First, they must become a collective being and burn all of their money. After that, they then must destroy the image of the self by burning all of their mannequin counterparts that had been placed on the wall. Their heads freshly shaved, their true spiritual voyage begins. Every individual has to face their fears, which reveals spiders, fighting dogs and being sprayed in the face by a figure with lactating Jaguar nipples. Meaning, nipples that are literally dual Jaguar heads spitting out a steady stream of milk. From there, everything leads to a twist ending that I dare not spoil but that is a glove-tight fit for the rest of the film.

The Holy Mountain brilliantly explores not only matters like mysticism and growing as a spiritual being, but also the many facets that corrupt our world. In *El Topo* and even *Fando Y Lis*, the focus is more centralized with peeks at the world at large that we live in. Issues like religious corruption are certainly touched upon in *El Topo*, but not quite to the vicious and accurate levels of *The Holy Mountain*. Each companion is someone who has taken some things that are pure and have spoiled them with personal greed and lust for power. Creating toys for children to specifically shape them in a harmful way is hideous but yet, such things certainly do exist in more subtle ways. The artist taking something sacred like creating and turning it into a crude product is another type of human pollution, not to mention the exploitation of the poor and working classes, especially in the case of both Lut and Fon. The former is screwing over his employees literally, while the other is making it so that it can happen figuratively. It just takes a handful of wrong-hearted, moneyed and powerful leaders to harm and contaminate millions. We see it every day, to the point that *The Holy Mountain* feels in some ways more timely now than ever.

The way that Jodorowsky integrates his messages is a revelation. The continual references to the Tarot, which reigns fiercely here, is a perfect example. In the hands of a master, there is zero danger for anything to feel like new age navel gazing or gross overstatements about the actual nature and meanings of the Tarot. Case in point, how many horror movies and TV shows have you seen where someone gets the Death card and it is instant-spooky-bad-omen time? Exactly. Meanwhile, it is actually a symbol of change and transformation, meaning it is more about spiritual death and rebirth than literal physical death. There's a fantastic scene early on where the Alchemist tells the Thief that "the tarot will teach you how to create a soul." Also, the Thief himself is basically a human version of the first card of the major arcana, The Fool. Jodorowsky is a legitimate expert on Tarot and has written books on the matter, as well as doing public showings of his human tarot. (For a taste of that, definitely check out Louis Machet's excellent documentary, *La Constellation Jodorowsky* (1994).

The Holy Mountain, like all of Jodorowsky's canon work, is a deliberate and fierce act of love. Real love. Not just the lovely, frills and fragrance end of it, but the many layers and strata. Some of it is going to hurt, while other times will leave you thoroughly enchanted. But it is real, it is honest, it is absolutely radiant and it is all right there on a platter waiting for your arrival.

THE SINS OF THE FAMILY
WALERIAN BOROWCZYK'S *LA BÊTE*

HEATHER DRAIN

Ghosts are often thought of as spectral beings in ethereal and monstrous forms waiting for us in dusty corners, creaked out floorboards and the cold glass of mirrors. However, it is the ghosts not used for fright that can be the most damaging. (Just ask Hamlet!) It's the dust of sin, the residual emotional and historical stains left behind from our very own kin that can haunt almost indefinitely. It is the shadows, those figurative demons never exorcised or fully perished that are fed through familial dysfunction and superstition. It is the saddest strain of our existence that always leads to the innocent

suffering for the crimes of their fathers, mothers, and ancestors. We are all haunted in ways that are rich and sick by blood and sadness. It is this theme that is explored with a poet's heart and an artist's mind, in Walerian Borowczyk's 1975 masterpiece, *La Bête*.

This is a film that single-handledly forever altered the career of its maker, a man whose origins as a skilled artist and illustrator moved him into the world of animation and then cinema. A respected man whose work had won multiple awards and nominations, most notably at the Berlin International Film Festival both in 1966 for his short, *Rosalie*, as well as in 1972 for the feature film, *Blanche*. Borowczyk's feature work got more evocative and decadent by the mid 70's, with his anthology film, *Immoral Tales* (1974) causing some waves and putting his very established reputation in the European art-film world at

275

risk. But if that effort was considered to be risky by some, then Borowcyzk ripped the lid off and took the heads of the respectable audience right along with it when he made *La Bête*. The opening alone lets you know that you are in for something alternately beautiful, ugly, raw and tonally dark.

A quote from Voltaire appears in white text on a black background, while the ominous sound of horses and not much else can be heard. The quote in question is, "Troubled dreams are in fact a passing moment of madness." An intriguing and seemingly cryptic note to start with, though as *La Bête* rolls on, it will all become a little more lucid.

After the title credits, the origin of the horse audio appears, as Mathurin de l'Esperance (Pierre Benedetti) helps herd the main stud closer to the mare for mating. The male trots around the female, who is blatantly in heat as if he's dancing in preparation for the inevitable act. The camera, with full honesty yet zero groin-dumbed titillation, reveals the act in full on explicit detail. As the male horse mounts, he bites her neck, giving us a faceful of the ugly, raw art of husbandry. The quick cuts all throughout help set the rough, rhythmic pace culminating with the male sort of sweetly cleaning up his mate's nethers post-completion, all the while Mathurin, a slight and shaggy man with deep sad eyes, looks on with an intense and yet unreadable look on his face. This is a man weighed down, right down to his injured arm and a physical gait that screams lost.

We soon get to meet Mathurin's father, Pierre (Guy Trejan) and his uncle, Duke Rammendelo De Bolo (Marcel Dalio). The two bicker back and forth about the upcoming nuptials between Mathurin and Lucy Broadhurst (Lisbeth Hummel), a lovely young Englishwoman who has come into a large estate thanks to the will of her recently deceased father. As Pierre tidies up the ornate and dusty tomb-like room, it is quickly apparent that the l'Esperance clan's richer days are firmly behind, leaving them only with the relics of the gorgeous but crumbling estate and the shadows of their ancestors.

Rammendelo, a crusty old aristocrat confined to a wheelchair, chastises Pierre, saying that this marriage will kill Mathurin and accuses him of putting money before his own son. Despite his protestations, Pierre needs him since due to the specifications of the will, Lucy and Mathurin's marriage must be blessed by Cardinal Joseph de Bolo (Jean Martinelli) and him alone. The good Cardinal is naturally Rammendelo's brother and since Pierre hasn't talked to him since Mathurin's birth, he needs him to act as expressor conduit. With the wedding scheduled within the next 48 hours, time is not the best resource to lose.

Rammendelo steadfastly refuses to help until Pierre threatens blackmail, as he still has the vial of poison that the Duke used to murder his wife, the Duchess, forty years ago. That does the trick, though Rammendelo gets one last snipe in about how Pierre knows about Mathurin's "nature," before leaving.

The local parish priest (Roland Armontel) arrives with two young altar boys, Modeste and Theodore, chosen for their individual talents with singing and playing the organ. The boys' presence around the Priest feels innately not right but is never addressed directly, just leaving a dim-shadow of a horrible hint. The Priest is concerned about the Duke, whose health has a looming question mark hanging over it, and mentions to Pierre, "We, frail humans, we are like animals, we suffer from the laws of nature." Indeed and the implications behind such a statement feel like the heaviest kind of lodestone.

A snail crawls up the Duke's hand, which he quickly swats away, vaguely disgusted. He does attempt to call the Cardinal, who has been out doing mission work in Africa, but the secretary hangs up on him as soon as he mentions his name. (Sullied reputations feel like the order of the day for nearly every character that graces this film.) Meanwhile, Pierre takes on the task of grooming his only son as Lucy and her Aunt Virginia (Elisabeth Kaza) are on their way to the estate. Driving through the province, Lucy joyfully exclaims "Beautiful France," as her sour faced, prim Aunt responds, "Beautiful France has always lived in lust."

The Priest waits outside the main bathroom door with his two young charges as Pierre informally baptizes Mathurin, an act he manages to con the Father into vouching for with promises that once the couple is wed, they will help repair the local church and provide it with a brand new bell. The deal is done, making the Priest as much of a dusty relic as the house itself.

Compelled by the beauty of rural France, Lucy has the driver stop so she can snap a few pictures of the surrounding flora and fauna. Her Aunt grumbles on about the melancholy of nature, making her niece respond, "Nature is serious but never sad." Brimming with youthful naivete and primal repression, with the latter itchingly more apparent when the driver, making a wrong turn, ends up on a street with two horses mating right in front of the car and flaxen haired Lucy immediately jumps out of the backseat and snaps a picture of the equine coupling.

The ladies finally arrive and are greeted by a friendly, if passive-aggressive Duke Rammendelo, who is all too happy to inform them that Pierre is grooming his son in the bathroom. Lucy, with childlike curiosity, inquires about ghosts in the chateau, referring to a book written by their ancestor, Romilda de l'Esperance (Sirpa Lane). The Duke immediately scoffs at the idea of there even being a book but there is one line from Romilda's words that truly exists.

"I met and overcame him."

Adding to the fascinating if thoroughly mottled family history is the fact that they have kept Romilda's torn corset, complete with claw marks, framed and on the wall in the den.

Before the Duke can further arouse more of Lucy's inquisitiveness (or her Aunt's visible discomfort), Pierre shows up and tries to laugh all of it off, with him even joking about the rumored curse that every 200 years, a beast arrives at their home. This "joke" seems to put their guests halfway at ease, though all the while, Mathurin's bohemian sister Clarisse (Pascale Rivault), makes love with the family's constantly being beckoned at servant, Ifany (Hassane Fall). In fact, they get interrupted mid-coitus courtesy of Pierre, leaving Clarisse so frustrated that she ends up humping the bedpost.

Mathurin confesses to his father, while the latter finishes grooming his son, that he is scared and that he is "ugly." The sad thing is that Mathurin is not ugly at all and while he might not be traditionally beautiful, like his fiancée, he has a warmth and wholly unique sort of handsomeness about him. The ugliness he thinks is his physicality is in fact, the multiple generations of familial dysfunction, that undoubtedly began long before Romilda, whose act (which will be explored here momentarily) has made her the victim-villain to rival Eve in the Garden of Eden. A convenient vessel of blame placed in a circumstance of never winning. Speaking of, Rammendelo begs Pierre one more time to halt the marriage, stressing that Mathurin is an innocent, but the fear of his family's legacy spiraling further down the tubes keeps the patriarch unmoved.

"It's the beginning of the end."

With the Cardinal's secretary remaining incommunicado, Pierre, in a fit of desperation, sends a telegram letting the Cardinal know that Mathurin has been baptized. Clarisse and Ifany begin to make love again, only to be the unlucky victims of seemingly infinite amounts of coitus interruptus. Ifany runs to his employers, while Clarisse briefly resumes her intimate act of bedpost frottage, before getting up and letting two little kids out of a locked closet. (And yet the family worries about Mathurin!)

Speaking of pent up sexuality, Lucy, momentarily by herself, starts to look at her photo of the two horses fornicating and becomes aroused, yet like Clarisse and Ifany, there is no resolution to her moment of lust. The chain of dysfunction grows weirder, as Rammendelo has Ifany collect a clump of Mathurin's hair and bring it back to him.

Despite Pierre's valiant efforts of masking the cracks of his estate, dinner does not go as planned, with Mathurin chewing his food like a squirrel, which sets his father off, further fueling the already skittish Virginia's second thoughts about the whole arrangement, despite Lucy's steadfast interest and quiet affection.

The ghosts of soiled lust of the l'Esperance family combined with personal need is a heady brew for Lucy. Admiring her body clad in a sheer white gown reflected in a three-way mirror, she grabs the rose that Mathurin had sent to her earlier, setting off a flashback of Romilda, looking lovely while playing the harpsichord on a sunny afternoon. Her pet lamb, whom she was watching while playing, wanders off, interrupting her musical practice, as she runs to go chase him. She does find him. Eviscerated. The very symbol of purity and sweetness ripped open like a brokenhearted failure and the grimmest sort of Valentine.

Back to the present, Pierre overhears Rammendelo trying to sabotage the upcoming nuptials while on the phone with the Cardinal. Blind with rage, he grabs a razor and murders his own kin. Sin in this family is nothing new and after that pseudo-Biblical twist, we are back with Romilda, who is being chased by the murderer of her beloved little lamb, a large looming Beast that looks and moves like the unholy bastard result of man and wolf. If the lamb was an appetizer, then the sweet female flesh of Romilda is the main course. More and more of her clothes gets torn off, exciting the Beast with every rip and tear. Her fear grows even more frantic after spotting the large erection looming at her from her pursuer. Blood is not the aim at this point, though Romilda manages to keep him momentarily at bay after accidentally pleasuring him with her feet as she precariously hangs on to a tree branch. Fleeing, the monster rubs Romilda's discarded powdered wig on himself, bringing to mind Clarisse's earlier ministrations on the bedpost.

Lucy, feeling bravely amorous, creeps in on a sleeping Mathurin, removing his shoe, only to get spooked and quickly runs back to her room. Grabbing the rose yet again, she starts to rub it all over her body, pressing the petals into her very sex. Romilda has steadily grown to enjoy the chase and is now engaging the beast directly, while Lucy is writhing in a near-painful looking frenzy. She gets up and checks on Mathurin again, only to run back to her room.

Bringing the Beast to total ecstasy, Romilda's passion unfurled literally slays the creature, leaving his large, once virile body now wholly lifeless. She has killed the Beast with the one thing that frightens many to this day—unbridled female sexuality. As she runs off, a snail slides off her shoe, bringing *la ronde* to earlier in the film when Rammendelo brushed a stray gastropod off of his hand. Oddly enough, the symbol of the snail crops up in some Tarot decks (namely the Rider-Waite deck) and can mean dealing with steady footing and bizarrely enough, progress. In the past, artists have used it as a symbol of resurrection, due to their nature to hibernate. Snails were also used as the Christian symbol of the deadly sin of sloth, as well as an example of punishment in the Bible.

Lucy visits Mathurin one more time only to find his supine form without heartbeat or breath. Naturally, she flips out and becomes hysterical. Virginia runs to comfort her niece, only to become emotively distraught herself at the sight of Mathurin's lifeless body being stripped to reveal a crude tail. The ladies quickly leave the estate for good, leading to one beautiful and near-mournful shot of Clarisse and Ifany looking out as a swirl of dead leaves blow around them. The Cardinal arrives just in time to see Lucy, still naked save for a fur coat (such a grimly appropriate choice of clothing, by the way) run out, dropping her horse sex photo, which he picks up. Flash back to Romilda, who attempts to cover the Beast's dead body with leaves, before departing, naked, shamed and changed forever.

Few films have examined the sins of the family and ancestry as boldly or as poetically as *La Bête*. It is a work that nearly defies comparison to anything else, yet it brings to my mind, George Romero's equally brilliant film, *Martin*. In the latter, the titular Martin is a mixed-up young man, far from evil despite the lines of bodies behind him, whose "vampirism" is more of a result of a "family curse" whose roots are less supernatural and more mentally and emotionally ill dysfunction. Anyone who has known of or been from a highly dysfunctional family will understand this all too well, as bad habits, attitudes, and downward spirals are usually acknowledged as either "normal" or a tragic, inescapable fate. Well, if any of it is ever acknowledged at all.

With *La Bête*, the curse is more fantastical, but like the fairy tales of old, the imagination is used to hint out that the darker side that is all too real. The sins of our fathers and mothers often end up hurting the innocent. (Let it be true of literal parents or the ones of a country who sends it young to filthen their hands and minds with war.) Pierre is not a wholesale villain, despite the fact that he did indeed sacrifice his only son, poor, beautiful and doomed Mathurin, in a heartbreakingly vain but well intentioned in the most fucked up way to save their family.

The real tragedy with *La Bête*, however, is not the film's story itself, but the critical aftershocks that forever damaged Borowczyk's career. Originally conceived as the fifth tale for 1974's *Immoral Tales*, *La Bête* was treated with all the outrage of the crudest 8mm stag loop instead of the work of bold art that it really is. In a world that demands qualities like edge and balls out bravery from art, most scatter in roach-like formation when they are actually graced with the real deal. The reaction to *La Bête* was no exception.

Films like *La Bête* are a litmus test for film critics and art crowds, but in a perfect world, no art should be any kind of litmus test at all. Borowcyzk continued to make films, including such strong entries as *La Marge* (1976), *Behind Convent Walls* (1978) and *The Strange Case Of Dr. Jekyll & Miss Osbourne* (1981), but his career was forever tainted, having gone from a respected artist whose work was once up for the Palme d'Or at the Cannes Film Festival to being lodged into the Erotica ghetto. (A field that should never be a ghetto, for what it's worth.)

At the end of the day, what matters is the work and Walerian Borowcyzk crafted one powerful, heavyweight, and heavyhearted film with *La Bête*. If it is too much for some, just watch the News and realize the world around us is far more offensive and frightening than any piece of art you will witness. Bless Borowcyzk for having the heart, mind, vision and fortitude to not treat any of us like simple minded veal in the form of art critics. If an artist creates something that rattles you, remember, this is often an act of true love and mental respect. Be grateful.

PALE BLUE EYES
RICHARD BLACKBURN'S *LEMORA: A CHILD'S TALE OF THE SUPERNATURAL*

HEATHER DRAIN

The world at large can be the most beautiful and magical world when you're a child. But as you come of age, colors can shift, shadows grow and certainty starts feeling not so certain anymore. Your world changes because you yourself are changing. Trying to wrangle with the fiery combination of hormonal limbo and the thinning veil of childhood is a journey that is as rich as it is hellish. Fairy tales of old were brilliant in a way because they touched upon this very real part of youth. The dark worldview and occasional dismemberment blood and guts shows of old combined with the fear of a world through a young girl's eyes are ripe material for horror. A film that forged these layers together was

LESLEY GILB y GHERYL SMITH
Dirigida por RICHARD BLACKBURN

Richard Blackburn's cult gem, 1975's *Lemora: A Child's Tale of the Supernatural.*

In the center of the strange, shadowy world of *Lemora* is young Lila, played to sensitive will o'the wisp gamine perfection by the late and utterly unforgettable Cheryl "Rainbeaux" Smith. Entering her early teens without a mother and a gangster father on the lam, life has already handed Lila a pretty complex hand. Parental discord aside, she blossoms into the singing star of the local church, whose Reverend, played by director/writer Blackburn, has taken her in, making him her proxy-father. Lila's world is about to get further shaken when she receives a letter from her now ill father, who is wanting to reconnect with his flaxen-haired long distance daughter.

Sneaking out, Lila goes to the bus station and after dealing with a ticket man (Steve Johnson) whose demeanor and presence is marginally more creepy than Peter Lorre in Fritz Lang's *M,* heads to where her father is staying. Arriving at the town of Astaroth, Lila is greeted with desolate woods, townspeople that have turned into deformed looking vampires and one intensely menacing old woman. (Naturally, since any town that shares its name with a demon that is commonly referred to as "The Great Duke of Hell," it is going to be predestined for some very bad things.)

Her salvation turns up in the form of the austere and charismatically regal Lemora (Lesley Gilb). Lemora gives Lila shelter and entrance into a world of night and strange feral children dressed up like tiny bejeweled bohemians. (Not unlike how the two super-fabulous former vampire hunters turned vampires were clad in Jean Rollin's phantasmagorical 1971 film *Shiver of the Vampires*). As the film unfurls, Lemora's interest in Lila veers into a foggy line between a mother-type wanting to groom her eldest and a different kind of admiration that crackles with a sensual tension that feels a bit impure. Things heighten as the mutant vampires in the town descend upon Lila, including her long lost father, resulting with the potential sacrificial lamb having to go into fight or flight mode. But when the heart faces what one has to do to actually survive it can be shattering, especially for a kid. As Lila grieves, Lemora comes back and gently bites her now-protege. When the Reverend shows up to rescue Lila, she implores him to kiss her, which he initially and weakly resists. But he ends up giving into the attraction that was hinted at in the beginning of the film. Not to erupt into a wholesale spoiler situation (too late), let's just say it does not go too well with the sexually repressed man of God.

Lemora is a rich film. Set in the 1930's, it has the visual look and tone of another time in an otherworldly version of small town America. Rich violets and blues are often used in the lighting, mixing well in watercolor smears with inky blacks and shadows. It is lush proof that you don't necessarily need a high budget to make an effective visual impact, especially in a genre film. You just need mental vision, a bit of heart and a great set of eyes for composition and lighting. Richard Blackburn clearly had all of that, as well as a strong script. The themes that are tackled here ring so true. Many children enter this life with not the best of circumstances given to them, much like Lila. Instead of absentee parents, they can have ones that would have been better off being out of the picture.

It's truly a shame that Richard Blackburn's sole feature film as a director is *Lemora*, though what a helluva credit! On a side note, Blackburn did get to co-write the extremely fabulous and bizarro-friendly 1982 Paul Bartel cult classic, *Eating Raoul*. Equally better, he had the good fortune of being part of a round table on the LA public access show, "Art Fein's Poker Party" in 1989. This was a round table that included the closest thing to a god, other than Lemmy, Timothy "Motherfucking" Carey. (My addition, not Mr. Carey's, who probably had a less of a potty mouth than your heart-in-the-right-place writer.)

The question that rings the loudest as the last frame unspools is the fate of Lila herself. The humans we see in her universe maybe not bloodsucking mutants or hypnotic vampire queens but are still predators of various stripes. There is her criminal father, the leering creeper at the bus station and ultimately the Reverend himself. The latter is fascinating because he is presented with some shades of gray while at the same time the film does not sugarcoat his unhealthy attraction to Lila, who is only 13 years of age. (Smith was actually around 18 years old when making *Lemora*, though her petite frame and aura of haunted innocence definitely belied that fact.) His act of taking her in was more than likely

done with honorable intention, but as Lila was blossoming in that weird cusp where you are not quite a child but still far from being an adult, his repressed desire becomes clearly triggered. Good intentions or not, Lila in the long term would have been no safer with the Reverend than being the lady-in-waiting in a house full of vampires. Probably less so. The one benefit of vampirism for her versus being human is that she is certainly given more empowerment from Lemora than from the patriarchal society of America in the 1930's. (Or the 2000's for that matter.)

Lemora, our titular alpha-female, is a riveting creature played hypnotically by the late and wonderful Leslie Gilb. Lemora's intentions with Lila criss-cross each other, with her being protective in parts but also preying on humans for a mesh of blood-as-food and flesh-for-fantasy. (You know, that thing that vampires do!) The ending only hints at motive, with the one truly lucid fact being that Lemora has gifted her "legacy" to Lila and is grooming her young charge. Whether the latter is due to Lemora wanting to have a daughter-of-sorts to possibly take her place for future reference or to have a beautiful eternal girl as her partner is something that is left for *you* to decide. Gilb has that oh so right mix of beauty, charisma, and menace that always makes a truly great lead vampire. (Also see Bela Lugosi, Christopher Lee, Patty Shepard, Ingrid Pitt, Robert Quarry, etc etc.)

Then there is Cheryl Smith as sweet and sweetly lost Lila. Though passing away at the much too young age of 47, Smith quickly made her mark as one of the most enigmatic actresses in modern cult film, with *Lemora* being her first prominent role. Ethereal in her beauty with blue eyes that hinted at an old soul with a young, fragile heart, Smith could not have been better cast as Lila. The moment she's on screen, you are not only captivated by her presence, but also feel immediately protective. Lila is an innocent in a world full of wolves in disguise, with the viewer being held captive as mere spectator to be paralyzed in thought and fear.

Lemora: A Child's Tale of the Supernatural is a bewitching film that is a wholly unique creature. Some films may have similar elements, with its closest kin perhaps being the equally brilliant Neil Jordan film, *A Company of Wolves* (1984), but that said, there is and forever will be only one *Lemora*. It's a spooky and simultaneously heart-sound work that makes one thrilled to live in a world where a film like this exists, but also sad for all the Lilas out there who are living in an existence devoid of supernatural magic and violet hues. If something hurts you, don't look away. Instead, do what you can. After all, supernatural vampires are the least of our problems. It's the ones with the still beating pulse we have to worry about.

LOVE IS THE LAW
THE SWEETEST CANDY SHELL WITH THE BITTEREST OF CENTERS IN ANNA BILLER'S *THE LOVE WITCH*

HEATHER DRAIN

The word "witch" has been a loaded one for centuries built upon centuries, screaming evil for some, a mystery for others and feminine power for all. It is condemnation and compliment all rolled into one cocoon of repression and expression. Indie filmmaker extraordinaire Anna Biller, who has been an underground gem of an artist since the mid-1990's, explores both that wicked witchcraft and feminine identity in her 2016 film, *The Love Witch*.

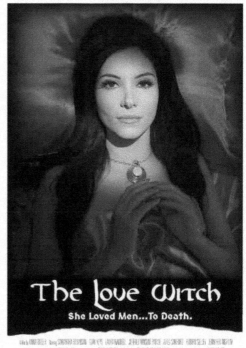

Witchcraft is inherently a sexy term, even though or maybe especially because it has been aimed with fear for centuries. It is a jubilant affront to the Judeo-Christian patriarchy, showing that women can be powerful without the help of an approved male god. In the current cultural climate where the battle for equality and the struggle to not let the percentage of mal-hearted and moneyed people bomb, either literally or metaphorically, us back into the age of internalized self-hatred, fear and externalized subservience, the appeal of witchcraft is absolutely sexier than ever.

The Love Witch is a film that has tapped into something very vital, both creatively and culturally. The plot revolves around Elaine (Samantha Robinson), who is on a bid to start a new life after her last relationship ended badly, with her ruminating on her "poor Jerry" (Stephen Wozniak) as she drives her maraschino-red retro sports car on a California highway. Judging by her flashbacks, Jerry's fate does not look too good on the living-side of things. Elaine arrives at her new place, a pad nestled inside a Victorian-era house that is so deliciously Gothic that both Shirley Jackson and Robert Smith would mutually hug each other and weep happy tears in its shadows.

She meets Trish (Laura Wadell), a British-born interior decorator who tries to befriend the beautiful and exotic newcomer. They go to a pastel-whipped-cream-dream of a tea room and discuss love, with Trish making noise about the dangers of playing into the patriarchy while Elaine is the architect of garnering and rewarding male attention. Their contrast is fascinating with Trish clearly

being compelled by Elaine, who looks and acts like a creature both of another time and yet of her own created time.

Elaine quickly makes her place in the town, selling her magically charged soaps through a local Wicca-tinged New Age shop called Moonrise Herbs. She quickly enchants Wayne (Jeffrey Vincent Parise), a hirsute English Literature professor who reeks of groovy alpha male-dom. He's the kind of guy who can quote some Keats before removing your day-of-the-week panties. Steak dinner and bedroom eyes seduction quickly takes a turn when Wayne starts feeling sick and actually cries. Elaine, while cooing words of support, intones via a voice over "What a pussy."

While disappointed that Wayne is not quite a "real man," she removes one of her hair pieces as well as her tampon, using the latter to make a spell. This latter move is so smart, not only for the utilization of something that is still viewed as gross and unclean by men but also the fact that a number of Pagan religions, including Wicca, view menstruation as a gift. This is to the extent that a woman is viewed at her most powerful when she is going through her menses.

Love is even more doomed for Elaine when she returns to a now deceased Wayne. Her response? She pees in a jar and digs his grave, noting that "I've buried people before." Soon, Elaine visits a burlesque club where she meets her old friend and dancer, Barbara (Jennifer Ingrum), as well as Gahan (frequent Biller collaborator, cohort and overall uber-tastic actor, Jared Sanford), a coven leader who has some vague and unhealthy power dynamics with Elaine. Freedom could be another word for nothing left to lose, or in the case of Elaine, everything in her vision and goals, to lose, as it is noted that women enticing men is a type of magic, too. Again, emphasis on feminine power being firmly tied to pleasing someone who happens to be a carrier of the penis.

The hanging cloud of controlling men from Elaine's past haunts her. Her dead husband, Jerry, can be heard berating her to "...step up your game..." Her own father cranks on that, "I have a crazy bitch for a daughter." (Note that if you call any person, male or female, a "crazy bitch," this is a good way to make that accusation become a fast reality!) Suddenly, Elaine's earlier statement about being "reborn through witchcraft" makes a lot of sense.

The cops are soon on her trail after the death of Wayne, even discovering her jar with her used tampon swimming within it. Hilariously, they don't even know what the bloody cotton feminine hygiene product is. More men who are patently clueless about the innermost workings of women in *The Love Witch* universe. Elaine's path of love-seeking continues, including Trish's sweet husband, Richard (Robert Seeley), which leaves him a sap and an addict, while the new object of his obsession is already bored.

Meanwhile, life throws an interesting curve ball when Detective Griff (Gian Keys), who is investigating the case, ends up sparking a connection with Elaine. The two go horseback riding and stumble upon the middle of a Summer Solstice celebration. The jubilant group, clad in Renaissance Faire-style clothing, end up staging a mock hand-fasting ceremony for Elaine and Griff. It's a genuinely sweet moment that is soon squashed by the fact that the qualities that have made Griff so attractive to her, like his alpha-male-Jack-Klugman-and-Hugh-Beaumont-had-a-handsome-but-don't-believe-in-magic-and-love-bastard-baby presence, are the same qualities that will make him reject both her love and way of life. Elaine's downward spiral results, leaving us with a film that visually evokes vibrant-occult-pulp beauty and Douglas Sirkian kisses of colored splendor from beyond, but is also far more rich than its frosting.

The Love Witch is a work that honors the complicated nature of the human condition, the oppressiveness of gender roles and how never being given a fair shot in this life can set one on the darkest paths. While Elaine can be calculated and so goal oriented that she does not and cannot let herself even think about the reverb of her actions on others, she is not the true villain—or heroine, for that matter. There is not a solid black or white with this character, amplified by a mesmerizing and empathetic performance by Samantha Robinson, who is aces high here. Many a write-up have praised her physical beauty and sex appeal, which yes, she's got both in bulk. But emphasizing those qualities about her is a bit of a disservice since there are plenty of beautiful, traditional-sexy looking people out there whose skill set does not lend itself to pulling off a complex role like Elaine. That said, it is fascinating because that short-sightedness is one of the things that the film itself feels firmly against.

Elaine uses her beauty and men's-magazines-from-the-1950's approach to coddling the male ego to snare herself a mate, yet she is never happy. Why? Either the men themselves do not fit the boxed in expectation of how a man should be or in the case of Griff, are so jocular that they have nailed themselves inside an emotional coffin. Their unifying quality is that none of them are interested in who Elaine truly is. They are only attracted to what she embodies for them as an archetype, not as an actual human being.

The real heartbreak is that Elaine, as a character, has boxed herself in too. Growing up with a background of men verbally abusing her, outlining every little-perceived flaw, any terra firma she can have as an adult is already shaky. She looks into the occult, or in this case a brand of witchcraft that comes across like a blend of both Gerald Gardener-styled Wicca and a dash of Aleister Crowley. (The famous Thoth tarot deck, created by Crowley and his dear friend and artist, Lady Frieda Harris, is visually referenced within the film.) Without getting too deep into either spiritual approach, both are infinitely more freeing to women in comparison to their Judeo-Christian counterparts. But like any belief system under the southern sun, it can easily be co-opted with the intent of, "Yes, ladies be free sexually—especially for any willing men nearby!" Not unlike how a lot of male hippie-type activists in the late 1960's were down with free love but would have women write down notes or serve them drinks during their meetings, instead of welcoming them as equals of a true sort.

Using beauty and sex to garner power is fleeting because, like most things attached to the human id, it is all mercurial. These can be sweet factors in living

but will always need something more stable to prevent a bitter taste. Things like common respect, heart and a basic understanding. Elaine has never presumably been shown such things, so she is left in a state of trying to connect, like we all do, but being held back by both her internalized issues as well as the external factors at hand.

Unlike so many films before *The Love Witch*, the occult as a factor is not wielded as some ooky spooky, road-to-straight-damnation tool. It is presented as both a beautiful ritual and source of power, but also, like anything else touched by mortal hands is not without some flaws. The weird and vaguely unhealthy dynamic between Elaine and Gahan points to this, though is not fully explored, which given that the film is mainly centered on her current quests for love, makes sense. On a side note, not enough words of praise can be heaped on Sanford, who is a total chameleon in all of Biller's works and is serving us some hetero-magical-semi-sleaze-Kenneth-Anger realness here. He is a magnetic actor who should be cast in innumerable projects.

Then, there is Biller herself. Being an underground darling for those in the know since the 1990's with her brilliant short films, then busting out her feature film debut with 2007's completely jubilant and equally complex VIVA, she has been one-of-a-kind from the get go. A juggernaut of a creative type not only directing the film, but also editing, musical composition, building and painting set pieces, creating the wardrobe and writing the script, Biller is the type of director that makes other directors look like mere Dungeon Masters at a poorly attended game of Advanced D&D. The fact that she also starred in everything she has released, minus *The Love Witch*, is just further proof of her being a firm art warrior to nod in respect to.

Something beautiful about *The Love Witch* is how the film itself is basically Elaine. Visually sumptuous, leading onlookers to think they are in for an ultra luscious and sexy-witchy ride, but once they get in, they are in for a much more layered experience. (That is, if their eyes and minds are fully open to it.) It's a subversive tactic that is not used enough nowadays and bless Anna Biller for not only having the vision and talent, but also the moral fortitude for making a brave film in the light of a world that will not let itself view men *and* women as what we are really all are, which are simply humans trying to find love, depth, fun and meaning in this beautiful mess of an existence.

THE BEAUTY THAT DEVOURS
NARCISSISM VS. NECROPHILIA, INSIDE *THE NEON DEMON*

JOHN SKIPP

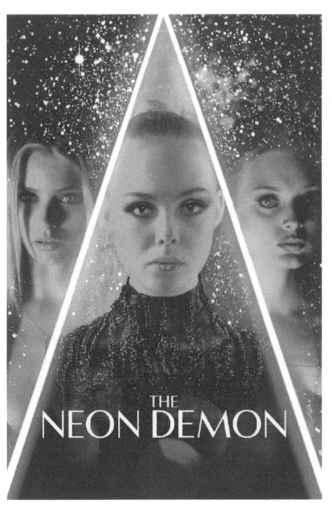

Let's talk, for a moment, about the intoxicating power of beauty.

The great Preston Sturges suggested there were three types of royalty in this world. First was *actual royalty* (being of a regal bloodline, as a prince or duchess or such). Second up were *the rich*, whose enormous wealth gave them power over and above that of most actual royalty, since the Industrial Revolution at least.

Finally came *the beautiful*: those beyond-precious few so profoundly appealing that they swarmed the senses, overwhelming rational mind to the point where its last vaguely-rational thought left was, "Oh, I want a piece of THAT!"

Yes, their power was fleeting. But while it lasted, at full flower, it didn't matter if their blood were regal or their bank account immense. Heads of state, heads of commerce—the most powerful people in the world—were often reduced to jelly by mere *proximity* to this primal power, which ran far deeper than their own. They knew it. And craved it.

And, of course, so did everyone else.

This has always put those genetically blessed and cursed with abnormal gorgeousity in a tricky position. Most extremely good-looking people would argue that, yes, it offers undeniable advantages. But do they feel like royalty? No. They feel more like perpetually-hunted prey. Like a food that everybody's decided is delicious. And their job, more often than not, is to *not get eaten* by every set of covetous teeth that leers their way.

Unless, of course, they take that power, stride directly up to the mouth of the Devil, and say, "Here I am. YOU KNOW YOU WANT IT."

Which brings us to *The Neon Demon*, Nicolas Winding Refn's blindingly gorgeous and weirdly profound meditation on L.A.'s glittering, ravenous fashion industry. It's an art film. It's a horror film. And it's one of the most sensorially-engulfing, lushly-mounted bizarro deep dives you are ever likely to experience.

Elle Fanning plays Jesse, the mysterious wide-eyed jailbait diva-in-waiting whose meteoric ascent is at the heart of our story. We meet her in repose across an elegant couch, impeccably coiffed and awash in her own blood, from a neat slit that runs the length of her delicate throat. She's an exquisite sacrifice to the camera gaze clicking away as it captures her, blank and unmoving. The fact that she has sacrificed *herself* only becomes clear when we next see her in the ladies room, trying to scrub the fake blood from her neck.

Jena Malone plays Ruby, the hungry makeup-artist-to-the-damned who first clocks Jesse as something special. Invites her to her first high-end Hollywood party, where she is immediately I.D.'d as a potential threat by super-creepy high-end fashion models Gigi and Sarah (Bella Heathcote and Abbey Lee, respectively). They icily intimidate the shit out out of young Jesse, whose greenhorn innocence quavers in stark contrast to their predatory composure.

But the next thing you know, Jesse's doe-eyed natural beauty is stealing jobs left and right from her surgically-enhanced competitors. The terrifying men who make the big decisions—reptilian high-powered fashion photographer Jack (Desmond Harrington) and palpitating unnamed Fashion Designer (Alessandro Nivola)—recognize that Jesse has that ineffable "It" that separates true aristocracy from the "merely" beautiful.

And, from there, the blood and existential soul-horror start pouring.

In terms of influences, my mind immediately leaps to the 1950 showbiz classic *All About Eve*, by way of David Lynch's landmark bizarro epic *Mulholland Drive* and Darren Aronofsky's equally brilliant *Black Swan*. But Refn's high-gloss fever dream is operating at a level of visual and sonic intoxication all its own, courtesy of cinematographer Natasha Braier, production designer Elliot Hostettor, and composer Cliff Martinez. There's scarcely a shot in this film that doesn't qualify as either gallery-worthy High Art, or at least the cover of Vogue, where astonishing colors and hypnotic textures reveal every bit as much as the story they frame. And the music—oh, the music—is right up there with *It Follows* in its electronic 21st-century capacity for deeply owning every speck of intense, suspenseful creepiness that befall our sodden senses.

Lest anyone suspect that this is just male-gaze misogyny, the script by Refn, Mary Laws, and Polly Stenham is searingly fem-accurate. The crazy shit these women say and do to each other ain't no male fantasy. These are women in the hell-hole together, for real. To a mind-blowing degree. And with barely an exploitable nipple onscreen, for all its insatiable tease.

Which brings us to the deeper level, where the corruptive narcissism of fashion and fame takes its shape as a neon triangle full of neon triangles. An image that makes no sense, until it reveals itself as a triptych of mirrors wherein the much-cherished notion of self-love takes its ultimate, grotesquely gorgeous plummet down the Devil's gullet, one onanistic French kiss at a time. SEDUCTION COMPLETE!

And then, of course, comes the knife-fellating, corpse-raping, ritualistically cannibalizing, designer eyeball-vomiting, and stun-tastically gushing river of menstrual blood under the cold gaze of the moon that give the third act its now-legendary transgressive street cred. If there's one thing I love, it's an art film OR a horror film where hapless audience members predictably, repeatedly walk out of every screening in disgust and dismay. One could call them candy-asses. But as both John Waters and Stephen King would say, that's pretty much *a standing ovation.*

Refn strode into the cinematic arena swinging hard, bringing a stunning combination of hyper-intense crime tropes, lush arthouse delirium, and *Texas Chainsaw* rawness, with increasing amounts of Jodorowsky thrown in (his previous film, *Only God Forgives*, was dedicated to the maestro). From the *Pusher* trilogy (1996-2005) and *Valhalla Rising* (2009), which helped launch frequent star and mad accomplice Mads Mikkelsen to well-deserved heights, and *Bronson* (2008), which did the same for Tom Hardy, Refn 's *enfant terrible* rep began to rival that of Lars Van Trier.

It wasn't until 2011's *Drive* that he hit the sweet spot of both Hollywood bankability and critical awe. At which point, he could have doubtlessly cashed in hard, latched onto the big budget franchise of his choice, and been gobbled by the actual neon demon called showbiz every bit as much as his unfortunate characters.

But as hyper-brilliant badass bizarro novelist Jeremy Robert Johnson (*Skullcrack City*) says, "I like that Refn follows up a mainstream success by saying, 'Fuck off!' (*Only God Forgives*), and then 'You're still here? Seriously?' (*The Neon Demon*)." It's always worthy of note when an artist finds his or her self right there at the precipice, and deliberately chooses troublemaking creative freedom over Easy Street.

As befits a life of such clearly defiant choices, critical and popular consensus on this particular flick are all over the goddam place. It got booed at Cannes, where it was up for the *Palm d'Or*. Many critics and friends, professional and otherwise, have found themselves wildly vacillating between "This movie is brilliant!" and "Fuck this shallow piece of shit!"

So please allow me to suggest that, just perhaps, *The Neon Demon* is confusing people because it's a profoundly deep movie about PROFOUNDLY SHALLOW PEOPLE. This creates a cognitive dissonance with the inarguably staggering artistry on display, leaving many stuck in the shallows of their own preconceptions, while the depths outrageously unfold all around them.

And while all of the performances are hyper-stylized perfection—including, swear to God, Keanu Reeves as the menacing shitbag manager of the sleazy Pasadena motel where Jesse awaits her imminent fame, while the world of rape howls all around her through the paper-thin nightmare walls of Hell—I've got to say that genuine top-ranked fashion model Abbey Lee gives one of the most haunted and terrifying portrayals of a certain type of ultra-gorgeous cold-blooded wannabe-alpha showbiz predator that I have ever seen. Hope to God she's not that scary in real life, but suspect she's spent her whole life as a phenomenal actress merely *masquerading* as a fantasy mannequin. Either way, she owns every spooky blue-eyed and cheek-chiseled frame she's in. A blood-sucking, Barbara Steele-worthy performance for the ages.

And just in case the point got missed, the closing credits feature the Last Model Standing, walking across a godforsaken desert landscape, while the pop singer Sia (whose controversial music videos for "Chandelier" and "Elastic Heart" featuring phenomenal tweenage dancer/inappropriate sex symbol/ legit phenomenon Maggie Zigler) brings that whole devouring-of-the-innocent conundrum full-circle like both everyone's and nobody's business.

The fact that I can't stop thinking about it pretty much confirms how swoonily I am in love with this film. Think it brilliantly nails that hideous part of our culture that fucks exclusively through its eyeballs. For whom beauty is not just everything, but the ONLY thing in this heartbreaking whorehouse of a town.

Maybe it's because I live so close to the mouth of the meat grinder, but JESUS did this hit some nerves for me.

THE BIZARRO ENCYCLOPEDIA OF FILM

I know a lot of ridiculously beautiful people here in Hollywood, relentlessly jockeying for that onscreen moment in which they are finally, truly seen. And do not envy them a bit.

Their struggles are both brutally matter-of-fact and frankly surreal: a fact that *The Neon Demon* gives allegorical dream-life to like nothing before, or—as of this writing—since.

DO YOU KNOW WHO YOU ARE?
DONALD CAMMELL & NICHOLAS ROEG'S
PERFORMANCE

HEATHER DRAIN

"You're a lashing, smashing hunk of man/Your sweat shines sweet and strong/
Your organs working perfectly/But there's a part that's not screwed on"
Rolling Stones *"Memo from Turner"*

"The only performance that makes it, that really makes it,
that makes it all the way is the one that achieves madness."
Turner *(Mick Jagger) in* Performance

Within the confines of cinema, there lies a playground for directors, writers, and actors to explore and explode social concepts and boxes, often in ways that few could be lucky enough to half-asleep-dream of. Gender roles and personal identity loom large and in charge in such a realm, especially since there was and still is so much confusion and forced damage from the status quo tied to it. Donald Cammell and Nicholas Roeg's 1970 film *Performance* explores this so smartly and unlike any other film, creating a work that is as brilliant as it is weird, giving it magickal fringes around the all too earthly blood, sweat, and violence tied to our lead character, Chas (James Fox.)

Vice. And Versa.

Mick Jagger.   And Mick Jagger.

James Fox.   And James Fox.

See them all in a film about fantasy. And reality. Vice. And versa.

performance.

James Fox / Mick Jagger / Anita Pallenberg / Michele Breton

THE BIZARRO ENCYCLOPEDIA OF FILM

The first section of *Performance* presents us a beautiful permutation of the gangster sub genre. Created in the ashes of the media blitz of real life English gangsters like the Kray Brothers (who by themselves inspired 1990's *The Krays*, starring real life brothers/musicians, Gary and Martin Kemp and the 2015 Tom Hardy vehicle *Legend*), *Performance* is less of a traditional film and more like a tapestry born and weaved from threads of blood, sexuality—some polluted and some sweet, Aleister Crowley-ian explorations and rituals, the influence of William S. Burroughs and most importantly, Jorge Luis Borges. You cannot simply view or break it down because it is not a simple film. But then again, anything worth nestling into and exploring will rarely ever be.

The sweet scent of high-grade fuel and violent sex begin the film, as images of jet planes and a big bad black car in the countryside are (brilliantly, as is all of the editing in the film) inter-cut with Chas having some aggressive, borderline murderous looking sex with his pretty girl of the night. In one flash

DROPPING OUT: Mick Jagger, the famed Rolling Stone, plays a straight dramatic role in his debut film, Warner Bros.' "Performance," changing from collar-and-tie establishmentarian to leatherjacketed cynic and finally to alienated longhair. James Fox stars with Jagger in the Technicolor drama, produced by Sanford Lieberson and directed by Donald Cammell and Nicolas Roeg.

ART 6

of a scene, we see Chas admire first his lady, Dana (Ann Sidney) while her head is burrowed in his lap, but then himself, in a shot of conflicted, haunted narcissism. Peeks into how macho-male image can bleed into homosexuality are laid out from the forefront, with Dana even jokingly calling Chas "a confirmed bachelor."

Chas meets up with his cronies, all of whom fit the bill of classic 1960's era English gangsters. Sharp and well tailored dark suit and a borderline-genial surface masking a shark-like-cold approach to violence are the order of the day. Lawmen and criminals are put side by side, as a discussion about the ill effects of violence in films upon children take place. The delicious irony of folks ignoring the ill effects of kids living in a violent world, while focusing on the shadow worlds of entertainment and mirror image of art.

Chas' boss, the charming but terrifying Harry Flowers (Johnny Shannon), warns him about mixing personal feelings with business and threatens him that, "You can get to love your work too much." The sadism burrowed in Chas' joy is not usually a huge problem but when it comes to the crew having to deal with Joey (Anthony Valentine), whose betting shop is about to be forced into a merger, he is warned to stay away. The nature of Chas' past dealings with Joey is a little murky, though whether it was a bad business dealing, a friendship ripped or something more intimate, he is put under strict orders to stay away. Joey's store, the love of his life, is wrecked, with Chas showing up during the aftermath. Making the air pregnant with confrontation, with Joey and a close mate of his attacking Chas within his apartment, including stripping and whipping him violently across the back. Bloody, bruised and seemingly down for the count, the two men let their guard down long enough for Chas to go full rogue and ultimately, gunning Joey down.

Letting the murdered ex-associates' mate run off, Chas goes on the lam. Given that Harry has referred to Chas as a "mad dog" that needs to be put to sleep, the police are the least of his worries. Overhearing a beautifully groovy rock guitarist talking with his mother in a diner about a basement he has been renting out from a reclusive musician that has gone into sublet, Chas takes a mental note of the address. Showing up at 81 Powis Square, he answers/ bluffs his way through a series of Caterpillar from *Alice In Wonderland*-like questions from an enigmatic and hazed out sounding woman. He is finally buzzed inside and fully enters a world that is a million miles away from his world of linear roles and poisoned ids.

Inside the building are walls painted in primary yellows and reds, Indian tapestries, esoterica objets d'arts and heavy curtains, preventing any stray rays of sunlight from gaining entrance. Chas meets Pherber (Anita Pallenberg), a lanky, leonine blonde who shows him to the basement. She takes his money, plus extra after Chas tells her that he is a traveling juggler—a "performer." Pherber tells her lover and Chas' new landlord, Turner (Mick Jagger), about their tenant. The latter is initially reluctant, wanting the new element out, but there is something about Chas that intrigues Turner. Polar opposites can see an anima/animus within each other, with Pherber and Turner edging Chas more into their world.

He gets fed a psychedelic mushroom that takes on near entheogen proportion with Chas having a vision that results in the incredible "Memo from Turner" sequence. Turner is the proxy Harry, singing such brilliantly written and nasty lyrics like "When the old men do the fighting/And the young men all look on/ And the young girls eat their mothers meat/From tubes of plasticon," while Chas' associates are ordered to strip their clothes off, which they all do, while occasionally echoing lines they had said in real life earlier in the film. The song and sequence are a massive highlight, featuring some killer slide guitar work from Ry Cooder.

Pherber and Turner dress Chas up in a long wig, makeup, and bohemian duds, turning the straight line gangster into a handsome-pretty dandy. After arguing with Pherber about how he is a "man's man," when the latter speaks of how there are those with masculine and feminine sides. However, change is on the

Story-in-Pictures   ''PERFORMANCE''   Photo 2

Turner's seedy establishment is invaded by Chas Devlin (JAMES FOX), an underworld enforcer on the run from both the police and his own gang. A top persuader in a lucrative protection racket, Devlin had discovered inherent perils in the extortion business.

COPYRIGHT © 1970 BY WARNER BROS. INC.

Printed in U.S.A.

rise when he ends up embracing and making surprisingly gentle love with Lucy (Michelle Breton), a lithe barely 18-year-old gamine lover of both Pherber and Turner. Chas remarks on her physical form, as they kiss, comparing her body to a "little boy's." Nope. Not questionable at all.

Chas' crime past does catch up with him, resulting in a bloody but incredibly ambiguous ending that calls into question what exactly is the nature of death in the cinematic and spiritual universe of *Performance*?

Like many a great and hard-to-pin-down work, the studio had no idea how to handle a movie quite like this. *Performance* was shelved for two years, with Cammell being cornered to re-edit the film. This kind of forced move usually results in a de-fanged work, but Cammell, along with editor Frank Mozzola, utilized some artistic alchemy and added *extra* teeth to the film. Flash forwards and fast cuts are tightly created here with a Swiss-watch precision. Mozzola does not get enough love as an editor. There are moves made here that require multiple viewings and that is just to give you a fighting chance of cracking the golden code.

When *Performance* was released, the two factors that were latched on to immediately, both by the public at large as well as the promotional machine

was the presence of Mick Jagger and the scenes of a menage-a-trois between Pallenberg, Breton and the Stones front man. Given that the Stones were reeling from the high of both *Beggars Banquet (1968)* and *Let it Bleed (1969)*, it was natural to focus on Jagger, in his motion picture debut. Jagger is quite good here, slinking about his absolute androgynous physical prime. He is the most beautiful female in the film. As for the sex? Of course, people were going to focus on that. We are creatures often ruled by our loins as much as our hearts and heads. The scene reportedly took several days to film and was described by Pallenberg as an "ordeal" in an interview that was featured on the Warner Brothers Archive DVD release of the film. It is a very earthy and for all of the furor, a fairly short scene. There is a fabulous story that outtakes from the threesome scene were submitted to an erotic film festival in Amsterdam and won first place. This is more likely urban legend since it's easy to find this rumor stated, but actual proof has yet to turn up.

So, yes, Jagger is a primed, shadowy peacock and the ambiance of illicit drugs and languid sex are all there, but the true hearts and stars of *Performance* are James Fox and the unbeatable duo of Cammell and Roeg. Fox is a barely contained tsunami of repression and pain and violence as Chas. It's an absolutely brave performance, as he is able to convincingly pull off rare moments of tenderness and Chas' glimmers of personal transition. His presence looms fiercely throughout, making it inconceivable to even imagine anyone else but Fox in this film. (The original script had Chas as an American gangster, with talks of Marlon Brando, an off/on friend of Cammell's, starring.) It is riveting to see how he plays off his character around the lioness-trickster of Pallenberg (who resembles her late lover and Rolling Stones architect Brian Jones in some scenes), the waifish-vulnerability of Breton and the childish satyr of Jagger himself.

Cammell and Roeg's direction and cinematography are bar none. It is a seduction with a lush kiss and a fist to the neck. The brutality and beauty at play here are evidenced in every shot, whether it is the firm editing, the vibrant color schemes and object composition, the music choices with range from twangy-dirty honky tonk to white noise and the characters themselves. This is a sensual world but it is one littered with as much bad mojo as it is good. On top of that, the lines between the blood and the seed are further blurred, but such is the life and death show.

Performance is vital, electric work of art that demands as much attention now as it did back in its original inception. To view it as a work that simply resulted from the sex, drugs and rock & roll clichés of the 1960's is viewing it with one damaged eye. It is deeper than that and is sitting down in an old, ornate velvet chair, waiting for you to arrive.

SELLING YOUR SOUL TO ROCK & ROLL
BRIAN DEPALMA'S
PHANTOM OF THE PARADISE

HEATHER DRAIN

*"Born defeated/died in vain/Super destruction
you were hooked on pain and though your music lingers on/
All of us are glad you're gone"*

"The Hell of It" Paul Williams

The world is not one always built for artists and few feel this as deeply and knowingly as other artists. Industries built to help them prosper quickly become the devices to help strangle and rob them. Just look at the music industry, which was perhaps at its rock dinosaur heights in the mid-1970's. A machine that produced some of the biggest flames of the decade while using some of its biggest burnouts and casualties as the fuel for the fire. Pretty dark stuff, eh? Especially for a movie musical, a genre usually described more in terms like splashy, fun, corny, hackneyed, sunny and zany, depending on the film and the critic in question.

313

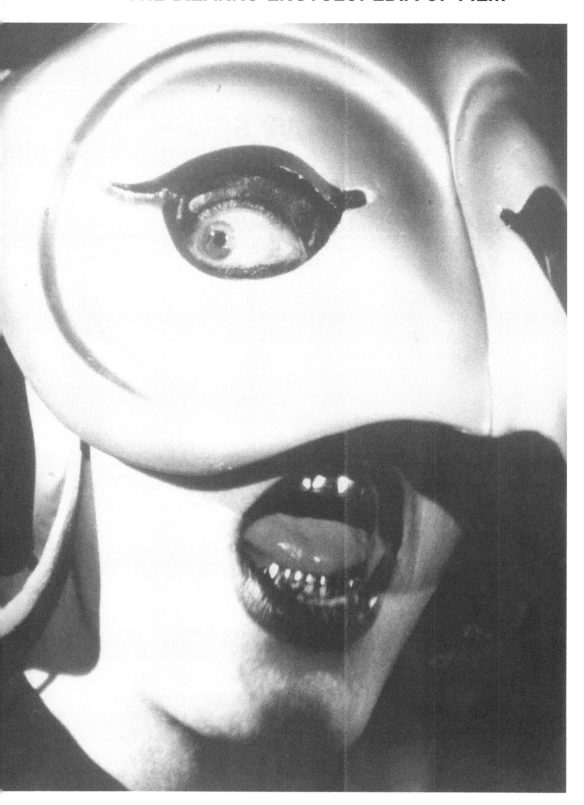

THE BIZARRO ENCYCLOPEDIA OF FILM

But what about dark? Intelligent? Heartbreaking? Border-breaking? Those are some descriptors that have rarely found a good home with musicals, barring the fairly gut-wrenching "Remember My Forgotten Man" sequence in Busby Berkeley's *Gold Diggers of 1933* and 95% of Bob Fosse's film and stage career. There's one more film to add to that to list and it is a stunner: Brian DePalma's 1974 *Phantom of the Paradise*.

Set in the dog-eat-dog world of rock music, *Phantom of the Paradise* or as it was originally supposed to be called, *Phantom of the Fillmore*, was DePalma's film after 1972's beautifully taut and twisted thriller *Sisters*. DePalma basically went from a tale of murder and physical deformity to yet another tale of murder and physical deformity, but *Phantom of the Paradise* is so much more. From its Rod Serling voiced-intro and opening retro-50's-styled rock-crooner "Goodbye Eddie" to the blood-stained live concert tragic bacchanal, it is clear that while this film has many elements utilized here and there, *Phantom* is singular in its creation and existence.

The film's heart is placed within a young, lanky singer-songwriter named Winslow Leach (played by one of the most criminally unsung character actors in all the hemispheres, William Finley). He auditions a song from his rock opera based on the legend of Faust for Rock & Roll impresario Swan (Paul Williams), who watches from a booth up above that is lined with one-way mirrors. Swan's main-man, Philbin (the late George Memmoli) doesn't understand Swan's interest in that "creep," but his boss implores him to "listen to the music."

Philbin goes down to talk to Winslow, laying down some grade-A record-industry-scum-type schmooze on the sharp but very bright-eyed young man. He's initially excited until Philbin lets him know, in wholesale used-car-salesman-conspiratorial mode, that he could be as big as The Juicy Fruits. (The pseudo-Sha Na Na band you see at the beginning, complete with greased up pompadours and false hewed nostalgia.) This sets him, grabbing Philbin, who is roughly two-three times Winslow's size, growling that he's "..not going to let my music be mutilated by those grease balls!"

Winslow's temper, not to mention a passion for his music, makes no dent and he ends up getting quickly hoodwinked by Philbin and his boss, Swan. Visiting the

Harbor Productions Presents
A Pressman-Williams Production

PHANTOM OF THE PARADISE
Released by 20th Century-Fox

PP/33 Swan (PAUL WILLIAMS) is the incredibly successful record producer and impresario who runs the paradise, the ultimate rock palace.

home of Death Records, Swan's label, Winslow is revealed to be on the list with the words "Never to be Seen" and gets unceremoniously thrown out.

(Quick trivia note: Death Records was originally named Swan Song throughout the film, after legal threats from the Led Zeppelin camp during post-production, with the reasoning being that it was too close to the band's real life Swan Song Records. Now, given Zeppelin's highly dodgy reputation of "borrowing" freely and frequently from other musicians, this is beyond ridiculous. Don't believe me, break out your Ouija board and ask Randy California.)

Passion and protectiveness is a fierce driver and Winslow ends up showing up to a massive audition at Swan's mansion for singers. Well, attractive, lithe, young and female singers. Arriving to a cacophony of crackling voices making ramshackle of one of his songs (one of whom is Los Angeles buxom-blonde-fame-revenant Angelyne), he picks up a sweet, velvet like voice, belonging to a plucky and equally driven singer named Phoenix (Jessica Harper.) Winslow is clearly moved by Phoenix and her voice, coaching her through his lyrics, despite noting how odd it is that Swan never notified him about his music being used. Eventually, she gets ushered into the "audition," only to run out crying, after Philbin lunges his heft towards her.

Dressing in highly questionable bohemian drag, Winslow bizarrely manages to gain entry into the audition, which consists of a gaggle of nubile beauties writing on a round bed in a room of mirrors. Strikingly, a sweet-faced blonde, played by the ethereal Cheryl "Rainbeaux" Smith, tries to embrace him, obviously unsure of the whole casting couch process. Swan emerges like the Wizard of Oz from behind a mirrored door and tells his security to get the "fag" out of there. This leads to poor Winslow getting beaten, bloodied and planted with hard drugs, which gives him a one-way ticket to Sing Sing.

Even worse, his teeth end up getting pulled out and replaced with metal ones, all in the name of saving the state money. Being the living definition of beaten not broken, it just takes hearing the Juicy Fruits on the radio and the DJ talking about them singing "Faust," to set Winslow full tilt off and land himself in a vehicle. Prison Break is just the beginning, with Winslow ending up back at Death Records, on a one-man path of revenge-rocketed destruction. Unfortunately, he ends up getting facially disfigured after getting his head stuck in a record press.

You can't keep a good man or artist down and through some brilliant POV camera work, we see Winslow enter Swan's residence and pick out a silver-hawk type mask and a black leather outfit. The Phantom is born and means business, something the enigmatic Swan

quickly realizes when his retro-styled 60's group, The Beach Bums, whose rehearsal is kibbushed due to an explosion during rehearsal. The pseudo-Beach Boys harmonies and DePalma's thumbprint use of split-screen, showing us both Swan's reactions, Winslow as The Phantom in action, the band singing and Philbin trying to calm one of the nervous Beach Bums by shoving pills at him and sweating sheer mook-dom.

Inevitably cornering The Phantom, Swan strikes a deal with him. At first, he helps fine tune a voice box to give him back his voice, after his vocal chords were mangled, presumably from the record press accident. His first words growl out in a static voice: "Phoeniiiixxxx," giving Swan the bargaining chip to edge Winslow into signing, in his own blood, a contract that is roughly the size of Gogol's Dead Souls. Life mirrors art in a perverse way, with Swan assuring Winslow that he will use Phoenix's voice with his songs to open the ageless power magnate's new theatre, The Paradise.

In a haze of seclusion, candles, pills, and thoughts of Phoenix, Winslow toils until the new songs are finished. Swan has him sealed in the studio (shot in the real-life Record Plant in LA, where many a rock group recorded, including Black Sabbath's seminal 1972 album "Vol. 4"), brick by brick, Poe's "Black Cat" style. (One of many mini-horror genre homages scattered throughout the film. This is Brian "Illegitimate Yankee Son of Alfred Hitchcock" DePalma we're talking about, after all.) A good man with a temper and a heart can bloom into a bomb if mistreated. A great artist who happens to also be a good man with a huge heart and a nuclear temper with an atomic core? It's Fat Man and Little Boy time. Needless to say, rousing from his pill and exhaustion-fueled slumber only to find his freshly written songs missing and a brick wall behind the door is met with an electronic scream of rage.

Further adding lighter fluid to the castle fire is the discovery that it will not be Phoenix as the main singer to debut Winslow's music at the Paradise, but instead, a glitter-rocker who makes the word "fey" look like Lee Marvin's scowl, inexplicably and beautifully named Beef (Gerrit Graham.) Realistically, there could be another chapter on Beef and Gerrit Graham's performance alone. Graham, one of the most skilled physical comedians and overall character actors in the business, took the instruction of making Beef "flamboyant," the latter being code for gay and made it something bigger, funnier and more balls out than what could have been a mincing rawk-diva. His Beef is thoroughly hilarious, unforgettable and shimmery in the ridiculousness of it all. When he hears the Phantom's screams and emerges out of his dressing room, resplendent in hair curlers and a belt that is adorned with antlers...excuse me. Fucking antlers. It's a belt with antlers. The man is wearing a belt with goddamned antlers. It's like discovering a new star system in the night sky, folks.

Anyways, when he emerges and lisps to Philbin, "What was that? " it is so simple and so funny, making Graham a golden alchemist of comedy. Speaking of Beef, while showering and rehearsing one of the big numbers from the upcoming show, "Life at Last," he gets an unexpected visit from The Phantom, making him the

Marian Crane to Winslow's Norman Bates. Instead of a knife, though, he gets a toilet plunger over his mouth with The Phantom telling him that his music was written for Phoenix only and that "anyone else who tries, dies!"

Not being stupid, Beef immediately tries to bail but is vamoose-blocked by Arnold "Pusherman" Philbin, who accuses him of being hopped up on speed. In one of the best lines in the film, Beef defensively states, "I know drug real from real real!" But Philbin is persistent in that way that all great stout-parasitical music industry vultures are and the show goes on. The opening number, The Undead, begins the proceedings with a German Expressionistic set and stage makeup, with a dash of Grand Guignol as they hack apart planted audience members who turn from flesh to dummy parts faster than the entire H.G. Lewis gore trilogy. The monster being sewn up behind them emerges to be Beef, with blonde ringlets, glitter-blood, and enough bisexual swagger to out the Starchild himself, Paul Stanley.

All is going well until The Phantom, who has been watching the proceedings from the catwalk up above with nearly-demonic glee, throws a neon bolt prop in the shape of a lightning bolt directly at poor Beef, who is hideously electrocuted on stage and in front of a large audience, who are ecstatic and thrilled by "the show." With the star now thoroughly cooked and wholesale dead, Phoenix, who has been relegated to background singer, is pushed up front and sings "Old Souls," reminding us all of not only the velvet on velvet beauty of her voice, but the beauty still resonates inside our deformed and now-murderous protagonist. All as if to let us know that the sins of the flesh can never truly tarnish the spark of the spirit, heart, and soul.

Phoenix is now the huge star, literally rising out of the charred remnants of Beef. Afterward, Winslow tries to warn her about the price, pointing out the legions of fans calling our her name, while a tiny handful mourns over the still-sizzling corpse of Beef. It only frightens her, making her run faster into the arms of Swan, who is all too ready to seduce her, body and soul. Despondent, Winslow tries to commit suicide, which doesn't quite take. Swan greets him, reminding him that under contract, Winslow cannot die until his boss, Swan, does too. Stabbing Swan, who is irritated but still very much unharmed, tersely reminds him that he is under contract too.

Faust is more than just a rock opera after all. Will Winslow be able to save Phoenix and his own very soul? What is the fate of The Paradise itself? Will Beef become a resurrection of the highest rock and roll order? There's a yes, no and a question mark answer for all of those questions, but if you have not already seen this film, watch it and then come back with the appropriate answers.

Harbor Productions Presents
A Pressman Williams Production
PHANTOM OF THE PARADISE
Released by 20th Century-Fox

PP/1   Phoenix (JESSICA HARPER) is the aspiring
songstress who gains stardom at the Paradise,
the ultimate rock palace.

Phantom of the Paradise is a scratch cake of inspiration, layers and with enough substance to make the frosting all the sweeter. Amidst the humor, some obvious and often black-frayed is a message, if not a full flag-on-fire for all artists. The under and over-current message here is that things like souls and heart are mere fodder for the grist mill of big business. The fire you see is not mere decor but with a closer look, a funeral pyre eternally stoked by the exploitation of fragile hearts born in a world that takes expression for granted. Before I start writing the rest of this chapter in my own blood on black paper while listening to The Cure's "Head on the Door" album on a loop, the film is surface-level lighter than this, making the big ugly message at hand nearly subversive. Which is even better. Just as healthy for you as a brownie laced with kale, but brought to you with respect and love, instead of pastry-born lies.

Hilarious as it is ultimately heartbreaking, the whole film is cinched together by a series of stellar performances and one of the best soundtracks of not only a rock & roll musical, but any modern musical. For a genre that has been extra prone to false-feeling dramatics (any post-*Jesus Christ Superstar* work by Andrew Lloyd Webber) and pie-eyed nostalgia (*Grease*), *Phantom Of The Paradise* neatly steps over the usual trappings. Having the twin brilliance of DePalma and Paul Williams working together helped spark this special film, with the latter often being credited to near-director status by the actors who were most involved in the musical aspects. Anyone who, foolishly, tries to write off Paul Williams needs only to watch and listen to this film. From the spot-on greaser-doo wop of The Juicy Fruits with "Goodbye Eddie" to the deeply dark "Old Souls" and ending with the infernal and exquisitely cynical "The Hell of It," it is a diverse soundtrack that matches and enhances every assorted tonal plot point within. On top of that, Williams' performance as Swan is pitch-perfect. Vain, nervous, cocky and ultimately haunted, Swan is such a strange cat, whose villainy is revealed to make him a victim just as much as Winslow. Albeit in some very different ways, but after all, both are "under contract." The reveal of how Swan ended up selling his soul is satirical and Williams pulls off a younger, more vulnerable man who was about to slit his wrists in a bathtub due to the fear of aging. Even pre-selling his soul, Swan was the antonym of a man like Winslow, who was tricked into his bad bargain.

Finley's Winslow, while relegated to being The Phantom for the majority of the film, is continually sympathetic and a prime example of the danger the wounded can wield. Finley, a willowy presence never to be duplicated, should have been granted more film roles, especially of the lead variety. His work in DePalma's delirious and Antonin-like *Dionysus In 69* (1969) is immense and equally worth seeking out. Matching Finley was the equally great and her own creature, Jessica Harper. The role of Phoenix was her first in a feature film and it is one that she made completely her own. Her voice alone is smokey and glorious but she infuses much heart and youthful spunk and naivete in the role, that you understand why Winslow is so taken with her. It's not just awkward man fawns over a pretty girl and thank god for that. Nothing that hackneyed. It's Phoenix's spark and talent, as well as her beauty, that captivates Winslow so deeply.

A special note needs to be made for Archie Hahn (another name that should be much bigger than it is), Harold Oblong, and Jeffrey Comanor, who play The Juicy Fruits, The Beach Bums, *and* The Undead. They are the closest thing to a Greek chorus and have unbelievable chemistry and talent. It would not be a complete film without this awesome trio. Also, start building your shrine to Gerrit Graham.

DePalma, Williams, and company created something special with *Phantom of the Paradise*. A film that is horror, comedy, musical and art-house with an art-heart. Remember kids, this world may not always be built for artists but it is the artists that help make the ride all the more rich and worthwhile. So let's all take care of and nurture the Winslow Leeches of this world.

CANDIDE ON SPEED
SCREWBALL SEX COMEDIES ON ACID IN ALEX DE RENZY'S *PRETTY PEACHES* TRILOGY

HEATHER DRAIN

Even in the wild wild west days of adult filmmaking, few directors were as bold and frankly, at times, batshit, as Alex de Renzy. Outre is a classier and equally accurate word to use, with de Renzy's work being interesting, talented, sleazy, exploitative and rarely boring. A fine example of this is his *Pretty Peaches* trilogy, starting with 1978's original *Pretty Peaches*.

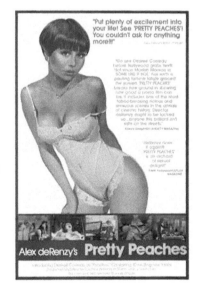

If one was to go by the original poster art, featuring a lifelike drawing of the film's star, Desiree Cousteau, looking like a curvy Kewpie doll in a cream colored teddy, you could easily assume that *Pretty Peaches* was another light-as-air adult sex comedy. Which is sort of true, but then again, this is a comedy by Alex de Renzy, so keep that remembrance sealed tight in your cranium.

The film begins with our titular Peaches (Cousteau) driving in a jeep and heading towards her father, Hugh's (John Leslie), wedding to her lovely, new stepmother, Lilly (Flower). Peaches, after several shots of hard liquor, gets jealous of not getting her daddy's attention, and she drives off in a huff. In fact, she leaves in such a huff that she ends up having an accident out in the country, leaving her physically unharmed but unconscious. Whether or not you believe in constructs like luck or fate, you will soon realize that if such things do exist, then our heroine has apparently done something so hideous on a cosmic level that she ends up being put through a series of misadventures that will start to read less like Penthouse Forum and more like the Personals in Nugget. Don't believe me? Keep reading.

While she is passed out, two young cads who had seen Peaches earlier at the gas station while dealing with a seat sniffing gas station clerk, stumble upon our beautiful and knocked out heroine. Kid (Joey Silvera) and his friend at first try to help. However, despite his friend being nervous, Kid immediately starts feeling her up and quickly graduates to mounting Peaches, who awakens right after the attack. In addition to essentially being raped back into consciousness, she also has a wicked case of amnesia. And if you're picturing the old school Conan O'Brien character, Clive Clemmons, waving the devil horns and playing electric guitar while a British voice screams out "Inappropriate!!!", then give your brain a high five because it is so right.

After the two try to run off with the amnesiac's van, she ends up tagging along and temporarily moving in with them. That scenario alone sounds like the most demented 70's sitcom plot to have emerged out of the first several strati of Hell. Still riddled with amnesia, she tries to find work, which leads to her getting an enema that is the Fleet equivalent to Vesuvius, in an often-censored scene, as well as being violated in a lesbian gang-bang that plays out like a Mack Sennett riot with gyrations, genitals, and one harrowingly sized dildo. Things get slightly brighter when she connects with a seemingly nice shrink (Paul Thomas.) They make tender love and then, as a romantic gesture, he brings her to one insane-o swing party which quickly turns into a huge oily mess of bodies. Little does Peaches know that daddy Hugh and his new bride will be there too. Will she get her memory back before something really life-altering and de Renzian happens?

Pretty Peaches pulls off some sort of strange alchemy where despite all of the depravity you are witnessing, the tone never veers off its screwball comedy path. It is way lighter than it should be, which makes it all the more compelling. A perfect example of this is when Kid sends Peaches to meet his "Uncle Percy," who is a "Doctor." This Doctor drags her into a hidden bathroom and after

borderline accosting her, he offers her a strange solution for amnesia. All in the form of an enema bag. Peaches immediately says "N.O.! No." His response? "Don't you want to be somebody?" It is that blurred line where hilarity and damage have the most awkward make-out session ever. Even better are some of the performances, from the eternally solid John Leslie to the underrated Flower, but this is Desiree Cousteau's show all the way. Her sweet face and curvy body rendered her a Betty Boop for the 70's, but with an "I Love Lucy" styled delivery. Nowhere is that more defined than in *Pretty Peaches*. Cousteau's performance is fun to watch and meringue-lite enough to keep you from calling your own sleazy-shrink.

Little under 10 years later, de Renzy returned to this singular universe with, what else, *Pretty Peaches 2*. In lieu of a continual storyline from the first film, the cycle is rebooted with young Peaches (Siobahn Hunter) having a sexual curiosity that is matched only by her pie-eyed naivete. Her domineering mother, Eunice (Tracey Adams, who looks as much like a "Eunice" as Bryan Ferry looks like a "Bubba"), is not much of help, with her making incidental cockblocking a borderline profession. This starts with Peaches' jock boyfriend Tommy (Peter North), whom Eunice ends up forcing to have sex with her via knife point. (The lady does not mess around!)

Beyond frustrated, Peaches goes to have a heart to heart with her father, Stanley (Hershel Savage). He encourages her to go out and explore the world on her own. She does just that and while hitchhiking, gets picked up by a trucker (Buck Adams.) But before she can lose her flower to a man who probably reeks of black beauties and Red Sovine tapes, a door-to-door hooker (!) (Jeanette Littledove) pops by and they quickly start to knock boots. Peaches watches with rapt fascination but never gets directly involved, which might be the result of the one synapse in her pretty but well-ventilated head that dictates common sense. Losing your virginity in a three-way with a strange trucker and the no-tell-motel version of a lot lizard is an ill-advised thing, not unlike having unprotected carny sex while a bible salesman watches. (Now there's a movie for you!)

Peaches soon reaches her destination of San Francisco, where she stays at the house of her Uncle Howard (Ron Jeremy), his newish wife (Ashley Welles) and his dorky son (Billy Dee.) This side of her father's family are all WAY too familiar with each other, to the point where she would be safer back with the trucker and his dollar-a-dance hooker. While staying there, she meets both

her uncle's exotic maid, Crystal (Melissa Melendez) and the superbly eccentric "Granny" (Jamie Gillis.) Yes, you read that correctly. Jamie Gillis is in grandma drag and yes, it is as wrong and amazing as you think it would be. Granny has Peaches don a skimpy teddy that is all the rage in France while schooling her on cleaning techniques. Soon, the big bad wolf comes out and after telling Peaches to keep the fact that she's a horny dude a secret, though no one on the "outside" is aware, Granny shows her the art of physical love.

After that, Peaches ends up in Chinatown, as her parents go to Uncle Howard's. While trying to find their daughter, they end up getting sidetracked by the ick-ick-icky family dynamic. Crystal ends up leaving and taking Peaches to "The Master" (also Ron Jeremy), where more education of the DNA exchanging occurs. But there is one more surprise in store for our heroine, all in an unlikely and yet, oddly expected form.

While *Pretty Peaches 2* lacks the screwball-comedy-from-Hell vibe of the original, it does make up for it with some strange plot decisions and terrific camera work. This is one well-lensed film and on top of that, there are some good performances here, namely from Savage, Adams and especially, Gillis, who completely steals the show as the lascivious "Granny." One would be hard pressed to think of a better "big bad wolf" than Jamie Gillis. Tracy Adams, who was often underused as an actress, has such a strong presence that she easily overshadows Siobahn Hunter. (Whom she was only older than by about 6 years. What is this? Hollywood?) Hunter does look lovely here and in the spirit of fairness, it's not like she is given much to do other than look pretty, bat her wide eyes and get busy.

DeRenzy ended up having one more "Peaches" film in him and in 1989, he directed *Pretty Peaches 3: The Voyage*. Returning from the last film is Tracey Adams as Peaches' mother, though her daughter is played this time around by super-curvy Keisha. For all intents and purposes, pretend that the last film didn't happen since this version of Peaches, while equally naïve as her predecessor is less concerned about sex and more focused on her spiritual journey. (The titular "Quest.") The fact alone that this is an Alex de Renzy film dealing with spirituality is pretty astounding.

Case in point, after being disturbed by her daughter having strange and erotic dreams, including one where two men claw through several pairs of tights and hosiery to get to a friend of Peaches, her mother arranges an appointment with a therapist. With some vague echoes of the original Peaches and her luck with salacious doctors, this incarnation goes to meet Dr. Thunderpussy (Rachel Ryan), who does exactly to her patient what you would expect someone with such a name would do. (Was Doctor LightningCervix too subtle?)

However advantageous, it is this encounter that sends our heroine on her journey. Will young Peaches find what she is looking for or only get used and chewed up in the process? *Pretty Peaches 3*, while not quite as well shot as the 2nd one or as bizarro as the first, does stand out for a number of reasons. For starters, it's a weirder animal, with some fairly funny and acidic commentary on religion in general. Whether it is a sleazy, Swaggart-like televangelist (more on him in a minute), lesbian "nuns," a yuppie New Age huckster or a Ray Ban wearing, "omm-ing" phony-guru, there is little chance for redemption or personal growth in this opportunistic world. The film's surprise ending is further proof of this. It would be heavy stuff if this film wasn't so goony and fun.

Speaking of fun, for starters there is Jamie Gillis as Reverend Billy Bob, crying on air when he's not running from the authorities or getting sidetracked by pleasures of the more Earthy variety. The image of Gillis in a white suit that is way too tight and wearing a cross the size of one of Rod Rooter's wind-chime-sized medallions is one that borders on the life-affirming. It is one of those moments where you can say, "You had me at Jamie Gillis playing a televangelist."

Keisha is surprisingly likable and warm in the title role, making her seem less cartoony than Siobahn Hunter's version. (Though Cousteau's Lucille Ball-esque performance is still miles ahead of both.) In some ways, she has more in common with the Cousteau version, since sex is something she is not so much seeking out as it is something that happens to find her. In a non-sex role, Jack Baker, whose resume ranged from *Happy Days* and *Kentucky Fried Movie* to *New Wave Hookers*, pops up, making the film instantly even better. Baker was an incredibly talented actor who really deserved a bigger career than he received but who always brightened up everything he was in. This is no exception. Mike Horner also gets a special nod for being really, really funny.

I would also be remiss if I didn't mention film legend Richard Pacheco turning up in a small non-sex cameo role as the most glorious wino in recent memory.

The original *Pretty Peaches* was only available uncut via gray market sources for years in the US, but thanks to the untiring and dedicated folks at Vinegar Syndrome, it is, along with the two sequels, available, uncut and looking better than ever. The original is now on Blu Ray and has some incredible supplementals, including rare footage of an interview with de Renzy himself. With the trilogy itself, it is a fun adult peek into cinematic chaos bordering on the surreal. It's not for everyone but if you are that person that is open to it, you will love it.

PLATES OF SHRIMP
AND OTTO PARTS
THE LIFE OF *REPO MAN* IS ALWAYS INTENSE

JOHN SKIPP

Oh, *Repo Man.* I love you so.

If movies were former paramours
I could travel back in time with,
onboard an unidentified flying
Chevy Malibu that was also — yeah,
you got it, a TIME MACHINE! — I
would never stop laughing and
rolling around with that beautiful,
hilarious, deliriously visionary film.

Repo Man is one of those movies
so jam-packed with fun, outrageous
ideas and preposterous tangents
that it not only defies, but *laughs in
the face* of any attempt to describe
it: a marketing nightmare for the
poor dumb bastards at Universal,
who almost killed this prime slice
of full-tilt Bizarro brilliance rather
than admit their own helplessness
in the face of its awesome power.

In the simplest terms, it's the story of Otto, a dumbass white suburban punk who stumbles sideways into infinity. As played to perfection by Emilio Estevez, he's a blank, cackling, quintessential fool, for whom the lowlife undertow of seedy Los Angeles is a launching pad for all the mysteries of existence.

Wandering back from a stupid cock-blocked punk rock party one early morning, Otto runs into Bud (the astonishing Harry Dean Stanton). Next thing he knows, he's a repo man with the Helping Hand Acceptance Corporation: a professional car thief, ripping the wheels out from under hapless "dildos who don't pay their bills".

But along the way, Otto finds himself increasingly entangled in the "lattice of coincidence" that underlies all things, as he is just-as-haplessly pinballed between decomposing aliens, shadowy government conspiracies, lobotomized mad scientists, rival repo gangs, bumbling liquor store heist aficionados with skinheads and bad Jimmy Cagney impressions, breathtakingly insincere evangelists, useless hippie parents, mystic acid casualties, plates of shrimp, The United Fruitcake Outlet, and the now sadly defunct *Weekly World News*.

Which ain't but the half of it.

It would be soooo easy for me to wax on forever about why *Repo Man* is one of my all-time most dearly beloved films. Or to explain why I think it's the very best movie about the secret, and therefore real Los Angeles, as I experience it day to day. Or to point out why I think it's also the most punk rock movie ever made (acing even writer/director Alex Cox's legendary follow-up, *Sid and Nancy*).

But why does it also rank amongst the greatest science fiction films of all time?

Possibly because there's more pure unhinged fucking Philip K. Dick in *Repo Man* than there is in any film that actually bears his name (with the possible exception of Linklater's *A Scanner, Darkly*). Shriek all you want: more than the brilliant *Blade Runner*. And certainly more than all the dimbulb action shitballs that Dick would have died before watching, had he lived long enough.

With a schizophrenic's helpless freeballing hyperconnectedness, and a master filmmaker's consummate control of the medium, Cox crams more salient and revelatory minutiae into every frame than most space opera stalwarts contain in their entire oeuvres. Which means that the movie is bristling with intelligence, even when the characters inside it are most decidedly not.

Never in the history of science fiction film has such systematic dismantling of reality-as-we-know-it been conducted with more casually anarchic glee. Like the same summer's *Buckaroo Banzai,* it's playful psychic subversion at its finest.

But unlike *Buckaroo*, there are no super-genius heroes on hand to save us. We're all bozos on this bus, as the comparably gonzo 70s comedy troupe The Firesign Theater once stated; and now that I mention it, that's as good a vintage pop culture comparison as I can make, in terms of tonality and countercultural intent. With a definite nod toward Robert Shea and Robert Anton Wilson's *Illuminatus* trilogy, so long as we're at it. And Rev. Ivan Stang's *Book of the SubGenius*, which underground cartoonist Jay Kinney quite accurately referred to as "staggering brilliance, masquerading as total bullshit."

But Cox's trump card—at least for me—is the way he grounds the whole wild mashup in street-level, bottom-feeding veracity. The people with whom we spend most of our time are as far away from godhead enlightenment or actual attainable human wisdom as a human being could get. Just like most of us. Scrabbling for clues in the chaos.

Alex Cox was a Brit expat –actually working as a repo man himself—when he first conceived of this glorious film. And he brings an outsider's wonder and awe to what was clearly an alien universe.

Like the best verbal historians—like Studs Terkel on weed and speed—he gets the dialogue *so right* that I have spent the rest of my life quoting it. It reeks deliciously of the actually-overheard: the random shit so crazy it has to be real. If not actually—from a content standpoint—true.

Were I composing a lazier piece, I'd just quote the motherfucker verbatim for 1,000 words and leave it at that. And you know what? It would be *waaaay* more entertaining than what you're reading right now.
But dialogue is nothing but scribbles on pieces of paper that nobody ever reads without great actors to deliver it. And like Preston Sturges, Billy Wilder, Quentin Tarantino, and the Coen Bros., Cox takes extra-special care to populate his screenplay in such a way that even the teeniest parts are stunningly vibrant with life.

THE BIZARRO ENCYCLOPEDIA OF FILM

Then he proceeds to stuff his motion picture with character actors so impeccably selected that you'd swear they were all born in that film. That they *couldn't possibly be anyone else* but the people they are in that crazily perfect hellish heaven on Earth.

How do you pick a performance, when *every* performance is so great? Fox Harris, Dick Rude, Vonetta McGee, Zander Schloss, and Sy Richardson are just the tip of the tip of an iceberg so huge it could easily gobble this book.

But pick I must, and so I follow my heart and the herd directly to Tracey Walter as Miller, the radiant sad-sack acid burnout and not-so-secret heart of *Repo Man*. Whether explaining the universe over a burning trash barrel, or explaining how he knows that "John Wayne was a fag," he's such a glistening gem—discarded by society at large, but treasured by the rest of us forever—that all must shield their eyes as they stare in wonder at his weirdly-but-truly glorious light. I KNOW I DO!

And so we come to the ending, about which I will say this: it's the only riff on Bowman's trip in *2001: A Space Odyssey* that simultaneously pokes and deeply embraces the wonder unveiled in Kubrick's own timeless masterpiece.

Repo Man? I would marry you. And in fact, already have, every time I watch you. Dozens of times, over the many years, with dozens and dozens more to come.

"Ordinary fucking people," Bud says. "I hate 'em." But the Alex Cox of *Repo Man* clearly does not.

Every single one of us has a key to the mystery.

And the universe is smarter than we may ever know.

THE BAUM WE DESERVE
BIZARRO FOR KIDS, THE OLD-FASHIONED WAY, AND THE GLORIOUS *RETURN TO OZ*

JOHN SKIPP

From the moment we're born, people tell us stories. And the stories told to children are some of the weirdest of them all. Myths, fables, fairy tales raised generations immemorial; now they commingle with endless cartoons and features, animated and otherwise, each in thrall to its corporate logo.

And in many ways, even the most cheesily-normative among them are Bizarro as fuck: full of talking animals and anthropomorphically transmogrified everythings, come to life to entertain us, stimulate our imaginations, and (most likely) attempt to teach us valuable lessons about life.

339

THE BIZARRO ENCYCLOPEDIA OF FILM

Since the 1930's, nobody has worked harder to define the parameters of childhood imagination than Walt Disney and the empire that bears his name. From the short theatrical programmer *Steamboat Willie* (1928) that introduced the world to Mickey Mouse, on through the latest Pixar extravaganza, only the comic book empires of DC and Marvel have ever begun to rival Disney's grip on the formative American psyche, nor spread it further around the world.

One year before little Walt was born, however, another young visionary United States citizen by the name of L. Frank Baum published a little book called *The Wizard of Oz* (1900). And by the marketing standards of the newborn 20th century, it was a phenomenal success. With the adventures of Dorothy, the Tin Woodsman, the Scarecrow, the Cowardly Lion, and the Wicked Witch of the West, Baum created a unique and enduring iconography for kids to fall in love with. The first American, I'd venture to say, to rival the impact of Lewis Carroll's 1865 classic, *Alice's Adventures in Wonderland* when it comes to creating a wholly original fantasy universe for children, one not hinged upon the folklore underpinning works like that of Hans Christian Anderson and The Brothers Grimm.

Baum, sadly, was not nearly the entrepreneur Disney turned out to be. Though he and his wife/business partner Maud launched a successful Broadway stage adaptation, and produced several silent films based on his numerous sequels—even planning an Oz-based theme park in 1905, fifty years before the birth of Disneyland—their considerable ambitions stumbled as often as not. And though the thirteen Oz novels he wrote himself (and the many more commissioned by Maud after his death) have never gone out of print to this day, it wasn't until 1939 that Oz got its next big break.

Of course, everybody knows about that classic MGM production, with Judy Garland and the nice singing Munchkins and such. It's a wonderful, charming film—again, Bizarro as all get-out—and it could be reasonably argued that the film did more to keep Oz alive into the 21st century than the books themselves. (Though I would not be the one to argue it.)

For Baum purists, however, the motion picture got as many things wrong as it got right. Garland, at 16, was waaaaay too old to play Dorothy. And for those who grew up on the original books, with their stunning artwork by W.W. Denslow and (more influentially) John R. Neill, it both visually and spiritually failed to match the magick of the original text.

Enter *Return to Oz* (1985): to my mind, the finest and most definitive Oz motion picture ever made. It only took forty-six more years for writer/director Walter Murch and his astonishing team to bring Baum's vision to vivid cinema life. And though it remains criminally underseen, it is very much an essential masterpiece.

But is it for kids? That's the question many parents have asked themselves. And the answer is *yes, if you don't mind scaring the shit out of your kids*. Because dispensed throughout—amidst the joy, adventure, and wonder—is some serious nightmare material every bit as grim as those aptly-named brothers used to fling.

For the first twenty minutes, we're stuck back in Kansas with little Dorothy (the astonishing Fairuza Balk, in her feature debut). She hasn't been able to sleep in the six months since the tornado that swept her to Oz. Aunt Em (Piper Laurie) is concerned about Dorothy's health, as well as the persistence of the girl's delusions regarding this "Oz" place she refuses to stop talking about.

A shooting star that delivers a key which is *clearly from Oz*—discovered by the hen Billina, a chicken one unlaid egg away from winding up as dinner—proves unpersuasive. And the next thing Dorothy knows, she's being taken to a terrifying asylum, where the condescending Dr. Worley (Nicol Williamson) and sinister Nurse Wilson (Jean Marsh) are gonna subject her to—I shit you not—*electroshock therapy*. It's a new technology the doc is pioneering. "It even has a face," he says, as he shows her the device. And indeed it does. THE FACE OF FEAR!

Allow me to assure you that none of this takes place in any Baum book. But damn if it doesn't make us fall in love with this brave, polite, unfailingly well-meaning little girl, as it reveals the genuine danger of the forces swirling around her (with Mario Bava levels of elegant menace).

So when a power blackout takes place just in time, and a mysterious girl sweeps in to rescue her, Dorothy flees into the raging storm outside. And pursued by Nurse Wilson, the girls wind up in a surging river that sweeps them downstream: Dorothy clinging to and climbing inside a makeshift wooden cage, the mystery girl vanished beneath the current.

Then, and only then, do we arrive in an amazing blend of Baum's second and third novels in the series, *The Marvelous Land of Oz* (1904) and *Ozma of Oz* (1907). There, Dorothy and Billina encounter a shattered Yellow Brick Road, leading to an Emerald City extinguished: all of its citizens reduced to stone statues, including The Tin Woodsman and Cowardly Lion. (Scarecrow, the new ruler of Oz, is nowhere to be found.)

They do, however, make some delightful friends in the form of Tik-Tok, the clankity robotic "Army of Oz", and a pumpkin-headed scarecrow by the name

of Jack Pumpkinhead. The former is not alive, and proud of it (the only reason he's not turned to stone); the latter is so only by virtue of "The Powder of Life", sprinkled vindictively upon him by the evil Princess Mombi.

Mombi, as it turns out, is just as evil as could be. Which is to say, insanely evil. Not only does she control the Wheelers (marauding henchmen with wheels instead of hands or feet). She's clipped all the heads off the most beautiful women in Oz—leaving them headless statues—and put all those heads in ornate glass cases that line her walls. At her whim, she can put on any head she wants. Look as sweet and unassuming as possible. But push come to shove, she always goes back to the O.G. Mombi (also Jean Marsh, and terrifying at every turn).

Stealing the Powder of Life, Dorothy and friends construct a new creature made of a two-sofa body, large palm fronds for wings, a broom for a tail, and the head of a Gump they find mounted on the wall. Though he doesn't know how, the Gump-couch flies them out the window to freedom...at least until he falls apart, and together they crash-land on the mountain of the wicked Nome King (also Nicol Williamson, to bring the whole thing around).

I probably should have mentioned that the Nome King is made of rock, and controls all the rocks and minerals of Oz. He therefore feels that the emeralds in the Emerald City were stolen from him, and is simply reclaiming what's his. He's the guy who turned everyone to stone. And much like Dr. Worley, he patronizingly frames their imminent destruction as a game for them to play. Because he's that kind of bastard.

This brings us to the thrill-packed conclusion, in which Dorothy and her new pals find an egg-cellent way to dispatch Ol' Nomey, render Mombi powerless, and bring Oz back to rollicking life in time for a really big party. (ALL movies should end with a really big party!) Then it's sadly time for Dorothy to return to Oz once again...only this time, she knows she can always come back, any time she wants. All she has to do is ask.

Again: is this a children's film? I'd venture to say that it's one of the greats. And while it doesn't have the non-stop feel-good whimsy of *The Wizard of Oz*, it does capture the genuine awe and magic of Baum. The warm-hearted sense of wonder. And the jaw-dropping sense of design (production designer Norman Reynolds, art director Charles Bishop, a mountain of special fx and visual fx designers, and Will Vinton in charge of the Nome King's stop-motion animation all deliver astonishing work).

I love the beauty and mystery composer David Shire brings from the very first notes, and sustains throughout. I love the tightness of Leslie Hodgeson's crackerjack editing: riveting during the action and adventure sequences, breathing just right in the pauses, and never going slack. I love every single one of the performances, both live and voice-over. I love the spectacular array of characters, in the wonderful script Murch spun out with co-writer Gill Dennis.

But if there's one single thing that nails the core of Baum, it's Fairuza Balk as Dorothy. Like the character, she was only nine years old at the time, and chosen after an exhaustive worldwide search. Murch said she was "absolutely great, a fantastic ally"; and watching her unwavering commitment on screen, I can only imagine he spent every second watching watching the dailies thinking "Thank God we found her. Thank God we found her." That little girl is in almost every single shot. And is a marvel of wonder, joy, fear, and courage in every single one.

Which brings us around to Walter Murch: himself a behind-the-scenes legend whose work as a sound editor, then film editor, then both, already included *The Godfather II, THX-1138, American Graffiti* (where he accidentally inspired the name R2D2), *The Conversation*, and *Apocalypse Now* (where he coined the term "sound designer", and won his first Oscar).

These were the achievements that put him on Hollywood's "Might Be a Hot New Director" list in 1980. And which put him in a room with a studio exec named Tom Wilhite. Who just happened to work for...wait for it...Disney.

And this is how Walt Disney and L. Frank Baum finally got hooked up. Because Walt always wanted to do an Oz film, but MGM had the rights tied up for the longest time. Once Disney finally acquired them, they struggled in vain for years to find a project that would fly. Walt died, but the desire remained. And their clock on the rights was running out.

So when Murch was asked, "What would you like to direct?", all he had to say was, "Oz."

Four years of arduous development later (with one year left on the clock),
Murch flew to England to shoot. Over the course of it, there were two regime
changes at Disney, one of them resulting in Murch getting fired mid-shoot. It

was only the fervent intervention of George Lucas, on Murch's behalf, that allowed him to finish the film. (Incidentally, in my opinion, the single best move Lucas ever made.)

In the end, *Return to Oz* was a financial and critical disappointment (as was the original *Wizard of Oz* upon its release, strangely enough). But over the years, its cult has grown, and will hopefully continue to do so. It sure as shit should!

Interesting side note: one of the storyboard artists was a young CalArts grad by the name of Henry Selick, who later went on to direct Tim Burton's *The Nightmare Before Christmas* (1993). Which featured a main character named Jack Skellington. Who bears a remarkable resemblance to Jack Pumpkinhead. A fact that totally makes me smile.

On a personal note: while I was far too old to experience this as a child, *Return to Oz* was the movie playing on this new-fangled doohickey called a "VHS machine" when my then-sweetheart Marianne went into labor with our first child, Melanie. I'm not blaming the film, mind you; I'm just saying that it has a pivotal resonance for me. That was in 1986.

And when my girls were old enough—I'm guessing little Mykey might have been at least three—we watched that crazy shit, along with *Bambi* and *Dumbo* and *Pinocchio* and, yes, *Alice in Wonderland*, on up through *The Little Mermaid* and *Beauty and the Beast* and the rest of what Disney ever had to offer. Along with *Pee-Wee's Playhouse*, and *The New Adventures of Mighty Mouse*, and Shelley Duvall's *Fairy Tale Theater*, and *Ren & Stimpy*, and *Powerpuff Girls*, and all the old Loony Toons and Betty Boop and Popeye shorts, and all the non-Disney features that aspired to the goal like *The Brave Little Toaster* and *The Land Before Time*.

That's not even counting *Mystery Science Theater 3000*, and the even-weirder treasure trove of "grown-up" stuff they would wander into throughout their lives. (I'm not even gonna pretend that they never saw *Meet the Feebles* or *Forbidden Zone*.)

Point being: little kids, from the time they're born, are bombarded with Bizarro. BIZARRO FOR KIDS! It's the first kind of story we're told, and we're told it from every direction.

I would like to suggest that this is not just a good thing, but a *wonderful* thing. That it trains us to imagine, even as "growing up" seeks to train us to abandon such notions. In that sense, growing up is a betrayal of magic. As if to say, "Remember all that crazy shit we told you? Well, FORGET IT. Childhood is when you get to be all whimsical and stupid. But now you're growing up. SNAP OUT OF IT, ASSHOLE!"

When Dr. Worley tells Dorothy that his electroshock therapy will "cure" her of her dreams, he's informing her that her dreams don't matter, and neither does she. Her adventures, her friendships, all the thoughts and experiences that make her *her* are an inconvenience at best, a problem at worst.

Rebellion against precisely this bullshit is what fuels artists — insider or out — to seek to tap the vast mystery strangeness underlying our normative lives. And it's what draws we as people to seek it out in our art-o-tainment. Reconnecting with our first impressions of the world.

In this and every other sense, I am madly in love with *Return to Oz*. And L. Frank Baum, for blazing that imaginative trail. And Fairuza, and Murch. And yes, Disney as well.

Sometimes it takes a vast corporate empire, taking a chance, to make something this magnificent. Give it life. And make it last across the centuries.

For every new kid ever born. Just like you. And me.

THE GAS OF GRACE AND SORROW
AND THE SOUL-PLUMBING ECSTASY
OF *SWISS ARMY MAN*

JOHN SKIPP

"Any sufficiently advanced technology
is indistinguishable from magic."
– Arthur C. Clarke

One of the reasons that people love movies is that they show us things ordinary life can't, making the miraculous appear before our eyes. It's a trick that we have taught ourselves, and have been playing with ever since.

We've always enjoyed telling each other stories, both to entertain and to teach with, or learn from. We're a fable-weaving species all the way. We want to understand why we're alive, and what that's supposed to mean. We tell each other stories to help explain life, insofar as we can, based on the evidence and our best conclusions; and in the absence of that, to make each other laugh at the grand incomprehension, our inability to actually part the mystery veil.

THE BIZARRO ENCYCLOPEDIA OF FILM

Telling stories is one thing; but making the impossible actually *visible to the eye* is a whole 'nother ballgame. The ability to sculpt physical objects, or paint or etch them in such a way that they show us in real space what our mind's eyes see makes it tangible in ways that talk does not. This is how the visual arts were born, doubtless long before the Lascaux Caves. This is where our imaginations began to get real.

Fast-forward to now, where the tools that we've created allow us to show each other things that would have made those cavemen shit. As outcast evangelical Whitney Pratney once said, before evidently being banned from *The 700 Club* forever, the motion picture technology of the 20th century has prepared us to witness miracles in ways that no previous generations ever knew. And the simple creatures we are have been forever changed by those creations.

Whether this is preparing us for some spectacular apocalypse or not, it's not for want of trying. Worst-case scenarios bombast us every day, in a seemingly-bottomless hunger for the closure of death. Of life *just being over*. So we don't have to worry, or think about it, ever again.

But there's that part of us that still hungers for life. That fucking *loves* life. That notices how the sunlight plays upon the leaves of the towering trees that loom above, the clear blue sky behind them. That relishes the experience of life, in all its infinite form, from the most sublime to the most ridiculous.

Which brings us, at last, to *Swiss Army Man*: the sweetest, most life-loving and thoroughly Bizarro film in this book. Written and directed by Dan Kwan and Daniel Schienert—otherwise known as Daniels—it's a technological marvel aimed directly at the simplest, most fundamental impulses we share. Which, for the sake of argument, are: to be seen for who we are. To care, and be cared about by others. To actually matter. And in the process, be given a reason to go on through this life.

When we meet Hank (the extraordinary Paul Dano), he's preparing to hang himself. Marooned on what appears to be some godforsaken island, shipwrecked and alone, he suddenly spots another body washed up on the beach. Getting down to check it out nearly kills his dumb ass. And when he discovers that the body is dead, incapable of nothing but post-mortem farts, he goes straight back to hanging himself, using the dead guy's belt as a new, improved noose.

But the corpse *won't stop farting*, totally wrecking the solemn mood Hank's trying to establish. And as the tide rolls in, and the body is washed back out to sea, those farts seem to propel it like a jet ski through the water.

Suddenly, Hank sees a way out of this. And harnessing the astounding fart power of this dead body, Hank rides it triumphantly away from the island, and toward freedom. The experience is so exhilarating that he loses control, tumbles off, and gets sucked back under the waves. (All this, just as we wrap the opening credits!)

He washes up on yet another beach, this one closer to civilization. And though tempted to leave the body behind, Hank recognizes it just might come in handy. And so he drags it along, in his pursuit of rescue.

Finally finding a cave for shelter from the rain that pours, he and the body huddle. And Hank starts talking to it, in slumber-party mode, trying to recreate some semblance of the life he lived before. Singing to it. Confiding in it. Then laying it across his lap for comfort. Not realizing that it has opened its eyes, water dripping from its lips.

The next morning, the rain has stopped, and a raccoon is licking the dead body's lips. Hank gives chase, but the raccoon gets away, and Hank knocks over the plastic cup full of his last fresh water, leaving him in despair.

That is, until the dead body starts *squirting water out of its mouth*, providing yet another useful quality for salvation. Which is great, until the corpse starts talking. And our fable weirdly, hilariously, beautifully deepens.

From this point on, it's about the mutual reawakening of Hank and Manny (the extraordinary Daniel Radcliffe, steering as far from his *Harry Potter* superstardom as he could possibly hope to go). The newly-resuscitated Manny is an absolute innocent, having to relearn what life is about from Hank, a young man who has run away from life because he believes himself to be an absolute failure at it.

THE BIZARRO ENCYCLOPEDIA OF FILM

In the process, we learn that Manny isn't the only one with extraordinary powers. As it turns out, Hank is a phenomenal artist (although this is never mentioned out loud): taking the litter strewn through the forest they travel and turning it into breathtaking objects and dioramas that most closely resemble Michel Gondry's mindblowing *The Science of Sleep* (2006). From trucks made of milk cartons with soda can wheels to a swimsuit issue of *Sports Illustrated* that launches Manny's prodigious boner (it's also a compass that can define true north!) to, ultimately, an imaginary bus made of wood and detritus wherein Hank transforms himself into a beautiful woman named Sarah Johnson — the woman he thinks he loves, now the woman Manny thinks *he* loves, so that Manny can remember what passion and desire were like — Hank uses his primitive tools to lushly recreate the world in the image of his own imagination, and pass it along as wisdom.

This kind of intimate devotion to each other, of course, can only result in love. The best result possible, but complicated by the notion of returning to the actual world. And the closer they get to "rescue", the more the world's bullshit intrudes on the genuine connection they have. So when Manny awakens to that bullshit, and fully feels the pain of it, all he wants is to die again, and be free of it once again and forever.

Which leads us to the elaborate grand finale, wherein the Daniels feel rightfully compelled to tie up every loose end. That's a lot to untangle; and speaking personally, I feel there's just a little over-thought fumbling in the end zone of the "real" world, which is what keeps it from quite hitting the emotional perfection of 70s counterculture favorite *Harold and Maude*.

That said, I honestly feel that *Swiss Army Man* IS the gender-melting *Harold and Maude* of the 21st century to date, in terms of bringing a couple of misfit oddballs to the ultimate meaning of life. It's a movie so lovely and funny and charming, so unmistakably heartfelt and sincere, and yet so utterly fucking delirious in both conception and execution that it pins the Bizarro-Meter to intoxicating levels of omigodliness. And the fart jokes, rather than cheapening the proceedings, elevate them to ecstatic proportions.

THE BIZARRO ENCYCLOPEDIA OF FILM

This is wholly on the shoulders of the Daniels, who blazed their trail with a string of staggeringly brilliant music videos like DJ Snake and Lil Jon's "Turn Down For What", where the technical shot-by-shot virtuosity was matched only by the insane energy and unbridled glee of every virtuoso shot. These are filmmakers on fire, with a style that takes the most glorious excesses of Fincher, Scorsese, Jeunet, and Danny Boyle, then melts them down into hyperactive globules for their own visionary cinematic lava lamp.

Swiss Army Man is overflowing with mastery, on precisely that level of high-end greatness. At the same time, it shows remarkable restraint, letting the story breathe between DP Larkin Seiple's breathtaking shots. Editor Matthew Hammon rides the rhythms like a Sufi/Jedi percussionist, knowing precisely when to speed or slow. The music by Andy Hull and Robert McDowell is such a sweet unfolding that I'm still wiping tears from my eyes, days later, every time I sing it to myself.

As mentioned before, both Dano and Radcliffe are beyond superb, with a two-man sustained performance so completely in the moment that you never doubt either one of them for a second, no matter how crazy shit gets. The rubber-faced more-than-dead Manny, enduring the longest sustained rigor mortis in film history, is a role for the ages. And Radcliffe is a constant radiant source of delight. It's a profoundly physical performance — the filmmakers were delighted to discover that keeping one eye at half-mast was a trick he'd long mastered beforehand, saving all kinds of makeup dollars and time — and yet his pure soul is never buried.

Dano, as the straight man here (though he spends roughly one-fifth of the film in frankly superlative drag), has a role every bit as demanding. This is Hank's story, after all; and his moment-by-moment, inch-by-inch transformation from soul lost to soul found is revelatory in every sense. The profound level of nuance he displays at every step — the multitudinous ways in which he becomes more and more beautiful — is acting of the very highest order.

End result being that I utterly fell in love with both of them. Which pretty much sealed the deal on utterly falling in love with the film.

But circling back to our initial premise: somewhere between the Lascaux Caves-worthy primitivism (courtesy of production designer Jason Kisvardey and art director David Duarte) and the cunningly integrated CGI (courtesy of a squad too huge to mention), *Swiss Army Man* delivers the heretofore-unimaginable visions of the Daniels so hard that I wish I could go back to cave-dwelling times and show them that shit. Watch their minds explode with possibility, a little bit sooner.

As it stands, I'm just glad that our still-unbelievably primitive present has been offered hieroglyphics of this extraordinary magnitude.

Witnessing miracles is just half of our job, from here on in. It's up to us to grow our souls accordingly.

And rise to that challenge.

PARTING IS SUCH SWEET SORROW THAT IT TOTALLY SUCKS
LLOYD AND BILLY GOT THEIR GUNN IN THE TIMELESS *TROMEO AND JULIET*

JOHN SKIPP

And so, at last, we come to Troma Entertainment. It would be impossible to do an encyclopedia of bizarro film—much less THE BIZARRO ENCYCLOPEDIA OF FILM (VOL. I)—without devoting at least one chapter to the self-described "longest-running independent production company" in outsider film history, whose library could singlehandedly fill a dozen well-stocked "Cult" sections without letting in a single other film. (Although most of them are—in the words of deranged filmmaker/impresario/ Tromatic founding father Lloyd Kaufman—"goat shit".)

Launched in 1974 by Kaufman and Michael Herz —who hilariously met as students at Yale (!), co-matriculating with party animals Oliver Stone and George W. Bush (!!)—Troma began as a way to emulate both low-budget hero Roger Corman and the company that launched him, Samuel Z. Arkoff and James H. Nicholson's legendary American International Pictures.

Starting with nothing but Kaufman's self-starring cornball second feature *The Battle of Love's Return* (1971) and a fierce desire to have control over their own creative destinies, they acquired an ugly little film by a guy named Joel M. Reed called *Zardu: Master of the Screaming Virgins*— subsequently retitled *The Incredible Torture Show* before Kaufman and Herz came up with the substantially-catchier *Bloodsucking Freaks* (1976)—and unleashed it (with no

small amount of personal shame) upon the sticky-floored grindhouses of the cinema world at large.

Its modest but undeniable success with the sleazy sickfuck crowd — weened on "Godfather of Gore" Herschell Gordon Lewis' pioneering splatfests *Blood Feast* (1963), *Two Thousand Maniacs!* (1964), and the case-specifically influential *Wizard of Gore* (1970) — showed them the distribution ropes, and set the stage for the madness to come.

After several disasters with shady business partners brought them to the brink of ruin, they made a string of "sexy comedies". The first, 1979's *Squeeze Play*, concerning the bodacious hijinks of a women's lib-tastic softball team, was flatly rejected by every distributor on Earth. But when one little theater in Norfolk, Virginia had a sudden hole in its double-feature schedule (paired with the Alan Arkin/Peter Falk-driven mainstream hit *The In-Laws*), *Squeeze Play* brought the house down. Suddenly, theaters all over the country were booking this goofy feature for its copious boobage and slapstick comedy, the *piece de resistance* being a softball wedged in some guy's bare ass. And AUDIENCES LOVED IT. It wound up raking in millions, putting Troma (and director "Samuel Weil", Kaufman's *nom de plume* for decades to come) on the map.

But when 20th Century Fox acquired and released fellow outsider maverick Bob Clark's *Porky's* (1981) to critical loathing and massive box office success, the big boys officially took over the party. And Troma's next three features sank like stones. Once again, they were faced with imminent doom.

As legend would have it, this was when co-Tromoid Michael Herz read an article in *Variety* stating that "Horror Was Dead". And his immediate response was, "We should make a horror movie."

Kaufman, who had meanwhile kept a roof over his head and garnered invaluable experience by working on the production end for filmmakers like John G. Advilson (believe it or not, the 1976 Academy Award-winning *Rocky* was edited entirely on Troma's hand-cranked moviolas), had such a shitty time as location manager on 1977's *Saturday Night Fever* that he equated horror with spending too much time in the new trendy "health spas" where upwardly-mobile narcissists spent more time sculpting their bodies than developing their souls.

The situation was ripe for horror. But Lloyd couldn't find a way into the story, until a sudden flash told him, "But what if it's a comedy?"

At which point, 1984's *The Toxic Avenger* was born. And—incredibly long story short—Troma's identity as a company specializing in raucous, subversive lowbrow splatstick horror comedy resulted in an ardent bizarro cult following that sustains to this day.

Speaking personally, I always admired the outrageous spunk and topical fuck-you spirit of *Toxie, Class of Nuke 'Em High* (1986), and their numerous sequels. Found them fun and inspiring. Laughed my ass off with alarming frequency. Was in awe of their promotional audacity. But never quite fell in love as hard as I hoped.

To my mind, it would be another decade before that formula resulted in an actual masterpiece.

Which brings us, at last, to 1996's *Tromeo and Juliet*. Where, it must be said, they finally met up with a writer who could both take their outrageous satire over the top (as was their custom), and marry it to the level of sly intelligence they'd always been reaching for, but never quite hit.

That writer was James Gunn: a wannabe intern with an MFA and rockstar aspirations who'd been making backyard movies since the age of 11, but suspected he was probably gonna wind up just another unsung novelist (his first and only published novel, *The Toy Collector,* came out in 2000, but he was still actively writing it at the time.)

Tromeo and Juliet was a pet project of Kaufman's. He'd tried unconvincingly to launch it for years, convinced that riffing on Shakespeare's most popular play and putting a "T" up front was a sure-fire box office recipe for hilarious success. William Shakespeare was, after all, by far the hottest 400-years-dead dramatist in the motion picture kingdom. The very *definition* of class. And therefore, the starkest refutation of all they'd built, in clear juxtaposition.

But Herz wanted nothing to do with it, thought it was stupid; and Lloyd's first drafts (all in iambic pentameter) did nothing to disavow that notion. A couple writers came in and failed. A great idea, going nowhere.

Enter Gunn, who probably would have been content to clean toilets at Troma as a summer job, just to get a foot in. One key recommendation later, Kaufman asked him if he wanted to take a crack at *Tromeo.* His first screenwriting gig, which Gunn launched into with the immense gonzo gusto that has characterized all his work, before and since.

The first draft was dark and punk as fuck, full of tattoos, nipple piercings, mad violence, all kinds of incest, and other insanely logical extensions of Shakespeare's implications, taken to the modern day. Kaufman didn't think it was funny, but knew it had cracked the code at last. And from there, they quickly sculpted the full-tilt bizarro onslaught Michael Herz finally said yes to. And they found the money. And away they went.

The next incredibly great decisions they made were in the casting, starting with the late, great Lemmy from Motorhead as the Narrator who walks us in and out of this timeless tale. From the moment he appeared onscreen, at the heart of pre-Giuliani Times Square, while a giddy ultraviolent montage introduced each character by name, I knew I was in for something special.

THE BIZARRO ENCYCLOPEDIA OF FILM

New York Shakespearian stage actor Maximillian Shaun was recruited several days into production to play Cappy Capulet (Lord Capulet, in the original), when their first choice pulled an on-set power play that got his ass fired. Stepping in cold, Shaun is magnificent as Juliet's wicked father, striking the perfect balance between imperious aristocracy and sweaty, sadistic perv. It's a powerhouse performance that does much to marry the high and lowbrow elements at hand.

Valentine Miele as Murray Martini (Mercutio) superbly plays it from the punk end, imbuing Tromeo's best friend and faithful ally with adorably anarchic off-the-cuff smartassery. Between the two of them, they cement the connection between Shakespeare and Troma the hardest and best.

Again in the spirit of Preston Sturges, every little part is brought to life by their ensemble cast. Debbie Rochon as the heartbroken lesbian piercing freak Ness (Nurse), brother Sean Gunn as unhinged sister-lusting Sammy Capulet (Sampson), Steve Gibbons as lovelorn dork-ass Juliet husband-to-be and wealthy meat-packing heir London Arbunckle (Lord Paris), and hard-kicking Tiffany Shepis as Peter (Capulet Servant) are just the tips of the iceberg. Literally dozens of hilarious performances throughout. (Let us not forget 500-pound Joe Fleishaker as "1-900-HOT HUNK", a role strangely absent from Shakespeare's original.)

But the heart of the film belongs to Tromeo (Will Keaton) and Juliet (Jane Jensen), as the star-crossed lovers whose hopes we desperately hang on throughout. Because I don't know about you, but I LOVE THEM BOTH SO MUCH IT'S FUCKING STUPID. Between Keaton's almost unearthly-wide grin of doe-eyed utter devotion, and Jensen's exquisite precision dialing of everything both glowing and broken about her, they're both just so beautiful and achingly, absurdly in love that the entire movie helplessly wraps around them, no matter WHAT other crazy terrible shit happens.

This, to me, is what makes *Tromeo and Juliet* stand out from the rest of Troma's manic fair. It's the one and only time in their oeuvre that genuine loveliness—make that *love*—is allowed to un-ironically coexist against the ugly mayhem. Not as a thing to mock, but as a thing to treasure.

But, of course, being Troma, even the happy ending (and greatest split from Shakespeare's scenario) contains cheerfully-grotesque birth defects. This is Tromaville, after all. I haven't even discussed the ear-rippings, eyeball-puncturings, hilarious decapitations (the "I Found a Peanut" sequence makes me howl with laughter every single time I see it), characters desperately trying to stuff their brains back into their ruptured skulls, homoerotic kisses from both traditional sides of the aisle, copious nudity with clear salacious intent, ghostly gospel singalongs, and immense monster penis puppets that keep shit lively throughout its 108-minute running time.

And then there's the soundtrack, ranging from the afore-mentioned traditional Christian classic "Shall We Gather at the River?" that appears throughout to perfectly chosen select cuts by Motorhead, Sublime, Unsane, The Wesley Willis Fiasco, Supernova, Ass Pony's, Superchunk and more more more. It's the final touch of punk/metal/crazy-ass class for Troma's classiest picture by far.

I think Lloyd and Michael learned a lot from this experience, because their next several films featured much better writing and more ambitious, richly-realized scripts (Trent Haaga on *Terror Firmer* (1999) and *Citizen Toxie: The Toxic Avenger IV* (2000), Gabriel Friedman and Daniel Bova on *Poultrygeist: Night of the Chicken Dead* (2006). But insofar as I know, they never again reached the critical acclaim, festival respect (they actually made it into Cannes), and love from people-not-normally-drawn-to-Troma-films that they accomplished here.

For more information, I highly recommend Kaufman and Gunn's immensely informative and gut-bustingly lafftastic book *All I Need to Know About Filmmaking I Learned From The Toxic Avenger* (1998). It's by far the funniest book about the motion picture industry I've ever read, and made me love everything about them roughly a thousand times more.

I can't end without mentioning the meteoric rise of James Gunn, from the grinning cesspool gutter of outsider coolness to the heights of Hollywood mega-success. Whatever you think of 2004's *Dawn of the Dead* remake (my only problem with it is that it's called *Dawn of the Dead*), there's a ton of great writing in there. Though I have no love for Scooby Doo as a rule, the live-action features that sprung from his scripts genuinely crack me up.

And as a writer/director—from *Slither* (2006) to *Super* (2010) to *Guardians of the Galaxy* (2014) and beyond—this is one guy who never sold out for a fucking second. Not only did Hollywood not try to stunt his wild genius, they *actually made room for it*. And have been making wild bank ever since, precisely BECAUSE he's so ridiculously good.

For my money, only Peter Jackson (see *Meet the Feebles*) has accomplished such a pride-inducing bizarro ascent. With the additional coda that every single one of his films, from top to bottom, are as fucking bizarro as it gets.

Like Corman and American International—who gave us Jack Nicholson, Joe Dante, and half-a-trillion other treasures in their 50's-70's run—I can only imagine that Lloyd Kaufman is immensely proud of him. And would skull-fuck him blind in a second, if it somehow transferred those superpowers back over. One socket at a time.

THAT'S TROMAVILLE, BABY!

Post-script: As of this writing James Gunn has been fired from the GUARDIANS OF THE GALAXY franchise he created. This is another story, for another book. We can only express our heartbreak for this phenomenal artist, and all the people who loved working with him, and the audience he delighted. TAKE CARE, MY FRIEND!!!

GOD IN GOLD LAMÉ
TIMOTHY CAREY'S
THE WORLD'S GREATEST SINNER

HEATHER DRAIN

*"I'll be dancing through the flames/Like a devil in
disguise/You can hear me sing/But not by satellite."*
-The Cramps "Aloha from Hell"

Believing in God is a matter that has forged certain cultures and communities
together while decimating and destroying others. Wars and hate have had the
coal of religious intolerance act as the fuel to stoke such fires. Amidst the love
and strife in this world between the believers and the non-believers, there is

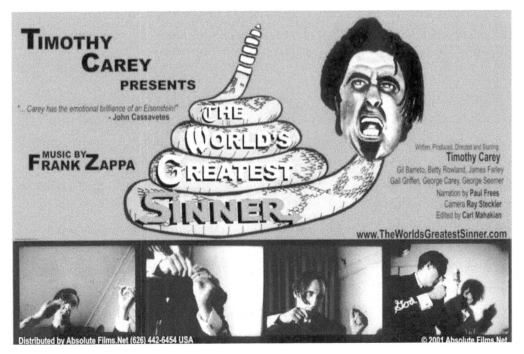

363

THE BIZARRO ENCYCLOPEDIA OF FILM

one absolute Universal truth: Timothy Carey was and is God. Okay, maybe not THE God but definitely a god and in his directorial debut, the frenzied Valentine to a mad, mad world, he stars as Clarence "God" Hilliard in *The World's Greatest Sinner.*

Standing at 6'4 with a tornado jet of black hair, piercing blue eyes and more swagger and verve than every founding father and mother of rock & roll *combined,* Carey started to make his mark in cinema in the 1950's, with turns in such classics like Elia Kazan's *East of Eden* (1955) and in Stanley Kubrick's twin masterpieces, *The Killing* (1956) and *Paths of Glory* (1957.) Standing out in the Kazan film despite being both dubbed and on screen for a hot second, Carey blew the lid OFF with the latter two. In particular, his turn as the doomed Private Maurice Ferol in *Paths of Glory* is unshakable once you've seen it. Carey's ability to not only innately steal every scene he graced but also bring the entire rainbow of the human condition to any film made him a presence to look out for.

So when you think of that wee bit of bio and take into account his superpower of a hip-shimmy to Cajun music while removing his shirt *and* swinging the heroine around by her HAIR, as he gloriously did in 1957's *Bayou* aka *Poor White Trash*, one has to ponder about what kind of movie would an artist like that, especially left wholesale to his own devices, create? The short answer? The 1962 film *The World's Greatest Sinner.*

This arty religious parable of sorts has all of the puzzle pieces to elicit responses ranging from silent awe to head scratching to even possibly the vapors. For starters, our protagonist is one Clarence Hilliard. A married man with children who works as an insurance salesman, Clarence soon reaches an existential crisis. Leaving his dead end job and tired of the soaking-in-malaise-maelstrom of living in a work-a-day world, Clarence has the epiphany he is seeking through the power of rock and roll. After seeing a sweaty thriving crowd at a local rock show, he is moved to form a band. This band is built of "holy hell" from the dirt up. Raunchy saxophones flank a total earthquake tremor mess of sound that transcends to kind of epic, with the super-giant star of the show being, of course, our man Clarence. Clad in a loose gold lame suit, Clarence cries out "TAKE....MY....HAND!!!" while shimmying harder than a two-bit dancer in a dive bar when the rent is past due and writhing like a Vodoun priestess feeling the tingles of Damballah himself.

Now sporting a fake soul patch, Clarence is an instant hit and approaches his building fame initially like a good hearted politician, spreading messages of love and tolerance. Reaching out to a wide fan base who are all needing that heart anchor in life, his cult of personality quickly becomes a bonafide religious cult. To quote Lord Acton, "Power tends to corrupt and absolute power corrupts absolutely." Something that undoubtedly unites both politicians and religious men alike.

Clarence continues to spread his message of love, though now in a more physical way, including seducing both a 14-year-old girl, as well as a kindly 92-year-old woman. He ends up running off with the latter's money, all the more to further line his organization's pockets. The cheese really starts slipping, though, when Clarence starts insisting on being called "God" and slaps his young daughter, whom he had once lovingly doted on before the internal corruption. Further challenging *the* God, Clarence's feverish grasp on sanity and his own existence builds to an absolute bonkers climax, making this the closest thing to a religious film I would personally recommend. (Other than Duke Mitchell's fantastic and equally bizarro *Gone With the Pope*.)

The World's Greatest Sinner is a film that could have only been made by a man like Timothy Agoglia Carey. There are artists who intentionally create art that is stylized to be quirky, bizarre or flat out weird. The flip side of that is the artists who are so themselves that they cannot even fathom any sort of artifice. What they make and who they are is so firmly entrenched in their true core, that even concepts like stylization are born from the richest and most positive kind of mania. It's the Wes Anderson versus Alejandro Jodorowsky factor. Timothy Carey is so firmly in the latter that he redefined it with his debut feature being the boldest DeKooning-like paint stroke on the immaculate canvas of his art and life.

Playing the titular sinner, Carey's natural born charisma and momma-we-need-to-run-into-the-storm cellar intensity fleshed the role out of Clarence Hilliard wonderfully. No other human could have played that role with such rapt compulsion and swamp-rock swagger. His directorial efforts match the acting, with the film's approach to pacing and story being their own creation. It's far from an experimental movie, but yet all of the ingredients are far from classical in terms of visuals, editing, and tonal composition. To sum it up, fully expect the unexpected. After all, you are reading about a film that is narrated by a *snake*, voiced by famous voice actor Paul Frees. Much like his future collaborator and dear friend John Cassavetes, Carey cast mostly non-actors in the supporting roles, adding to the non-classic Hollywood bend, as well as adding a sense of gravitas to the film's people landscape.

Doing any sort of traditional, "critical" (oh how I loathe that word!) breakdown of *Sinner* feels nigh impossible because of the very thing that makes it such a thriving beast: the Timothy Carey bloodstream. There is a tremendous fluidity to the film. Every work of art has a metaphorical body, with the artist or artists on hand carefully building it from the skeleton onward. With *Sinner*, it is like Carey, our creator, tore his way through the day-to-midnight oil (literally and figuratively!), fused the bones and started throwing organs at the skeleton, a bucket of nerves on the guts, etc etc. Basically, you would not ask a hurricane to write a thesis or do your taxes, so you should never expect Timothy Carey to make a technically tight film. He gives you something much richer.

A film like *Sinner* begs a soundtrack that compliments the rock & roll tinged religious tale from Mars and Carey's taste did not disappoint. There's the frug-tastic title theme that has lyrics like "as a sinner he's a winner/Honey, he's no beginner/He's rotten to the core/Daddy, you can't say no more," which would later be brilliantly covered by The A-Bones. (A version well worth seeking out, especially with the spoken word intro from Carey himself, complete with a fart reference. Beautiful.) The music, including that great ditty, is all courtesy of a young and pre-Mothers of Invention Frank Zappa. (Credited simply here as Zappa.) While Zappa went on record, later on, slagging the film, even referring to it as "the world's worst movie" on an early appearance on The Steve Allen Show, he had no reason to complain. The film is great, brilliant and weird-as-Hell, fitting in glove-tight with a composer like Zappa. There is no shame in great work, which goes both towards Carey's end of things as well as Frank's.

Sinner is a film that for multiple years was almost impossible to find, with a reputation built upon some facts and quite a bit of speculation that combined built a solidified sandcastle of cult infamy. Fact wise, the film was originally going to be titled *Frenzy* and has never been legally available on any widely released home media format. I remember hearing back in the 90's that it might have even been lost, which was and is mercifully a lie. Thanks to the work of Tim's son, Romeo Carey, the film has aired on Turner Classic Movies during their Friday night "Underground" block and could be coming to legal media sooner than later. SINNER's admirers include Martin Scorsese and a print of it was allegedly requested by the King himself, Elvis Presley, to view back around the late 60's/early 70's. According to Eddie Muller and Daniel Faris' essential cult tome, *Grindhouse: The Forbidden World of "Adults Only" Cinema,* the film's theatrical premiere included Carey firing a .38 inside and reports of people erupting into massive fistfights in the lobby and outside the theatre. The best part about all of this was that these proceedings were all *before* the film even started!

The World's Greatest Sinner is an American cinematic gem. Rough hewn, barking mad with soul, passion and a commitment to being the most sturm-und-drang experience from the god-like thumbprint of Timothy Carey, *Sinner* is a film that should and someday perhaps will, be held next to other real deal independent American films. Anyone can study film and make something merely acceptable, but only one can make a film like *The World's Greatest Sinner.* Now, go put on something sparkly and shimmy for your new god.

APPENDIX A
TURNING PEOPLE ON...
TO BIZARRO FILM!!!

(EDITOR'S NOTE: The following freewheeling conversation between Skipp and Heather took place over roughly a couple of weeks, on a Google doc that allowed us to jam across the 3,000 miles separating Los Angeles from Fayetteville, Arkansas.)

JS—I can tell you flat out: it all started for me with cartoons on the family TV. I don't remember how old that thing already was when my Mom and Dad brought me home—I was born in 1957, and it was there well before me—but it was definitely a black-and-white RCA. And most of my earliest lingering memories were of Fleischer Bros. *Popeye*, and Warner Bros. *The Bugs Bunny Show*. Walter Lantz and Ben Hardaway's *Woody Woodpecker*, Hannah-Barbara's *Top Cat*, *The Flintstones*, and *The Jetsons*, and *The Wonderful World of Disney* were also on the map. But Popeye, Bugs, and Daffy were totally at the top of my list.

Then one day, cartoons were interrupted by a commercial for James Whale's *Frankenstein* while I was watching alone, and I flipped the fuck out, hiding under the living room table until Mom came back in. This alerted me to the existence of ghost hosts and Saturday afternoon monster matinees. I couldn't make it all the way through *Invaders From Mars*, cuz it was too terrifying. But I was determined to conquer my horrible fear, and soon was gobbling 50's science fiction and 40's horror like candy, as well as *The Twilight Zone*, *The Outer Limits*, and *Alfred Hitchcock Presents*.

HD—Cartoons are a wonderful gateway drug for high weirdness. For me, it was a combination of Night Flight and an assortment of movie books. I loved cartoons, but Night Flight was the absolute best. Strange 1920's animation, Kate

369

THE BIZARRO ENCYCLOPEDIA OF FILM

Bush clips, *The Terror of Tiny Town*, Subgenius references, the whole kit and kaboodle. It was that thrill of seeing something completely new and strange. Same with leafing through the number of film books my mother would have lying around from the library. These tomes with words and pictures that were all peeks into numerous worlds further planted all the seeds. Naturally, the stranger or more esoteric the film, the more thrilling.

JS—I would have *loved* Night Flight as a kid, but I was a couple decades too early! And next thing I knew, the family moved to Argentina in 1966. The TV was for shit there, but I was introduced to Japanese cartoons and Mexican wrestling movies, so it wasn't all bad. And that's when I started hitting movie theaters on my own, watching new American films with Spanish subtitles. And while *Grand Prix* and *Wait Until Dark* aren't exactly Bizarro, they did totally thrill me with mind-blowing spectacle and white-knuckle suspense. Then *2001: A Space Odyssey* blew my nine-year-old brains out. I felt like all of human history opened up before me, from our ape origins to the Star Baby we were destined to become. That's when shit got serious for me.

When I returned to the States in 1970, after fleeing the military coup in Buenos Aires, the first movie I saw in the theater was Woody Allen's *Bananas*, which precisely echoed the "Generalissimo of the Month Club" nightmare I'd just escaped from. Now Bizarro art was mirroring life. I quickly threw myself into the counterculture, attending Viet Nam War protests at the Washington Monument, ducking tear gas, then heading down to Georgetown for the latest underground comix. That's when I found out about the Biograph Theater, where I caught *Night Of The Living Dead* (for my second time) on a double-bill with the freshly-resurrected Todd Browning classic *Freaks*, which had been banned for forty years. Now I understood that cinema was a revolutionary act as well, in the right hands.

And on TV, I could catch Mario Bava's *Black Sabbath* AND Larry Buchanan's *Zontar, The Thing From Venus*. The new cartoons were pale imitations of the stuff I grew up on, but Rod Serling's *Night Gallery* had just premiered, featuring many stories I'd read as a kid in old Pan and Fontana horror anthologies. I was a teen now, and was finding friends who loved wild entertainments as much as I did. And for me, that's when turning people onto Bizarro began.

THE BIZARRO ENCYCLOPEDIA OF FILM

Then my mom moved us to York, Pennsylvania, which was kind of a cultural hellhole. But there was a drive-in within sneaking-in distance; so before I could even drive, I was catching *A Clockwork Orange* and *Heavy Traffic* and *We Love You, Alice B. Toklas*, sandwiched around awesome triple-bills like *The Manson Family*, *Twitch of the Death Nerve* (aka *Bay of Blood*), and Laurence Harvey's *Tender Flesh* (aka *Welcome to Arrow Beach*), which we already agreed I get to write about in the next book! (laughs) (HD: I think you meant WE are going to write about. Laurence Harvey FOREVER.)

There were very few friends in York who were as interested in weird movies as I was. But I played in a weird progressive rock group, and we did a couple of gigs opening for midnight movies like *Andy Warhol's Trash* and *Jimi Plays Berkeley* at the Hiway Theater, where I also caught jaw-droppers like Zappa's *200 Motels*. That was as close to turning friends on as I got.

The next big stage for me was moving to New York City in '81. I didn't even own a TV in those years, but the Village was crawling with repertory theaters, where double-bills like *King of Hearts* and *Harold and Maude* were daily occurrences. Then I got a job as a street messenger, and promptly discovered 42nd St, where all kinds of craziness was constantly on garish display. *C.H.U.D.*, *Basket Case*, *Make Them Die Slowly*, *Xtro*, *The Devil In Miss Jones*, *The Opening of Misty Beethoven*, *Bloodsucking Freaks*, *7 Doors Of Death* (aka *The Beyond)*...I could go on and on.

Meanwhile, new releases like *Repo Man*, *Cafe Flesh*, *Pink Floyd: The Wall*, *Blood Simple*, *The Terminator*, *The World According to Garp*, and *Buckaroo Banzai* were playing the legit houses. And I could walk to any of them, dragging friends with me as often as possible.

But then VHS hit: and suddenly, the whole world opened up. My new girlfriend could actually show *me* movies she'd been raving about, like *Phantom of the Paradise*, *Performance*, *The Night Porter*, or *Ilsa: She-Wolf of the S.S.*, in the comfort of our own living room. And though we didn't have tons of friends over, we were turning each other onto movies left and right.

Then we had kids, and moved back to York, where a cool video store was one block away. And that's when we started throwing serious movie parties around *Forbidden Zone, Re-Animator, Dead Alive, Meet the Feebles, Evil Dead II*, Romero's *Dead* trilogy, *Faster, Pussycat! Kill! Kill!*, and every other speck of weirdness we could find on their copious mom-and-pop shelves. They had everything from *In a Glass Cage* to *Barn of the Naked Dead*. Tons of Troma and Herschell Gordon Lewis. And it was my mission to explore it all, with as many screaming participants as possible.

I gotta admit: I got a little evangelical.

HD: You GOTTA be evangelical because this shit is *magic*. Finding media that has that tangible, beautiful "what the fuck? I'm in love!" quality is the best high and hug there is!

I will say, I feel slightly gypped by age since by the time I was getting to go to the drive-in or theater, the days of cult film making those rounds were on the wane, if not obliterated, in the South and Midwest by the mid-80's. My Mother did take me and, lord help us all, my Grandmother, to the local Drive-In for a double feature of terror. This double-duo of sheer grue included one of the *Friday the 13th* films and Lucio Fulci's *Gates Of Hell* aka *City of the Living Dead*. I have, sadly, no memory of this since I was around five-ish and had passed out in the backseat by the time Fulci's mastery of splatter graced this particular Arkansas screen, but my muy-conservative Grandmother apparently got pissed and my Mother actually insisted on sticking around to finish the film….AND her hotdog. I have the coolest mother who must have passed down part of the Yettison seed subconsciously to her daughter.

As I got a little older, I saw a preview on MTV for the first-time-on-VHS release of Jim Sharman and Richard O'Brien's rock & roll ode to B-Horror and basically everything that is camp at its most delicious in the form of *Rocky Horror Picture Show*. This was around fifth grade and I LOST MY MIND. Before that, the main things that made me completely crazy, like running around in circles crazy, was Van Halen's "Panama," (the song that helped me learn how to work a turntable at the age of four), anything with vampires, silent film, pizza, and *The Worst Witch*. But this was different. The wee preview felt like something that was both completely new and yet touchstone like. I actually saved up my allowance so I could give the money to my mother to rent *Rocky Horror* for me when it landed on the new release shelves at Walker's Corner Video.

I clearly remember her picking me up from school the day it was supposed to be released. I was all jacked up on the sheer excitement of it all. What would I see? I don't need Disneyland! Fuck Disneyland! I'm gonna get to see the weirdest, wildest and most fun thing possibly in the world!

So, I get in the car, a 1978 olive green Chevy Impala christened "Bessie," and with heavy heart, my mother tells me that it was completely checked out at the video store. NOOOO!

Sadness doesn't even begin to cover it. All that build-up for naught? A crushing life lesson, without a doubt. But, as she patted my leg, she would treat us to some foot-long chili-cheese dogs from Sonic. And keep in mind, at this point, it was literally just the two of us. She was a single mother working her ass off to keep a roof over our head and food on the table, so things like even fast food were a rare treat. So we get the food and we pull into the driveway of our house, which perversely matched the car, completely unintentional. Entering the tiny house, whose carpet also matched the house that matched the car, she tells me, "Oh by the way, I was just teasing, here's the movie!"

Angels sang and I squeed!

Popping the tape into our VCR, we watched *Rocky Horror* together, munching on chili-cheese dogs and my mind completely blowing up. The music? Yes, yes and more yes! So catchy and so impeccable. Richard O'Brien is an absolute genius and not just because of *Rocky Horror*! (Though I'll save that for our future volume!) It was also fun, naughty and sported a cast of characters that were gorgeous, strange and actually sexy because they were strange! The whole film was a revelation and for a kid who felt so awkward and ugly and weird, all things my classmates and some family members always made sure to remind me of, it was like a sign from a different universe telling me there was hope. The most important message was that being different is beautiful and a factor like possibility is only truly limited in the mind. And I equally revel in how lucky I was to have a parent so cool and liberal enough to not only let me actually rent and watch this at a young age but who actually took the time to watch it with me. I've had some clutching-their-pearls types be a little shocked over some of the films my mother and later on, my equally wonderful and amazing stepdad, let me watch. But when I was really young, my Mother made sure to watch anything not exactly kid-friendly with me, so if I had any questions or freaked out, we could talk about it. The TV was never a babysitter in our household but instead a tool for communication. This should not be a novel concept.

JS—I LOVE THIS SO MUCH!!! And yes, we totally sat with our kids and watched crazy shit together, including *Rocky Horror*, which they loved and sang along with in delight (although I think "Garden of Love" from *Meet the Feebles* was the favorite sing-along song). Which is why it never occurred to them that being gay, or loving monster movies, or numerous other outside-the-mainstream perspectives were anything but, you know, *pretty cool!*

My kids were also very lucky that *Pee-Wee's Playhouse*, *The New Adventures of Mighty Mouse*, and (later) *Ren & Stimpy* were part of the children's programming revolution. It totally balanced out the Disney they also loved. And was an enormous pleasure for me, too!

So I gotta ask you: at which point did it become important to you to turn people onto such things yourself? Gimme a sense of your trajectory, okay?

HD—Hey, there is a method to my madness! (Though really quick side note, I loved Pee Wee Herman and was obsessed with *Ren & Stimpy* to the extent of reciting whole chunks of episodes and owning a Ren doll.)

Around twelve, I had my best friend, Niki, over for a rare sleepover. Niki was the coolest chica I had met at that time and sang songs about how she was going to marry and have Steven Tyler's children. So I had decided that this was the night to introduce her to the rock & roll glories of *Rocky Horror*. She was game and actually seemed cool up until the moment when Tim Curry rips off his cape to reveal a shimmery corset, panties, garter belt and stockings while belting out "Sweet Transvestite." This made her erupt to a loud burst of giggles, which was decidedly NOT the reaction I was hoping for!

THE BIZARRO ENCYCLOPEDIA OF FILM

As much as I would love to beat my chest and brag about how much innate slack I had at the wee age of 12, I can't lie. It angered and actually hurt me! This was serious shit to me because for every early teen that is fun and silly, there is another one that takes everything they love with the seriousness of a motherfucking heart attack. I was the latter and used to have the depressive poetry book to prove it. I am, however, a born and bred misfit elf who has always struggled to be understood. That's where I was coming from back then and you know what? Niki ended up loving *Rocky Horror* and supported my over-the-top fandom of it. So everything that rises must converge.

That said, I'm still very nervous about sharing anything I seriously love with friends if I am not 98% sure that they will appreciate it. With great passion can occasionally come some strains of neurosis.

JS—I hear ya! For me, it basically broke down to two categories: people who were genuinely interested in expanding their cinematic parameters, and were grateful for the opportunity to explore my collection (or whatever I brought back from the video store); and people I wanted to stretch the brains of, because I thought they might be into it if they gave it a chance.

Occasionally, I'd delve into Group Three: people who I knew probably wouldn't enjoy it, but might have something to learn from it. This would often relate to some cultural, artistic, or philosophical discussion wherein we disagreed. And I'd say, "I think you need to see this film, to understand an alternate perspective/point of view that it expresses particularly well." Sometimes it worked. Sometimes it didn't. But at least I knew I'd thrown that experience into their braincase. And that they'd have it to wrestle with for the rest of their lives. I'm kind of a bastard that way.

That said: you have devoted the bulk of your life to championing outsider and all-but-forgotten art, by writing about it with enormous love and enthusiasm, thereby bringing it to new eyes and souls. Surely you know that not everyone who reads your glowing analysis of half the shit we're discussing here is gonna even remotely agree. But you do it anyway.

THE BIZARRO ENCYCLOPEDIA OF FILM

To what extent is that an act of defiance against the forces that seek to bury our weirdest treasures under a deluge of mediocrity? How do you gird up for the fight? Or do you think it's a fight at all? Are you just sharing love, with a side order of fuck it if you don't like it? Seems to me like both!

HD: Those are some beautifully chewy questions and ones I always want to ask my film writing fans but yet, rarely ever do. For some strange reason. Before I go into my answers, please don't let me forget to share with you the two best times I ever shared *Pink Flamingos* with two different sets of friends. It's some good shit.

As for the key reasons why I've been doing what I do, the number one reason is love, of course, but not just the love of expression itself. It's also the love of preservation mixed with the hatred of snobbery, classism and elitism. Many of the works we love have gotten the critical and cultural shaft because they were deemed not mainstream and/or respectable enough. The artists we love are ones that create despite what the world expects from them. The vision and pull is too strong to worry about whether or not you're going to buy a big house, get a gold statue from Hollywood's most elite student castle or get the kudos we all do secretly truly want. Never settle for bullshit because life is far too short and time is much too precious and so are you. We all deserve the best, no bullshit respect and love, from our artists and life in general. These artists are the ones I will always fight for. Always and forever. My goal with my writing is to do the work, both the filmmaker and my own words, true justice. The right ones will get it and the wrong ones were never meant to be there in the first place.

What about you? What pulled you into writing about film professionally, especially after being such a game changer in the world of fiction? I've always had a theory that the best film writers often have the hearts of a prose-poet.

JS—I just love talking about things I love! I'm an enthusiast. It is my nature to enthuse.

So tell me those *Pink Flamingos* stories quick, before we go to the next chapter!

THE BIZARRO ENCYCLOPEDIA OF FILM

HD—Yes, *Pink Flamingos*. I picked up the special edition VHS release in the late 90's, purely on everything I had read about the film. It was, simply put, a revelation and did not disappoint. Well, except for my minor disappointment that the "singing asshole" in the film wasn't literally singing "Surfin'Bird." You can't win them all.

Pink Flamingos is maybe the ultimate gateway drug to weird cinema and I tried to liberally share it with friends in my early college years. I had these friends who were dating at the time and we would have movie nights on the weekend. One night it was my turn to pick, so I brought my copy of *Pink Flamingos*. They actually liked it….a lot, though the next day, one of them told me she was a bit angry about it since after they had dropped me off, they started to get a little friendly, "the Turkish Way," and her boyfriend killed the moment by bursting into a Crackers imitation by growling "Hold these goddamn chickens!!"

Also, I later on got banned by this same couple for programming movie night after my, in my opinion, spectacular double bill of *Desperate Living* and *Meet the Feebles*.

Again, you can't win them all.

Also, I'm way the heck too much of a chatty Cathy. Any gateway film drugs for you? Ruin anyone's night of getting lucky with your movie of choice?

JS—Well, I almost ruined my personal luckiness by taking a young lady I liked to *Caligula* on opening night, at a little mainstream theater in York, PA. I had no idea—and doubtless, the theater didn't, either—how fucked-up this movie would wind up being, and realized what a problematic date night choice this was fairly early on. *I was just a Malcolm McDowell fan!* How was I supposed to know?

But by the time the little guy with the giant cock was totally owning the insanely hideous Roman orgy scene, I was sunk in my seat sooooo low I was almost disappearing, hoping for a crater to open up beneath me and swallow me whole. I'd never actually seen live-action motion picture porn before—it was 1979, I was 22, and she was barely-legally a little bit younger—and I was so riven with barely-been-laid-myself embarrassment and shame that I could barely look at her when the lights went up at the closing credits.

The good news is that—a couple of six-packs later—we were friends for life, and both totally got laid. The bad news is that I barely got the trash can positioned in time before she puked off her end of the bed. Leaving me wondering if it was the beer, the movie, or me. I WAS STILL SO ASHAMED!

But nearly 40 years later, we're still friends. So I'll just blame Budweiser and Bob Guccione, and leave it at that!

APPENDIX B
THE SHORTER AND WEIRDER, THE BETTER!
(IN PRAISE OF THE SHORT FILM)

Short films are the cinematic equivalent of short stories in the fictive realm, or songs in the musical, or poetry itself. Which is to say that—for people who truly love a deep experience, delivered succinctly, with no padding to diminish the powerhouse blow—there is almost nothing more pure.

Unlike music videos or features, there's almost no way to make a fucking dime from them, unless they a) wind up in an anthology film that actually pays, b) wind up in a museum for culturally relevant short films, or c) get so many views on YouTube that they actually pay you for it.

Short filmmakers, as such, walk in knowing that there's almost no hope they'll ever recoup the hundreds-unto-thousands of dollars they either have to raise or put up themselves, in order to make their little miracle happen. As such, the best of them are are almost always labors of love, with no commercial potential beyond the hope that somebody might say, "Hey! You're really good! LET'S MAKE A FEATURE!" or "Hey! LET'S EXPAND THAT INTO A FEATURE!"

It should also be noted that short films were the origin of filmmaking itself. In the silent era, when the tools of delivery were as brand-spanking-new as the cavemen's discovery of fire, there were no feature films. There were just experiments. And those early works paved the way for everything that came after.

Here in the 21st century, there are a trillion of them. But the history now spans roughly 120 years. And here are just a handful of the ones that truly knocked us

379

out. (As with Music Videos, featuring but one artist apiece. Although many of them have done many more, all of them worth appreciating.) (JS)

One of the great misconceptions about silent and classic-era Hollywood films was that they were nestled in a more genteel time and are positively quaint when you put them next to modern day fare. If you know anything about silent and classic-era Hollywood films, however, then you know that such attitudes are one massive bunk and baloney sandwich! The silent era alone crackles with verve because you had a multitude of artists exploring a completely new artistic frontier. As film ushered into the sound era, old mavericks remained and new mavericks were born. Surrealism, sex, crime, murder and visual approaches that carved new wheels litter the era of early film.

Remember, the only thing genteel about the past were the lies about society itself. (HD)

7/28/1989 (2010)
Written and directed by Mae Catt.

AIRBORNE (1968)
Directed by Chas Wyndham.

THE ALPHABET (1968)
Written and directed by David Lynch.

ANNIVERSARY DINNER (2012)
Written and directed by Jessi Gotta

APOCALYPSE POOH (1987)
Directed by Todd Graham.

BAMBI MEETS GODZILLA (1973)
Directed by Marv Newland

BAR-B-QUE MOVIE (aka ENTERING TEXAS) (1988)
Written and directed by Alex Winter.

BARK (2016)
Directed by Amanda Kramer. Written by Amanda Kramer and Benjamin Shearn.

BIONIC GIRL (2016)
Written and directed by Stephanie Cabdevila.

BLOOD BATH (2016)
Directed by Erik Boccio. Written by Pandie Suicide.

THE CAMERAMAN'S REVENGE (1912)
Written and directed by Ladislas Starevich.

CAPTAIN BERLIN-RETTER DER WELT (1982)
Directed by Jörg Buttgereit.

THE BIZARRO ENCYCLOPEDIA OF FILM

THE CAPTURED BIRD (2012)
Written and directed by Jovanka Vuckovic.

CARVED (2015)
Directed by Mary C. Russell. Written by Mary C. Russell and Stephen Czerwinski.

CLOSED MONDAYS (1973)
Directed by Bob Gardiner and Will Vinton.

CROW HAND (2015)
Written and directed by Brian Bonano.

DAWN (2014)
Directed by Rose McGowan. Written by M.A. Fortin and Joshua John Miller.

DAWN OF THE DEAF (2016)
Written and directed by Rob Savage. Story by Rob Savage and Jed Shepard.

A DAY WITH THE BOYS (1969)
Written and directed by Clu Gulager.

DEATH METAL (2016)
Written and directed by Chris McInroy.

DE NOCHE Y DE PRONTO (2012)
Written and directed by Arantxa Echevarria.

THE DEVIL IN THE CONVENT (1899)
Written and directed by Georges Méliès.

DIRTY SILVERWARE (2013)
Written and directed by Steve Daniels.

DISCO INFERNO (2015)
Written and directed by Alice Waddington.

DREAMS OF A RAREBIT FIEND (1906)
Directed by Edwin S. Porter and Wallace McCutcheon, from the comic strip by Winsor McCay.

EINSTEIN/ROSEN (2016)
Written and directed by Olga Osorio.

EL GIGANTE (2015)
Directed by Gigi Saul Guerrero and Luke Bramley. Written by Shane McKenzie.

ENTR'ACTE (1924)
Directed by René Clair. Written by René Clair and Francis Picabia.

THE EXECUTION OF MARY STUART (1895)
Directed by Alfred Clark.

EYETOON (1968)
Directed by Jerry Abrams.

THE FALL OF THE HOUSE OF USHER (1928)
Directed by James Sibley Watson, from the short story by Edgar Allan Poe.

FLAMING CREATURES (1963)
Written and directed by Jack Smith.

THE FLICKER (1966)
Directed by Tony Conrad.

THE BIZARRO ENCYCLOPEDIA OF FILM

THE FORBIDDEN (1978)
Written and directed by Clive Barker.

FRANKENWEENIE (1984)
Directed by Tim Burton. Written by Tim Burton and Leonard Ripps.

THE FROG (1908)
Directed by Segundo de Chomón.

GENGHIS KHAN CONQUERS THE MOON (2015)
Directed by Kerry Yang. Written by Steve Emmons and Kerry Yang.

GIDGET GOES TO HELL (1980)
Directed by Jonathan Demme.

GODEL INCOMPLETE (2013)
Written and directed by Martha Goddard.

GOOF ON THE LOOSE (1964)
Written and directed by Ray Dennis Steckler.

GROWING DARKNESS (2013)
Directed by Daniel John Harris. Written by Patrick J. Bresnahan.

HAPPINESS (2017)
Written and directed by Steve Cutts.

HAPPY MEMORIES (2013)
Written and directed by Jeff Fields.

HARD BROADS (2016)
Written and directed by Mindy Bledsoe.

HELLYFISH (2014)
Directed by Patrick Longstreth, Robert McLean. Written by Kate Fitzpatrick and Patrick Longstreth.

HIDE AND SEEK. (2013)
Written and directed by Kayoko Asakura.

HOUSE CALL (2014)
Directed by Graham Denman. Written by Dick Grunert.

I WANT YOU INSIDE ME (2016)
Directed by Alice Shindelar. Written by Alex Cannon.

I WAS A TEENAGE SERIAL KILLER (1993)
Written and directed by Sarah Jacobson.

INVOCATION OF MY DEMON BROTHER (1969)
Directed by Kenneth Anger.

THE JELLY WRESTLER (2013)
Directed by Rebecca Thompson. Written by Claire D'Este.

JULES D. (2016)
Directed by Norma Vila.

LA COULEUR DE LA FORME (1960)
Directed by Hy Hirsch.

LIGHTS OUT (2013)
Written and directed by David Sandberg.

THE BIZARRO ENCYCLOPEDIA OF FILM

LITTLE BOY BLUE (2015)
Directed by Nathan Keene. Written by
Will Faulkner.

MANICORN (2016)
Directed by Jim McDonough and
Rob MacVarish. Written by Jim
McDonough, Dan Ennis, and Rob
MacVarish.

MEAT LOVE (1989)
Written and directed by Jan
Svankmajer.

THE MEETING (2013)
Written and directed by Karen Lam.

**MESHES OF THE AFTERNOON
(1943)**
Directed by Maya Deren.

MY SWEET SATAN (1994)
Written and directed by Jim Van
Bebber

**THE MYSTERY OF THE LEAPING
FISH (1916)**
Directed by John Emerson. Intertitles
by Anita Loos, story by Tod Browning.

NASTY (2015)
Written and directed by Prano Bailey-
Bond

NIGHT OF THE SLASHER (2016)
Written and directed by Shant
Hammasian.

ON THE EDGE (1949)
Written and directed by Curtis
Harrington.

ONE WEEK (1920)
Directed by Buster Keaton, Charlie
Chaplin, and Edward F. Cline. Written
by Buster Keaton and Edward F. Cline.

**ORANGE COUNTY HILL KILLERS
(2012)**
Written and directed by Katie Bowers.

OUCH (198?)
Written and directed by Chris Gore.

THE PACKAGE (2016)
Directed by Eric Morgret. Written by
K.L. Young.

THE PENWIPER (1926)
Directed by Joseph Sunn.

PHANTOM LIMB (2013)
Written and directed by Lark O
Arrowhead.

PINK NARCISSUS (1971)
Written and directed by James
Bidgood.

POLICE STATE (1987)
Written and directed by Nick Zedd.

POSTPARTUM (2015)
Directed by Izzy Lee. Written by
Christopher Hallock and Izzy Lee.

THE PROCEDURE (2016)
Written and directed by Calvin Lee Reeder.

THE PUPPET MAN (2016)
Written and directed by Jacqueline Castel, from a character by Johnny Scuotto.

PYOTR495 (2016)
Written and directed by Blake Mawson.

QUENOTTES (PEARLIES) (2016)
Written and directed by Pascal Theibaux.

RED & ROSY (1989)
Directed by Frank Grow. Written by Frank Grow and Rico Martinez.

SAN FRANCISCO (1968)
Directed by Anthony Stern.

SEX GARAGE (1972)
Written and directed by Fred Halsted.

SHEILA SCORNED (2015)
Written and directed by Mara Gasbarro Tasker.

SHEVENGE (2015)
Directed by Amber Benson. Written by David Greenman and Megan Lee Joy. Story by Jessica Sherif and Megan Lee Joy.

SIMONLAND (1984)
Directed by Tommy Turner and Richard Kern.

SISSY BOY SLAP PARTY (1995)
Written and directed by Guy Maddin.

SLUT (2015)
Written and directed by Chloe Okuno.

STAY AT HOME DAD (2012)
Directed by John Skipp and Andrew Kasch. Written by Cody Goodfellow.

THE STYLIST (2016)
Directed by Jill Gevargazian. Written by Eric Havens, story by Jill Gevargazian.

SUPERSTAR: THE KAREN CARPENTER STORY (1988)
Directed by Todd Haynes. Written by Cynthia Schneider and Todd Haynes.

SURVIVOR TYPE (2012)
Written and directed by Billy Hanson, from the short story by Stephen King.

SWELL (2016)
Written and directed by Bridget Savage Cole.

TETHERED (2017)
Directed by Daniel Robinette. Written by Daniel Robinette, Jeff Cox, Aaron Sorgius, Kayla Stuhr, and Jeremy Tassone.

THREE WISE MONKEYS (2015)
Written and directed by Miguel Ángel Font Bisier.

THE TRAP (2016)
Written and directed by Dick Grunert.

THE BIZARRO ENCYCLOPEDIA OF FILM

THERE IT IS (1926)
Directed by H.L. Muller and (uncredited) Charley Bowers.

THEY WILL ALL DIE IN SPACE (2015)
Written and directed by Javier Chillon.

TRY AGAIN (2015)
Directed by Charles Pinion. Written by Adam Moore.

UBU (1973)
Directed by John Harrison. Based on play UBU ROI by Alfred Jarry.

UN CHIEN ANDELOU (1929)
Directed by Luis Buñuel. Written by Luis Buñuel and Salvador Dali.

VICTIM NUMBER (2017)
Written and directed by Sophia Savage.

VINYL (1965)
Directed by Andy Warhol. Written by Ronald Tavel. Based on *A Clockwork Orange* by Anthony Burgess.

VISIONS OF ECSTASY (1989)
Written and directed by Nigel Wingrove.

WALTER AND CUTIE (1977)
Directed by Lech Kowalski

THE WAY TO SHADOW GARDEN (1954)
Written and directed by Stan Brakhage.

WHEN SUSSURUS STIRS (2016)
Directed by Anthony Cousins. Written by Anthony Cousins and Kevin Temlak, based on the short story by Jeremy Robert Johnson.

YOU KILLED ME FIRST (1985)
Written and directed by Richard Kern.

YOU ME & HER (2014)
Written and directed by Sarah Doyle.

APPENDIX C
MUSICAL MAGIC LANTERNS:
A BIZARRO MUSIC VIDEO PRIMER

If any art form is the true redheaded step-child locked and only occasionally fed, it is the music video. (And coming from someone who is a dyed-in-the-wool red-headed step-child, I know from what I speak. Though mercifully I was not stowed away in any V.C. Andrews type homestead!) Why has such a young form that combines the visual with the sonic in a stand-out way gotten the critical shaft with little-to-no preservation efforts?

One reason is that it has often been viewed more as a means of promotion than creative expression. Let's face it, the cold world of advertisement is one that is looked at for having as much artistic merit and human pull as any and every Michael Bay movie. That said, given that the bulk of mainstream cinema and music are often made for the almighty, unholy dollar, it feels strange and frankly unfair that music videos have been so poorly regarded compared to its big brothers and sisters in the movies. Especially given that, again like their more respected and established bigger picture siblings, for every music video made to nab your dollar, there are two or three more that were made for balls out creation.

But hey, one of the strongest impulses for us in creating this tome is to help right the wrongs of cultural and critical neglect. We here at the BIZARRO FILM ENCYCLOPEDIA will never play you for a chump and serve you what WE think you want.

Listen, this ride is always too short and at the end of the day, what rules the most is what is in the heart and what is nestled in individual truth. While we will further delve into this very special and underlooked-at format in Volume Two, here is your amuse bouche of numerous key, cool, fascinating, brilliant,

THE BIZARRO ENCYCLOPEDIA OF FILM

darkly sexy and weird-as-a-goose-at-Dennys to get you properly started on this art-sonic journey. (HD)

1. **"Icehouse" Icehouse (1980)**
Directed by Russell Mulcahy.

2. **"When the Lady Smiles" Golden Earring (1984)**
Directed by Dick Maas.

3. **"Look Back in Anger" David Bowie (1979)**
Directed by David Mallet.

4. **"Jeopardy" Greg Kihn Band (1983)**
Directed by Joe Dea.

5. **"Do it Again" Wall of Voodoo (1987)**
Directed by Stephen Sayadian.

6. **"Joan Crawford" Blue Oyster Cult (1981)**
Directed by Casey Movies.

7. **"Believers of the Unpure" Christian Death (1986)**
Directed by Luca Pastore.

8. **"Self Control" Laura Branigan (1984)**
Directed by William Friedkin.

9. **"Ebony Eyes" Bob Welch (1977)**
Directed by Unknown (*Ed. Note: Yes, I know this is schmaltz, but this video is weirdly creepy. The AOR-ness of the song only enhances it. Don't believe me, imagine the worst human horror set to the Little River Band's "Reminiscing." Exactly.*)

10. **"Worlock" Skinny Puppy (1989)**
Directed by Nivek Ogre

11. **"AEIOU Sometimes Y" EBN-OZN (1984)**
Directed by Luis Aira and Ed Steinberg. (Ed Note: This video is my Zapruder Film.)

12. **"Nothing Bad Ever Happens To Me" Oingo Boingo (1983)**
Directed by Francis Delia.

13. **"Nova Heart" Spoons (1982)**
Directed by Robert F. Quartly.

14. **"You Are What You Is" Frank Zappa (1981)**
Directed by Frank Zappa.

15. **"Der Adler" Udo Kier (1985)**
Director Unknown.

16. **"Lay it Down" Ratt (1985)**
Director Unknown. *(Ed. Note. The only music video where the little boy is CREEPIER than the clown. Seriously, I fear for that poor party clown every time I see him next to Satan Junior.)*

17. **"Rainbow in the Dark" Dio (1983)**
Director Unknown.

18. **"Trashed" Black Sabbath (1983)**
Director Unknown.

19. **"Dog Police" by Dog Police (1984)**
Directed by Jill Mulharon.

20. **"You're a Zombie" by Norm Norman (1983)**
Director Unknown.

21. **"Feet Don't Fail Me Now" Utopia (1982)**
Directed by Todd Rundgren.

22. **"Mein Teil" Rammstein (2004)**
Directed by Zoran Bihać

23. **"Hello Skinny" The Residents (1978)**
Directed by Graeme Whifler.

24. **"Love Without Anger" Devo (1978)**
Directed by Gerald V. Casale.

25. **"Arroyo" SWA (1986)**
Directed by Merrill Ward.

26. **"Cruising" Michael Nesmith (1979)**
Directed by William Dear.

27. **"Beyond My Control" Mylene Farmer (1992)**
Directed by Laurent Boutonnat.

28. **"Dancing With Myself" Billy Idol (1983)**
Directed by Tobe Hooper.

29. **"Mask" Bauhaus (1981)**
Directed by Christopher Collins.

THE BIZARRO ENCYCLOPEDIA OF FILM

Meanwhile... Skipp here! And I'd just like to say that there's no WAY I'm lettin' this go without adding a few of my own near and dears. So without repeating any musical artists (cuz God knows that many many, both above and below, are repeat offenders in the Bizarro music video sweepstakes), I brazenly insist upon including the following.

Should also note that music videos, like short films, are where many filmmakers hone their chops on their way to features (although generally at far larger budgets, because record labels are more than happy to spend the money they'd otherwise have to pay the actual musicians).

And while much contempt has been ladled on mere music video directors, daring to attempt to parlay those skills on a larger narrative pallette (because, yes, they are not the same form, as completely unalike as epic novels and haiku), there's no denying that the wild imagination expended therein has expanded the visual vocabulary of ALL motion pictures. And those who have successfully transitioned (Michel Gondry, David Fincher, Spike Jonez, and The Daniels, for example) have enriched the world of movies to a staggering degree.

Music videos are a very specific merger of music and visuals. And the dance between music and visuals is eternally key. It's an art form I am madly in love with, and requires no justification whatsoever. CHECK 'EM OUT, BABY! If you haven't already. And you'll see what we mean. (JS)

30. **"Human Behavior" Bjork (1993)**
Directed by Michel Gondry.

31. **"Come to Daddy" Aphex Twin (1997)**
Directed by Chris Cunningham.

32. **"Dope Hat" Marilyn Manson (1994)**
Directed by Tom Stern. *(Ed. note. Extra bonus points for featuring my daughters Melanie and Mykey, and lifelong friends Chris and Max Cirigliano, as the kids imperiled on this Willy Wonkoid expedition. As a result, it was heavily censored on MTV. But the uncut version is online, and incredibly fun in ways that Marilyn's increasingly dark-as-fuck videos never went again.)*

33. **"I Fink U Freeky" Die Antwood (2012)**
Directed by Roger Ballen and Ninja.

34. **"Three Little Pigs" Green Jello (1992)**
Directed by Fred Stuhr.

35. **"Sober" Tool (1993)**
Directed by Fred Stuhr.

36. **"Black Hole Sun" Soundgarden (1994)**
Directed by Howard Greenhalgh. *(Ed. note. When first released, audiences were awed by the subtle, terrifying use of CGI fx. As a result, some genius decided to throw more money at the fx, resulting in cartoonish bombast that killed the subtlety of the original. I was furious. But the original is still astounding, and the bombastic one's still pretty fucking cool.)*

37. **"Fish Heads" Barnes & Barnes (1980)**
Directed by Bill Paxton. *(Redheaded Ed. Note. How I forgot to list ANY Barnes & Barnes is a total mystery. I worship at the altar of these guys and my personal video pick would be "Pizza Face." Also, note that the late and always great Bill Paxton both starred and directed the clip for "Fish Heads.")*

38. **"Land of Confusion" Genesis (1986)**
Directed by John Lloyd and Jim Yukich.

39. **"Cry" Godley & Creme (1985)**
Directed by Kevin Godley and Lol Creme.

40. **"Turn Down for What" DJ Snake + Lil John (2013)**
Directed by Daniels.

41. **"Chandelier" Sia (2014)**
Directed by Sia and Daniel Askill.

42. **"Lullaby" The Cure (1989)**
Directed by Tim Pope.

43. **"Mr. Krinkle" Primus (1993)**
Directed by Mark Kohr.

44. **"Sharkey's Day" Laurie Anderson (1984)**
Director unknown.

45. **"Once in a Lifetime" Talking Heads (1980)**
Directed by Toni Basil.

46. **"The Diplomat" Pig Destroyer (2012)**
Directed by Phil Mucci.

47. **"Don't Come Around Here No More" Tom Petty (1985)**
Directed by Jeff Stein.

48. **"Weapon of Choice" Fatboy Slim (2000)**
Directed by Spike Jonze.

49. **"Fantasy" DyE (2011)**
Directed by Jeremie Perin.

50. **"Who Was in My Bed Last Night" Butthole Surfers (1993)**
Directed by William Stobaugh.

51. **"The Unified Field" IAMX (2013)**
Directed by Chris Corner and Danny Drysdale.

52. **"Deep Down Low" Valentino Khan. (2017)**
Directed by Ian Pons Jewell.

53. **"Big Bad Wolf" Duck Sauce (2014)**
Directed by Keith Schofield.

54. **"Army Dreamers" Kate Bush (1980)**
Directed by Keith MacMillan. (Redheaded Ed. Note. Kate Bush deserves her own solo chapter.)

55. **"Money for Nothing" Dire Straits (1985)**
Directed by Steve Barron.

56. **"Girls Just Want to Have Fun" Cyndi Lauper (1983)**
Directed by Edd Griles.

57. **"Manifesto" Burning Ghosts (2016)**
Directed by Travis Flournoy.

58. **"Don't Let's Start" They Might Be Giants (1987)**
Directed by Adam Bernstein.

59. **"She Blinded Me With Science" Thomas Dolby (1982)**
Directed by Thomas Dolby.

60. "Hot Rod Worm" The Slow Poisoner (2013)

Directed by John Skipp and Andrew Kasch. *(Ed. note. You can call bullshit if you want. But capturing both the musical and visual magic of psychedelic swampabilly one-man-band Andrew Goldfarb (aka The Slow Poisoner) felt like a sacred duty. And you can't say he ain't Bizarro as fuck! The whole point of doing* it was to get people to discover how cool he is. Which was always, frankly the point of making music videos in the first place.) (Redheaded Ed. Note. I absolutely love this video and song. Music video is its best when the visuals are completely intertwined with the music and this is a fabulous example. Plus, the percussionist is EN FUEGO!)*

APPENDIX D
WE'RE ALL MONSTERS
A TRIBUTE TO GEORGE A. ROMERO

HEATHER DRAIN

Love, like all of our innately weird and wondrous emotions, has many shades and expressions. But the one linchpin for love to have maximum impact is the Terra Firma of truth and respect. If that's in your soul and soil, then you're going to grow the richest of gardens and that is exactly what George A. Romero did with his work.

Romero was the rarest breed of artist: the true blue game changers. With the horror genre, Romero didn't just add a new spoke to to the wheel but created an entirely new wheel, one that numerous filmmakers have worked hard to copy copiously ever since. (Some better than others!) Romero's horror, most famously his zombie films, including all-holy triad of *Night of the Living Dead* (1968), *Dawn of the Dead* (1978) and *Day of the Dead* (1985), have been praised for their mix of social consciousness, occasional dark humor and some of the best gore effects seen in American cinema.

All of this praise is completely justified, of course, and on top of that, nestled in the very core of all of Romero's key films is the darkest and most terrifying truth there can be. WE are the monsters. In the Romero universe, no zombie (the *Dead* series), biological weapon (*The Crazies*) or possible vampire (*Martin*) is as scary and more dangerous than humans. That's not to say that his worldview was all encompassing in cruel nihilism and cynicism. Far from it! His work has the kind of heart that comes with real love and respect. If we're ever going to grow for the better in this world, then we have to absolutely face the best and worst aspects of our species and with that, ourselves. He let us know this, why? Because he genuinely cared and gave enough of a shit to take risk after risk to do so.

Villainy is a more complicated creature in Romero's work and bless him for that, because that is honest. The man never ever took an easy way out, which is perfect for horror because it snatches any possible tension relief from your sweaty little hands. Life rarely has any easy and pat answers, so why should horror? George A. Romero continually played it smart and made us think while still hitting us occasionally on a more gut level. He tapped into the visceral and cerebral like the maestro he was and will always be. This world feels a little less magical without him in it, but his trail of personal stardust is widely available for all of us to see, feel and absorb. I miss the man greatly, though I never had the good fortune to meet or correspond with him. Yet, he feels like the uncle I always wished for, except even better. Instead of Christmas presents, he gave us films like MARTIN, which has a permanent place in my heart and list of top five favorite films ever. A man and artist like George A. Romero not only raises my expectations of other directors, but also of myself. We love you, Sir and will always fight for your memory and art till the absolute living end.

THE REAL DEAL
WHAT GEORGE A. ROMERO
HAS ALWAYS MEANT TO ME

JOHN SKIPP

[EDITOR'S NOTE: Below is the Facebook post I wrote the night George Romero died. 7/16/2017]

John Skipp hasn't cried this hard since Bowie. And will not be able to comment at length here tonight, because everything I have to say may take a couple of days. (Let's just say I started drinking a little early.)

But in a life full of great art heroes, who taught me to TELL THE TRUTH AS HARD AS POSSIBLE, IN EVERY SINGLE THING YOU DO, WHETHER ANYBODY FUCKING LIKES IT OR NOT, nobody has ever inspired me harder than George A. Romero. Who we lost today. But have forever.

Just yesterday, Jonathan Maberry, David J. Schow and I were at Dark Delicacies, signing *Nights of the Living Dead*, which George and Jonathan co-edited. and which was released just a couple of days ago.

And though I knew from reading the galleys that it was gonna happen, it was kind of surreal to see that the book had actually been dedicated to me.

I'm too sad and hammered to put the actual dedication up. But it was one of the proudest moments of my life.

And one of the last things we did at that signing was to take this picture, below, holding up our book that we did together. HIS BOOK, which we were lucky enough to be a part of.

He specifically requested this picture. Jonathan sent it straight away. So I'd like to think he got a chance to see it. See how happy and proud to be there we were.

It's the closest thing we'll ever get to saying goodbye.

I'm gonna go a little Tibetan Book of the Dead here, and just say,,,as if he could hear it, and it might help, on his way from here to there...

I LOVE YOU, GEORGE!!! You fought and fought to say things that mattered, in a genre that often only cared about the next kill scene. You got fucked and fucked and fucked again, while the visions you created got cashed in on by a gazillion people, almost none of them you.

You have always been one of those artists who never stopped pushing, because you never stopped caring. Not just about the art, but about the social conditions afflicting us. Decade after decade, ahead of the cultural conversation. Sometimes provoking it. Sometimes utterly ignored.

You have always cared. And I trust you will take that to wherever next you go, being a glorious thorn in the side of all those forces who seek to keep us asleep, and obedient, and unaware of how much we truly matter to each other.

I would neither be the artist nor the human being I have become without you. And can never, ever thank you enough.

THE BIZARRO ENCYCLOPEDIA OF FILM

Every single thing I ever did, tried to do, attempt now, and do from now until I'm dead bears the mark of your honor, and sincerity, and devotion. I could not be more proud of you, inspired by you, or more lovingly grateful for all you've done and been.

Now go rock the next slice of multiverse you land in. YOU ARE SOOOOOOO LOVED. My greatest sorrow is how much this world's unlove hurt.

So please, as you go, feel the love so many many of us have. I'm really glad you've always known how much I fucking love you, and thank you. Cuz I was never shy about that.

And that will have to do.

Now, if you'll excuse me, I'm gonna cry some more.

Yer pal in foreverness,
Skipp

ACKNOWLEDGEMENTS

We'd like to thank all of the kind people who helped us over the three-anna-halfs years spent dreaming up this book, and putting it together. From suggesting films to giving us access to photos, we could not have done this without you. (And if we didn't mention you, feel free to sternly waggle your finger at us, and we'll get you on Volume II, okay?) THANKS!!!

Leslie Sternbergh Alexander
Suzie Ayala
Anna Biller
Prano Bailey-Bond
David Beckham
Patricia Beller
Scott Bradley
Brian Bubonic
Chris Burdick
Leza Cantoral
Romeo Carey
Nathan Carson
Nick Cato
Garrett Cook
Jason Crane
Andrea Dawn
Nicholas Day
David Del Valle
Eli Dorsey
Ron Fiasco
Julie Finch
Anthony Gambol

Jill Gevergizian
Andrew Goldfarb
Cody Goodfellow
Jim Hassinger
Will Huston
Erika Instead
Shawn Jones
Del James
Sabrina Kaleta
Joshua Knapton
Jonathan Lees
Marc Levinthal
Tim Lucas
Jim McDonough
Allison McGillicuddy
Shane McKenzie
Lisa Millraney
Bob Murawski
Nicholas Patnaude
Christoph Paul
Lawrence Person
John Peters
Lisa Petrucci

Charles Pinion
Jeff Prettyman
Gregory Robert
Martin Roberts
Lauren Salerno
Alan Scott
Bill Shafer
Jeremy C Shipp
Amelia Shugrue
Janna Silverstein
Melanie Skipp
Danger Slater
Sean Smithson
Ricky Snyder
Marc Thorner
Ant Timpson
Marvin Vernon
Rudy Vile
Darren Villeneuve
Mike Watt
Lee Widener

Image Credits

BiOS

John Skipp is a Saturn Award-winning filmmaker (*Tales of Halloween*), Stoker Award-winning anthologist (*Demons, Mondo Zombie*), and *New York Times* bestselling author (*The Light at the End, The Scream*). He's a compulsive collaborator, musical pornographer, black-humored optimist and all-around Renaissance mutant. His first anthology, *Book of the Dead*, laid the foundation in 1989 for modern post-Romero zombie literature. And he's editor-in-chief of Fungasm Press. From splatterpunk founding father to bizarro elder statesman, Skipp has influenced a generation of horror and counterculture artists around the world. His latest book, aside from this, is *The Art of Horrible People*.

Heather Drain is a writer from the Bible Belt Babylon hinterlands of Arkansas. Exploring and championing various fringe artists and art is her passion and one that has led to writing for both print periodicals like Video Watchdog, Paracinema, and Art Decades, as well as for websites ranging from Diabolique to Dangerous Minds. She lives with her painter husband, Chuck, under the tyrannical rule of their two cats, Ziggy and Davey Boy Roberts, and three pet rats, Giles, Brother Nero, and Matt Hardy.

Paula Rozelle Hanback is an overeducated and underpaid artist and art professor who is perpetually tired and usually covered in cat hair. An aging post-punk, she was Goth before Goth was a thing, and regularly forces her family to listen to The Cure. She wishes she could wear a gown every day.

Lightning Source UK Ltd.
Milton Keynes UK
UKHW030626181120
373624UK00009B/1006

9 781621 052951